John Dickenson
Senior Lecturer in Geography, University of Liverpool

with a Foreword by

J. M. Houston
Chancellor of Regent College, Vancouver

Brazil

Longman London and New York

'É tudo um mundo
que se desvenda
aos olhos do leitor'
(*Caio Prado Jnr*).

Longman Group Limited
Longman House, Burnt Mill, Harlow,
Essex, England
Associated Companies throughout the World.

Published in the United States of America by Longman Inc., New York

First published 1982

British Library Cataloguing in Publication Data

Dickenson, John
Brazil. — (The World's landscapes)
1. Brazil — History
I. Title II. Series
981 F2521

ISBN 0-582-30016-9
ISBN 0-582-30017-7 Pbk

Library of Congress Cataloging in Publication Data

Dickenson, John P.
Brazil.

(World's landscapes)
Bibliography: p.
Includes index.
1. Brazil — Economic conditions. 2. Brazil — Social conditions.
3. Landscape — Brazil. I. Title. II. Series.
HC187.D66 1982 333.73'0981 81-20827
ISBN 0-582-30016-9 AACR2
ISBN 0-582-30017-7 (pbk.)

Printed in Singapore by
Singapore National Printers (Pte) Ltd.

Contents

Part III

Part IV

List of maps

List of illustrations

Foreword

by Dr J. M. Houston, Chancellor of Regent College, Vancouver

Despite the multitude of geographical books that deal with differing areas of the world, no series has before attempted to explain man's role in moulding and changing its diverse landscapes. At the most there are books that study individual areas in detail, but usually in language too technical for the general reader. It is the purpose of this series to take regional geographical studies to the frontiers of contemporary research on the making of the world's landscapes. This is being done by specialists, each in his own area, yet in non-technical language that should appeal to both the general reader and to the discerning student.

We are leaving behind us an age that has viewed Nature as an objective reality. Today we are living in a more pragmatic, less idealistic age. The nouns of previous thought forms are the verbs of a new outlook. Pure thought is being replaced by the use of knowledge for a technological society, busily engaged in changing the face of the earth. It is an age of operational thinking. The very functions of Nature are being threatened by scientific takeovers, and it is not too fanciful to predict that the daily weather, the biological cycles of life processes, as well as the energy of the atom will become harnessed to human corporations. Thus it becomes imperative that all thoughtful citizens of our world today should know something of the changes man has already wrought in his physical habitat, and which he is now modifying with accelerating power.

Studies on man's impact on the landscapes of the earth are expanding rapidly. They involve diverse disciplines such as Quaternary sciences, archaeology, history and anthropology, with subjects that range from pollen analysis, to plant domestication, field systems, settlement patterns and industrial land-use. But with his sense of place, and his sympathy for synthesis, the geographer is well placed to handle this diversity of data in a meaningful manner. The appraisal of landscape changes, how and when man has altered and remoulded the surface of the earth, is both pragmatic and interesting to a wide range of readers.

The concept of 'landscape' is of course both concrete and elusive. In its

Anglo-Saxon origin, *landskift* referred to some unit of area that was a natural entity, such as the lands of a tribe or of a feudal lord. It was only at the end of the sixteenth century that, through the influence of Dutch landscape painters, the word also acquired the idea of a unit of visual perceptions, of a view. In the German *landschaft*, both definitions have been maintained, a source of confusion and uncertainty in the use of the term. However, despite scholarly analysis of its ambiguity, the concept of landscape has increasing currency precisely because of its ambiguity. It refers to the total man-land complex in place and time, suggesting spatial interactions, and indicative of visual features that we can select, such as field and settlement patterns, set in the mosaics of relief, soils and vegetation. Thus the 'landscape' is the point of reference in the selection of widely ranging data. It is the tangible context of man's association with the earth. It is the documentary evidence of the power of human perception to mould the resources of nature into human usage, a perception as varied as his cultures. Today, the ideological attitudes of man are being more dramatically imprinted on the earth than ever before, owing to technological capabilities.

Brazil lends itself well to the landscape approach undertaken in this work. In its colonial history there are traceable, differing perceptions of land and landscape which have left their mark on the contemporary scene. Dr Dickenson has identified succinctly the principal factors involved in the shaping of the Brazilian landscapes, in a country that is the fifth largest in the world. As he points out, the very spaciousness of the country has encouraged a wasteful presumption of riches and an instability of occupance that have scarred Brazil, with cyclical stages of colonial landscape evolution: brasilwood, sugar, gold and coffee. Each was responsible for the settlement of a particular area in distinctive ways. Today, over half of Brazil's population is classified as 'urban', and the range of these urban landscapes likewise reflects the stages and functional activities of modern economic life. Dr Dickenson concludes his survey with a series of suggestive insights on Brazilian attitudes to landscape and its shaping in regional fiction and the image-making of modern tastes and values. The sheer scale of Brazil's territory and its apparent wealth has encouraged profligacy in its use, and fantasy in its image-making. The book is well illustrated and it is an illuminating study that should be of interest to a wide range of readers.

J. M. Houston

Acknowledgements

Grateful acknowledgement is made to the following for permission to use material in the production of maps and photographs:

Fundação Instituto Brasileiro de Geografia e Estatistica *Atlas Nacional do Brasil*, 1966 – II–1–Hipsometria (Map 2); II–11–Vegetação (Map 3); III-6-Colonização (Map 7); Carta do Brazil 1:50:000 Maringá, Folha SF-22-Y-D-11-3 (Map 15); A. Franca (*Amarcha do café e an frentes pioneiras*, 1960 p. 16 (Map 6).

P. Petrone 'Povoamevito e colonização' in A. Azevedo *Brasil, terra e homen*, Editoria Universidade de São Paulo pp. 131, 134, 139, 145 (Map 5).

Smithsonian Institution Press from *Smithsonian Institution Bureau of American Ethnology, Bulletin 143*, vol. 1, 'The marginal tribes', p. 12, Julian Steward, ed., Washington, D. C. 1946 and vol. 3, 'The tropical forest tribes', p. xxvi, Julian H. Steward, ed., Washington, D.C. 1948 (Map 4).

Aerofilms for our Fig. 6.6.

The Brazilian Embassy for our Fig. 6.18.

All remaining photographs are by the author.

Introduction

This study derives from the combination of three factors – my field observations during geographical research in Brazil over the past two decades, the rising interest in perception studies within geography in recent years, and the opportunities afforded by the approach and format of the 'World's Landscapes' series. My interest in the Brazilian landscape began when I undertook doctoral research on the industrial geography of Minas Gerais, in south-eastern Brazil. As a newcomer I spent a good deal of time looking at the landscapes of Brazil with a geographer's eyes. In addition to my detailed field studies in Minas Gerais, I was able to travel in other parts of the country. Subsequent visits to Brazil, to research, to teach and to attend conferences, have enabled me to travel extensively, so that I have a reasonable familiarity with the North-east, South-east and South regions of the country, and some acquaintance with the Centre-West and Amazonia.

My interest as a geographer in place and landscape has been heightened since the early 1970s by the growth of the field of perception studies, stimulated in particular by the writings of David Lowenthal, Hugh Prince, Yi Fu Tuan and others. In consequence my more recent visits to Brazil have had the dual function of pursuing my interest in geographical aspects of economic development, and of attempting to identify, appreciate and interpret the landscapes of the country.

The broad area of perception studies encompasses a number of sub-fields which relate to different scales and techniques of analysis and description, not all of them relevant to the study of landscape. The term landscape itself has a range and ambiguity of meanings. The 'World's Landscapes' series facilitates some exploration of these ambiguities within the frame of its general concern for what James Houston describes as 'the tangible context of man's association with the earth'. (Houston 1970: v–vi)

The opportunity to write the present volume has provided the spur to read more systematically within the growing literature of perception studies and to develop and apply the ideas contained in this literature to the Brazilian landscape. During the writing of this volume two new books provided particular

Fig. 0.1 A rural scene in central Minas Gerais

stimulus and encouragement – D. W. Meinig's *The Interpretation of Ordinary Landscapes* and E. B. Burn's *The Poverty of Progress.* The former has been a particular challenge and reassurance, in articulating clearly approaches to landscape which I was tentatively trying to explore in a Brazilian context. Among the essays included, that by Lewis on axioms for reading the North American cultural landscape touches on a number of themes relevant to Brazil, while Meinig's exploration of the way we look at landscape – as nature, habitat, artifact, system, problem, wealth, ideology, history, place, and aesthetic – confirms the diversity of approaches available. His case for the study of symbolic landscapes is also apposite in the Brazilian case. Samuel's discussion of the biography of landscape, of the virtue of seeking to identify the makers of landscape is also relevant, as is his counter-argument that the biographers of many landscapes are not identifiable, as these have been shaped by millions of unknown and unknowing individuals. This argument links closely with that developed, in a specifically Latin American context, by Burns, who explores the roles of both the élite minority and the impoverished majority in the development process, and thus in landscape change.

At a late stage in my writing also I came across the work of the Liverpool businessman William Hadfield, author of several books on Brazil in the latter part of the nineteenth century. Writing from the other bank of the Mersey he observed that books on Brazil should avoid 'the Scylla of extreme succinctness and the Charybdis of needless diffuseness' – salutary warning indeed! (Hadfield 1854: 88). The present volume does not seek to be a comprehensive survey of the Brazilian landscape, for the sheer scale and diversity of the subject is incompatible with the limited space available. Instead, what I have attempted here is to build up a portrait of the present-day landscape of Brazil, using a range of approaches rather than a single one. The objectives set are twofold – primarily to describe and interpret the landscape or landscapes of Brazil as they have evolved and currently exist, and secondly to explore and demonstrate the viability of differing approaches to landscape description and analysis. It is also hoped that this work will prompt further work on these themes, for in its preparation many lacunae in the literature on the Brazilian landscape and landscape-shaping factors were evident.

The book follows an evolutionary approach, examining the perceptions of land and landscape held at different times in Brazil's history, giving particular emphasis to elements which persist in the landscapes of today. If the contemporary landscape is a palimpsest, built up by the generally slow process of change in the physical environment and more rapid change brought about by man, then the 'layers' can be viewed from different perspectives as man has perceived, used and created the landscape. In the past, as Hugh Prince has noted (1971), there were real, imagined and abstract worlds, and these have helped to shape the landscapes of the present. Hopefully I have identified at least the principal factors involved in the shaping of the Brazilian landscape.

For our purpose the physical landscape of Brazil may be treated as a *tabula rasa*, since, in historical terms, man appears to have been a relatively recent immigrant into what is now Brazil. This therefore permits us to describe the physical environment in essentially scientific terms, giving as far as possible an objective portrait of the natural landscape within which and upon which man has operated to create the landscapes which currently exist.

The legacy of early man in the Brazilian landscape is limited. The Amerindian in Brazil appears to have been less advanced than his counterpart in Andean or Meso-America. He was less numerous and less civilized, and in the face of European expansion after 1500 the number of Indians has declined and the area occupied has dwindled, so that the present contribution of the Indian has diminished both absolutely and relatively. The impact of the Indian has been, almost literally, little more than a scratching of the surface of the land.

The phase of Portuguese occupation is an important one, representing one of the pioneering phases of European imperialism, and we can see, from the colonial period, both the vision and the exploitation of 'far places'. During this period, of the sixteenth to eighteenth centuries, major elements in the pattern of settlement and land ownership, urban fabric, demographic mix and economic organization were laid and persist to the present.

After independence in 1822 Brazil became closely enmeshed with European powers engaged in the Industrial Revolution and with their economic expansion overseas. This did not result in new formal colonial links, but European influences had a profound effect on Brazil's development and thus on its landscape. Several aspects of these influences are explored in Chapter 5. In the early nineteenth century the Brazilian élite deliberately sought and consciously aped the fashions of Europe. During the colonial and early post-colonial period Brazil's development was dependent on slave labour, but with the abolition of slavery alternative labour sources, in the form of European immigrants, became important. These groups were attracted to Brazil by images presented by recruiting agencies, they created distinctive ethnic landscapes in the areas in which they settled, and left some record of their reaction to the New World in the tropics in which they found themselves.

Increasing involvement in international trade also brought foreign investors to Brazil. Their views of the country's economic potential afford a differing perspective on the landscape and their actions were important in the shaping of the late nineteenth-century landscape, through the provision of infrastructure and urban services and in directing the nature of economic development. This was also a period of travel and exploration by European gentlefolk and scientists in Brazil, and their writings provide us with an external impression of the country and are responsible for some of the persisting images held of Brazil by foreigners.

In the twentieth century, in common with other Third World countries, Brazil has sought to develop and modernize. Efforts have been made to secure economic advance, diversify the economy and improve the living standards of the population. In this process the State has been a major element in shaping the path and structure of development, and thus having an impact on the landscape. The role of the State in landscape modification, particularly in non-socialist countries, appears to be little considered in the landscape literature. Furthermore, landscapes of economic progress in general seem to be neglected, presumably because factories, chimneys, gas works, power stations, railroads and highways are the very antithesis of aesthetically pleasing landscapes. Yet, in a developing country, such features provide new and distinctive elements in the landscape, and contrast with the natural landscape and the more slowly evolved and conservative rural landscapes. In addition, such developments are powerful stimuli to other landscape changes, in the fostering of urban growth as people find employment in factories or migrate in search of it.

Economic progress has brought substantial change to the Brazilian landscape, with movement from a rural, primary product-based economy to a more diversified urban one. By 1970 over half of Brazil's population was living in places defined as urban. The urban landscape has become both the objective and the norm for many Brazilians. In addition Brazil has sought to create specific urban landscapes, whether through simple and small-scale company towns, built for factory workers, or larger and more ostentatious projects.

Brazil's economic progress in the period since 1945 culminated in the 'economic miracle' of the late 1960s and early 1970s. The instigators and beneficiaries of this miracle are the principal shapers of the contemporary landscape and the arbiters of landscape 'taste'. Yet this group represents only a minority of the population. Many people have not benefited greatly from this advance, and comprise the urban and rural poor, who live in landscapes of relative or absolute poverty. In spite of rapid urbanization it is estimated that one-third of the population in 1980, some 40 million people, live in rural areas, either in established farming areas or on the persisting dynamic frontier. Non-urban land still constitutes the bulk of Brazilian territory. These landscapes of development are explored in Chapter 6.

The study concludes with a series of shorter essays on attitudes to landscape and the shaping of landscape tastes. Increasingly the landscapes we see or believe we see are shaped or created by the media. The field of literary landscapes is an established one in perception studies and indeed pre-dates it in

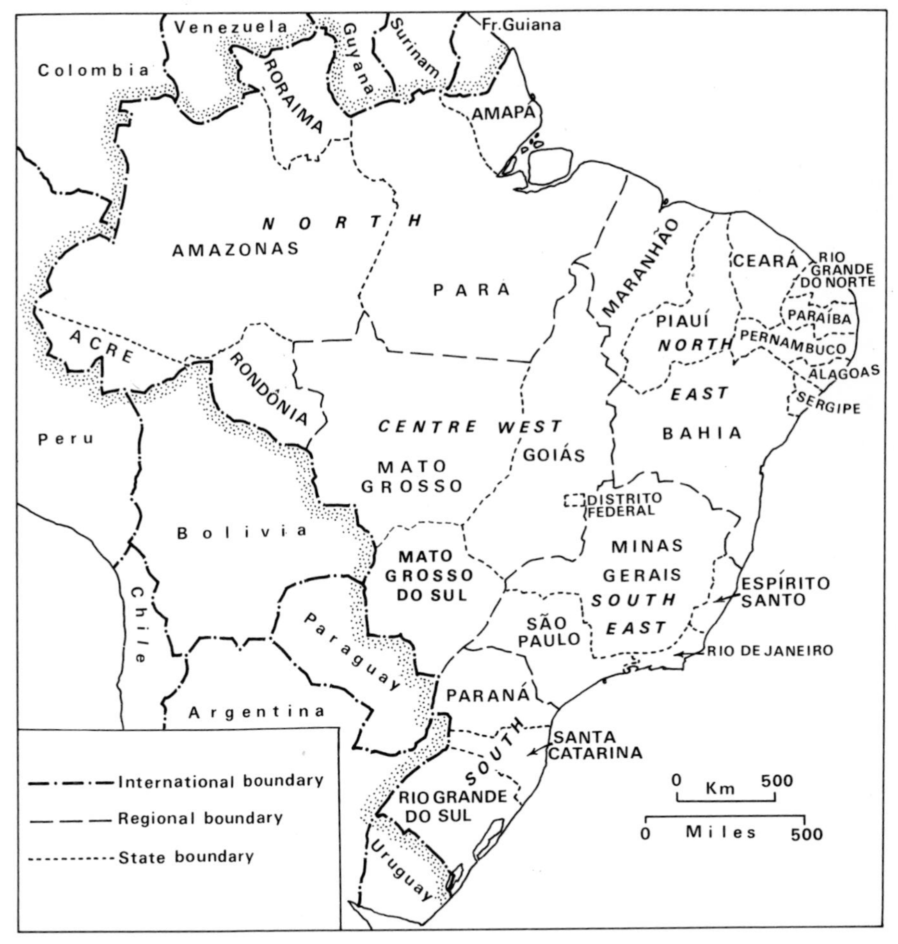

Map 1 Brazil: regions and states

'regional' writing. In Brazil there is a substantial body of such regional fiction. The country's close involvement with the capitalist model of development has involved increasing acceptance of many of the image-making trappings of capitalist economies. A good deal of development has been linked to upper class acceptance of the aspirations and artifacts of capitalist consumer society, particularly via the activities of multi-national corporations, so that 'universal' elements intrude increasingly into the Brazilian landscape. A significant area of growth in recent years has been the rise of domestic and international tourism, which both projects and creates distinctive landscape images. In the development process the State has played an increasing role, modifying old landscapes and creating new ones, and has also sought to create images of Brazil both internally and overseas. Influences such as this shape the landscape we see or promote its modification.

During the preparation of this book I have incurred many debts of gratitude. The University of Liverpool has provided funds and facilities for research and writing, and the technical staff of the Department of Geography made available their diverse and considerable skills. Alan Hodgkiss and Sandra Mather drew the maps, Douglas Birch, Ian Qualtrough and Chris Roberts produced most of the photographs and Joan Bell transformed part of an untidy manuscript into a neat typescript. I am grateful also to Jean Lowe for working a similar miracle on the remainder. At crucial times in the writing, and in varying ways, Cristina Ortiz, Heitor Vila Lobos, Maria Bethania and Len Brown have provided valuable inspiration. Stephanie and Maria have blithely ignored the notice on the study door that 'É favor não incomodar', while Bonnie braved the book-strewn chaos in order to sustain me (and the Brazilian economy) with coffee.

Part I

1

The natural landscape

Man is a relatively recent arrival in the lands which have become Brazil, and for much of his occupance his numbers have been small and his technology simple. In consequence man's impact on the physical landscape before 1500 was limited. With the arrival of Europeans, modification of the natural landscape became more substantial but man's perceptions of the landscape and the changes to which he has subjected it since that time are fairly well documented. In these circumstances we have some notion of the pre-Cabralian landscape, which permits a reasonably objective and scientific outline of the unmodified physical landscape which has subsequently been subject to appraisal, utilization, destruction or rejection by man.

At the broadest scale Brazil presents an apparently simple pattern in its physical geography. Much of its land consists of the geologically ancient rocks of the Brazil and Guyana shields overlain in limited areas by later materials, and separated by the recent deposits of the Amazon basin. The essentially tropical nature of the environment, in which nine-tenths of the national territory lies within the tropics, is reflected in the climate, soils and vegetation.

A crucial element in the geography of Brazil is the sheer fact of size. With an area of 8.5 million km^2 Brazil ranks as the world's fifth largest country. Size offers space, a potential for expansion and growth and, at least implicitly, the possibility of a range of resources. Yet this very spaciousness and presumption of riches has perhaps fostered the instability characteristic of man's use of the Brazilian land over the past five centuries, as people and the foci of economic activity have moved from the apparent waning of one resource to the seemingly waxing possibilities of another.

In addition to the basic element of size, Brazil is also distinguished by the continentality of her territory, in that only one-fifth of the land is within 250 km of the sea, and over one-third, a higher proportion than for any of the continents, is over 1000 km from the sea. Of a total periphery of some 23 000 km only 7400 km is coastline, the remaining two-thirds being land boundaries with other South American countries. The absence of a west coast, compounded by environmental obstacles, may have been a deterrent to the penetration and occupation of interior Brazil, in that there was no Pacific seaboard to act as a spur, matching that of North America's 'manifest destiny'.

Several authors have remarked on the absence from Brazil of environmental constraints which occur elsewhere in the world. Few areas of the country are too wet, or too dry, or too cold to be put to economic use. There are few mountainous areas, or slopes too steep to cultivate, nor is the land subject to geologic instability. Although resource surveys are incomplete it is apparent that there is a diversity and wealth of resources available for exploitation and development. Yet Brazil remains a country of unfulfilled promises, for while it is true that development has not been constrained by environmental extremes, there are facets of relief, drainage, climate and soils which have so far inhibited full utilization of the land and its resources.

Shields, sediments and surfaces

Brazil's geological pattern is derived from an ancient complex of pre-Cambrian rocks, deformed by later earth movements, and partially overlain by a sedimentary cover of variable thickness. These sediments occur mainly in a series of depositional basins and have been affected by uplift and erosion.

The pre-Cambrian crystalline complex occurs in two major shield areas, the Guyana and Brazilian highlands, and the small Riograndense shield in the far south. The Guyana area consists of a single bloc with little more recent cover but the Brazilian shield is considerably masked by later sediments. The shield areas consist of Archean and Algonkian materials. The oldest rocks – granites, gneisses and similar rocks – occur mainly in the Guyana highlands and more sporadically in the Brazilian highlands. The Algonkian rocks are less extensive and more scattered, the main occurrences being in Minas Gerais and Bahia. They include sedimentary, metamorphic and granitic rocks and contain important sources of minerals.

Paleozoic and more recent sediments occur in zones of subsidence which were little disturbed during the depositional phases, such that the strata are mainly horizontal. The principal depositional areas are Amazonia, the Middle North and Paraná basins and the lesser São Francisco, Recôncavo and Pantanal basins. The basins cover differing spans of the geological time scale and consist of material of marine, lacustrine and aeolian origin. Sandstones of various dates are particularly extensive but other rocks occur, including Silurian limestone in the São Francisco basin. The three major basins contain Carboniferous rocks, but only the Paraná basin has yielded workable coal. Cretaceous sediments are also extensive and contain some significant mineral resources, including Brazil's major known petroleum reserves, in the Recôncavo basin. Tertiary sediments are limited to Amazonia, the coastlands and a number of small interior basins, while Quaternary clays, sands and pebble beds are found mainly in the major river valleys and the Pantanal.

In its tectonic history Brazil has been affected by orogenic movements in the pre-Cambrian and Caledonian periods, when warping separated the Middle North and Paraná basins. Subsequent movements have been epeirogenic, giving rise to warping of both the basal complex and sedimentary rocks, and creating rifts, fault lines and similar features. These include the rift valleys of the São Francisco and Paraıba, and the coastal 'Great Escarpment' which forms a major obstacle to penetration into interior Brazil. In the upper Mesozoic such movements resulted in considerable faulting in the south and the outpouring of extensive basaltic materials, which cover an area of 1.2 million km^2 in the Paraná basin. The basalts reach thicknesses of up to 1500 m and provide the parent material for fertile *terra roxa* soils.

In general the lack of profound disturbance has resulted in the Brazilian lands being subjected to prolonged erosive activity, and extensive erosion surfaces have been identified, dating back to the Jurassic. These surfaces, particularly the older ones, are characterized by extensive planated surfaces, upon which remain uneroded sedimentary residuals in tabular form, known as *chapadões* and *chapadas* or, on a smaller scale near the coast, as *tabuleiros*. These surfaces have been most fully described in south-eastern Brazil, but are also identified in other parts of the country.

Relief and drainage

In spite of Brazil's territorial extent, its relief range is relatively limited, with less than one-tenth of its area being more than 800 m above sea level. The highest areas are in the south-east and the far north. Lowland areas below 200 m constitute 40 per cent of the national territory and are found mainly in the Amazon basin, the Pantanal and along the coast from Piauí to Espírito Santo and, less continuously, further south.

The most extensive relief forms are the upland plateaux, or *planaltos*, at between 200 and 800 m, which represent particularly the planed erosion surfaces. Extensive plateaux at below 500 m occur in the eastern Guyana highlands and the western part of the Brazilian shield, where they form the interfluves between the south bank tributaries of the Amazon. The higher plateaux occur mainly in the south-east and south, and include areas of up to 1200 m in the Chapada Diamantina and the serras Geral, Mantiqueira, do Espinhaço and do Mar. There are also small *planalto* areas at these elevations in the Guyana highlands, and it is here that Brazil's highest point, the Pico de Neblina (3014 m), is located.

Within these upland plateaux there are contrasts in detail. In central Brazil the *chapadões* are tabular sedimentary residuals left by erosion on the crystalline shield. Tabular forms and cuestas occur in the Middle North and Paraná basins in consequence of the erosion of horizontal sediments. In the north-east there are isolated hills and uplands upon the extensive level surfaces, while the south-east has single or multiple scarp barriers along the coast, and in the interior the highlands of the Serra do Espinhaço.

At a smaller scale the forces of erosion and climate working on the various

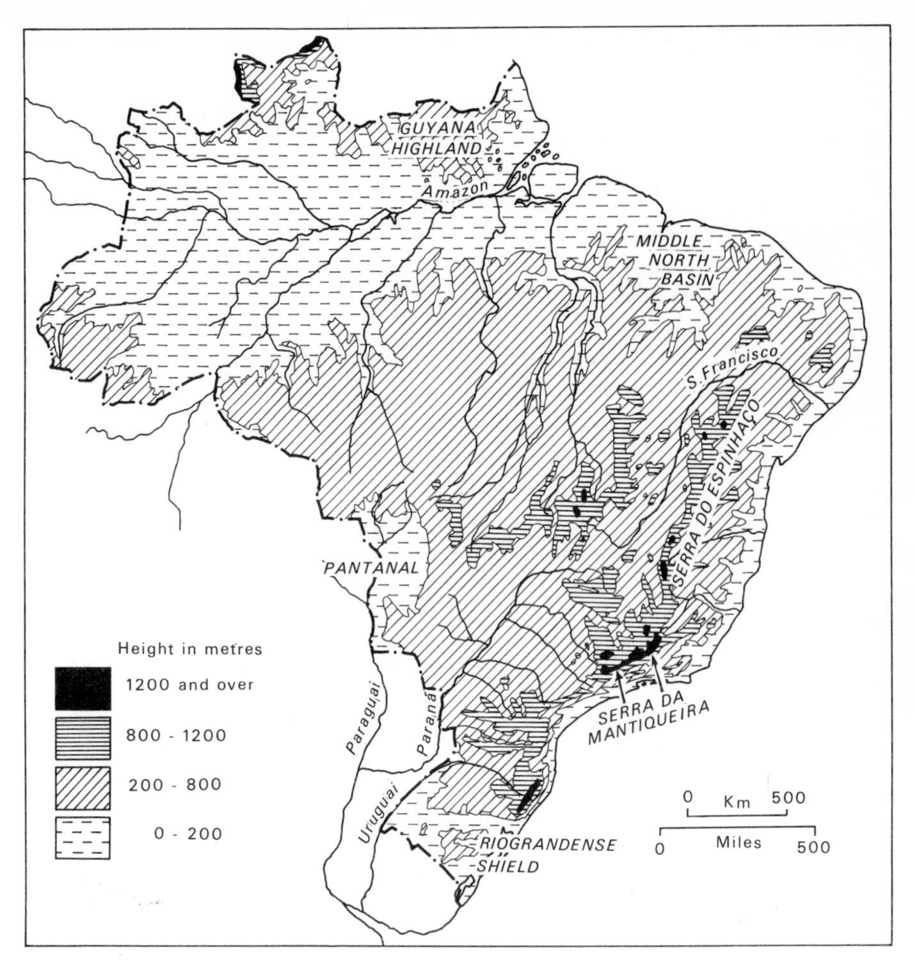

Map 2 Brazil: relief and drainage.

rock types have given rise to distinctive land forms. Amongst the most startling are the rounded forms of the igneous rocks, such as Sugar Loaf, the inselbergs of the north-east, and the karstic forms of the Silurian limestones of Minas Gerais and Bahia.

Brazil's river system is a vast, dense and powerful one. Five major systems, the Amazon, São Francisco, Paraná, Paraguai and Uruguai, have all or part of their basins within the country, and account for 80 per cent of the drainage. There are a series of smaller basins, mainly draining the coastal areas of the north-east, south-east and south.

A major contrast may be made between the rivers of the lowlands and those of the *planaltos*. The former, principally the Amazon and Paraguai, have very limited and smooth gradients. They present considerable potential for navigation but offer limited possibilities for the generation of hydro-electricity.

Fig. 1.1 Landscape of the *sertão*. The open, caatinga-covered plain of the *sertão*, broken by inselbergs. In the foreground the small town of Quixadá, Ceará.

Conversely the *planalto* rivers have steeper gradients and are broken by falls and rapids, restricting use for navigation but providing considerable hydro-electric potential.

With the major exception of the Amazon, Brazil's rivers do not penetrate directly inland but have long and circuitous routes to the sea. This is particularly true of the rivers of the Paraná–Paraguai system, many of which rise close to the Atlantic seaboard but flow west and south to the Plate estuary. The short streams draining more directly to the Atlantic also have broken courses and are not significant navigation or overland communication lines, though some have been tapped for energy.

The regimes of the rivers vary considerably with the rainfall patterns of different parts of the country. In the equatorial conditions of Amazonia seasonal fluctuations are of limited significance, but the rivers of the tropical areas have a more marked seasonality, with high water during the summer and low levels in autumn and winter. In the semi-arid north-east this pattern is so marked that the rivers, with the exception of the São Francisco, are intermittent, their courses being largely dry in the dry season. In southern Brazil seasonal contrasts are less apparent.

Climate

The climatic pattern of Brazil derives from its largely tropical location, the influence of the general circulation, particularly equatorial and tropical air masses over the Atlantic and the South American continent, and from topographic features. In view of its inter-tropical location much of the country experiences high annual average temperatures. Only under latitudinal influences in the south and altitudinal influences in the uplands of the south-east and centre-west does the average temperature fall below 22 °C. In these areas also the seasonal variation in temperature is more marked than in Amazonia and the north-east. In its rainfall pattern the bulk of the country receives between 1000 and 2000 mm per annum, but the range is from below 400 mm to in excess of 4000 mm per year.

The elements of temperature, rainfall and other climatic features give Brazil a pattern of climatic types which accords generally with the 'normal' pattern of tropical latitudes. Over much of the north and centre of the country there is a tropical wet climate with abundant rainfall and little or no dry season. Temperatures are high and the diurnal temperature range is more significant than the seasonal. Similar conditions of high temperatures and rainfall are found along the east coast.

Increasing occurrence of a dry season marks the transition to the more seasonal rainfall pattern of the tropical savanna climate. The area of the Planalto Central and the Middle North has a pattern of summer rain and winter drought, with over 80 per cent of the rain falling between October and March. Seasonal temperature contrasts are also more marked in the equatorial areas.

In the north-east the rainfall diminishes, giving a semi-arid climate in the interior *sertão*, characterized by a rainfall of less than 700 mm, high evaporation levels and high temperatures. In addition to the limited amount of rainfall, its occurrence is largely confined to a two to three month period. Rainfall in the *sertão* is limited and variable in amount, markedly seasonal in occurrence, and occasionally fails absolutely. Such failure gives rise to severe drought, and intense problems for the inhabitants of the region. In the present century major droughts have occurred in 1900, 1902–3, 1915, 1919, 1931–33, 1951–53, 1958 and 1970. The coastal strip of the north-east is not affected by this deficiency and receives significant autumn and winter rains, as do the uplands within the *sertão*, and both act as areas of refuge in time of drought.

Much of south-east Brazil is associated with a tropical climate modified by altitude, with a concentration of summer rain, and altitudinal modification of temperature, to a winter average below 18 °C. The southern states lie outside the tropics and in consequence of their latitude experience sub-tropical conditions, with average temperatures below 20 °C, and cool winters. Seasonal temperature contrasts are more pronounced, but the generally abundant rainfall of over 1500 mm has no seasonal component. The region is also subject to frost, occurring on average on ten days a year over most of the south, which also experiences occasional snowfall.

Vegetation and soils

The vegetation cover reflects the influence of climate, relief, altitude and soil; and in response to the diversity of these and other elements of the physical environment the vegetation pattern is one of considerable variety. A basic contrast can be made between areas of forest and grassland, but within these there is a range of vegetation types and transitions.

The Amazonian forest is one of the world's largest continuous woodlands, and covers some 40 per cent of Brazil. Associated with high temperatures and substantial precipitation throughout the year, it is a luxuriant vegetation type, with tall trees, a range of lower strata, lianas and epiphytes. It has a great diversity of species with an estimated 2000 indigenous tree species. Although its internal character is incompletely known, sub-types are recognized associated with variations in altitude and drainage conditions. The upland forest is the most typical, with tree species up to 60 m tall. The *várzea* forest is subject to seasonal flooding and is transitional between the upland forest and the riverine *igapó*, which is subject to more continuous flooding, and is lower and less dense.

In the east and south-east the tropical forest is more open in character and poorer in lianas and epiphytes. Along the east coast higher rainfall gives rise

Fig. 1.2 The tropical rain forest, Amazonas.

to a dense forest cover with a rich diversity of species. In the sub-tropical south the distinctive Araucaria pine forest has the Paraná pine as a dominant in a tree cover with several strata.

The non-forest vegetation also shows considerable diversity. The most extensive type is the *cerrado*, which covers about one-fifth of the country, particularly in central Brazil. This area has a distinct seasonality of rainfall and the vegetation is mixed in character, with a strata of dispersed, low contorted shrubs and a herb layer. The origin of the *cerrado* is controversial, and suggested influences include water deficiency, poor drainage, poor soils or fire. The *cerrado* is also diverse in detail and a number of sub-types, depending upon variations in shrub density, are recognized.

In the semi-arid north-east the vegetation is of a scrub character, known as *caatinga*. In this area the trees lose their leaves in the dry season and most are adapted to conditions of seasonal water shortage, with cacti and xerophytic

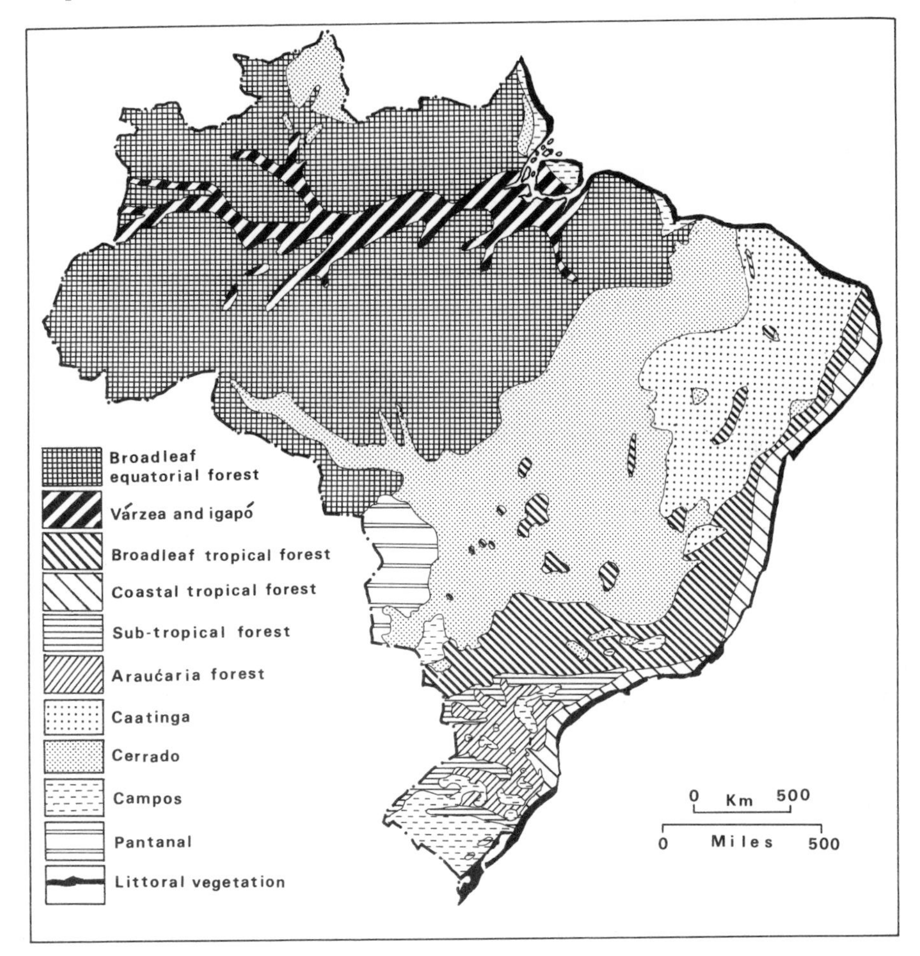

Map 3 Brazil: the vegetation pattern.

plants being common species. The *caatinga* exhibits a capacity for rapid recovery with the ending of drought, and flowers rapidly once the rains return.

In the plainlands of the south an open grassland – the *campos* – occurs, an extension of the pampas. Small grassland areas also exist in northern Amazonia and the higher parts of the south-eastern highlands. The lowland basin of the Pantanal has a distinctive and complex vegetation cover of trees, grass and marshland associated with seasonal flooding. Along the coast a number of distinct vegetation types occur – mangrove swamp, sand dune and salt marsh.

The nature of Brazil's soils is still incompletely known, and there is a general lack of detail as to the soil pattern. It is apparent however that over large parts of the country the soils are of low fertility. These poor soil types include latosols, red-yellow podsols and regosols. The latosols are most extensive in humid tropical Brazil and are found over wide areas and diverse parent rocks, and under both forest and *cerrado* vegetation. They are intensely and deeply weathered, and are deficient in both minerals and organic material. Red–yellow podzolic soils are also extensive. They occur under humid climatic conditions where the dry season is not marked, over various rock types, on undulating topography and under a forest cover. In the sub-humid areas red-brown Mediterranean soils occur, while in the south, under subtropical and temperate conditions and grassland vegetation, brunizem and red prairie soils, with dark, organic-rich surface horizons are found. There are also various azonal and intra-zonal types in the uplands and in areas prone to seasonal flooding or poor drainage.

During the Age of Discovery these 'empty' lands became available to the Portuguese and their descendants. The Amerindian population had made scarcely any impression on this natural landscape. Most of the change induced to date on these natural environments has therefore taken place within the past five centuries.

2

The Amerindian landscape

Man was a late arrival in the lands which have become Brazil. Knowledge of pre-European activity is limited, because of the lack of oral traditions among the Amerindians and the extensive disruption of their society by the Portuguese. There is also a seeming lack of Indian artifacts. These were few and simple, with limited use of stone or other durable materials, so few implements or utensils have survived the effects of the tropical environment. Habitations were also simple and impermanent and have similarly disappeared. In addition, Brazil's vast size, forest cover and the still incomplete exploration and survey mean that the total legacy is imperfectly known.

Much evidence of the activities of early man has to be derived from the records of Europeans at the time of conquest, and from the practices of Indian groups which survive to the present. Dependence on such sources may give a distorted picture, as many tribes were destroyed, displaced or disrupted by Europeans in the early decades of the sixteenth century. Other groups have survived into the twentieth century without direct contact with Europeans, though their life-style may have been modified by post-discovery Indian migrations and the diffusion of European artifacts by warfare and trade. Knowledge of the pre-European landscape is therefore imperfect and incomplete, and carries a peculiar time–space perspective, in that it derives from European interpretations of Indian life in the sixteenth century, from records of subsequent contacts, and from recent observations of tribes whose traditional practices survive within the same territory as the skyscrapers, factories and jet planes of 'modern' Brazil. In broad spatial terms our knowledge of the Indian landscapes of the coastlands derives from historical records; those from interior Amazonia are based on recent observations.

Such limited evidence as is available on pre-European Brazil is open to differing interpretations, but there is general agreement as to the broad historical and spatial patterns. Man was an immigrant into Brazil, part of the migrant streams of people of Asian origin who moved into the Americas via the Bering Strait land bridge during the last glacial period. The earliest human remains discovered in Brazil are less than 10 000 years old. There is no evidence to suggest that Brazilian Indians developed civilizations to compare with those of the Incas and Aztecs, and it is improbable that the Indian population ever reached more than 3 million inhabitants.

The early immigrants were small bands of hunter-gatherers, with limited technology and few artifacts. The precise pattern of movement into Brazil is uncertain, but the impact of early man on the environment, so long as he remained dependent on food gathered from the forest, hunted, or caught in the rivers and coastal waters, was limited. The extensive nature of this simple subsistence economy and increase in population encouraged the evolution of an annual subsistence cycle which utilized the seasonal variations in food availability over the tribal territories.

In spite of the relative isolation of these tribal groups scattered over such a vast territory, with considerable environmental contrasts, the Amerindians of Brazil developed a basically similar type of economy in which hunting, gathering, fishing and garden agriculture provided the means of subsistence. The dating of the development of more sedentary cultivation is uncertain but some evidence suggests that bitter manioc and maize were being cultivated about 3000 years ago. Use of agriculture was linked to lesser mobility of the group and, with more dependable food sources, some increase in numbers. Practice of agriculture provides the basis for a simple division of the Indians into hunter-gatherers and village farmers. Such a dichotomy is probably too crude, as there are considerable variations in the relative significance of these activities within the tribal groups, and significant intermixing in their spatial distribution. On a broad scale a distinction might be made between the hunter-gatherers of the more open plains and the semi-arid plateaux and the cultivators of the tropical forest, but the relationship between culture type and geographic area is not precise.

The *Handbook of South American Indians* used four basic criteria to define the tropical forest village culture: the cultivation of tropical root crops; particularly bitter manioc; the use of river craft; the use of hammocks; and the manufacture of pottery. Although described as a forest culture, these people were riparian rather than sylvan, concentrated along the river banks and coasts rather than in the forest interior. In the interfluve areas and those beyond the Amazonian and coastal rain forest were the less advanced hunter-gatherer groups. These represent the successors of the earliest migrant groups and of tribes pushed into these peripheral areas by later migrations and more advanced societies.

The hunter-gatherer groups lived in the economically more marginal areas and were dependent on simple food-collecting techniques. Thus dependence on hunting and the collection of fruits, nuts, plants, insects and honey greatly restricted the numbers of people which could be sustained and the level of culture which evolved. Dependence on sparse, dispersed food sources encouraged a nomadic life-style, which sought to take advantage of such resource diversity as was available by movement over considerable territories, and to avoid total depletion of these resources. This nomadic existence discouraged both the production of material goods and the construction of substantial

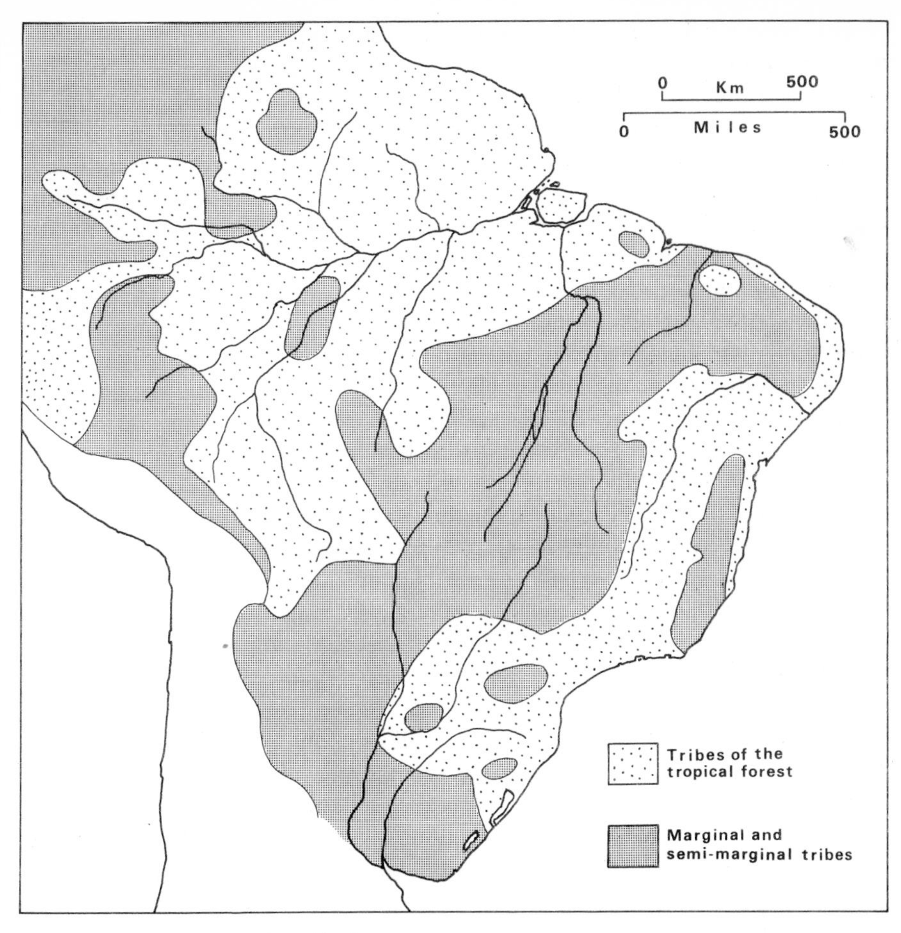

Map 4 Brazil: the distribution of Indian groups.

dwellings. Houses were often simple lean-tos or beehive huts, making up village clusters of perhaps five to 30 huts. In such larger clusters there was often a regular layout of a circle or semi-circle of huts around a central plaza.

The life-style of the hunter-gatherers was, and remains, in delicate balance with the physical environment. They were dependent on the latter for their survival, but the simplicity and transience of their activities made negligible impact upon it. Present-day hunter-gatherer groups constitute the survival of the simplest form of Brazilian society and, because of their occupation of lands less accessible to European penetration, one which has experienced least change since 1500.

The more advanced tropical forest culture was associated with the domestication and cultivation of plants. There is in fact a gradation from dependence purely on collecting, through incipient cultivation and mixed hunter-gatherer-farmer economies, to those dependent primarily upon crops.

The essential element in tropical forest culture was the slash and burn cultivation of a range of crops, particularly manioc, maize and beans. These and other crops were supplemented to varying degrees by forest gathering of fruits, insects and honey, and by protein obtained from hunting and fishing. This economy was closely adjusted to the environment, and though it did not sustain large populations or advanced civilizations, it provided a viable solution to tropical living. There was insufficient food surplus to sustain specialization, but many groups developed skills in weaving, basketry and pottery.

The slash and burn techniques were used to clear garden plots in the forest for cultivation. Vegetation on a suitable site was cut down by simple implements and after being allowed to dry was burned just prior to the rainy season, and crops planted in the partially cleared plots. The gardens were generally irregular in shape, uneven, and covered with ash, tree stumps and charred logs. These techniques have come to be seen as destructive of the environment, but as practised by the Indians seem to have been a careful adjustment to tropical conditions. As clearing of the forest cover was only partial, some protection of the soil from the effect of sun and rain was maintained. Tree burning provided ash as a fertilizer. The crops planted were mixed, mirroring the heterogeneous nature of the forest vegetation, making differing demands on soil nutrients and, as harvesting was staggered, limiting exposure of the bare earth.

The abandonment of gardens after three to five years has been claimed to indicate the destructive nature of these practices, but available evidence suggests that soil depletion may not have been the sole or principal cause of plot abandonment. There are numerous examples of long-term use of gardens and it is unlikely that the small groups would have totally exhausted the soil. In many cases plots were not weeded; this helps to maintain plant cover, but faces crops with increasing competition over two or three seasons, due to weed invasion and forest re-establishment. In such circumstances it was easier to clear a new plot from abundant land nearby, so that tribes exploited virgin forest on a sequential basis, or practised long-term land rotation, allowing plots to fully recover.

Cultivation was associated with more permanent settlement but the periodic movement of the village did not necessarily reflect soil exhaustion. It could reflect rationalization of the choice between rebuilding the village nearer to new plots or walking increasing distance to them, or the decay of communal dwellings and the need to replace them. Hostility of neighbouring tribes, fissioning of the village group or the death of a chieftain also encouraged movement. Where tribes retained some dependence on hunting, depletion of game in the vicinity of the village might determine movement of its site long before nearby cultivable lands were exhausted.

In some parts of Brazil the pattern of tropical forest agriculture was more permanent. In the *várzea* areas along the banks of the Amazon and its tributaries, the soils are annually rejuvenated by the deposition of silt during seasonal flooding. This sustained high yields and permanent cropping, while the rivers provided fish, turtles and their eggs, and water birds. There was a seasonality in the availability of food, but the Indians developed storage techniques for the season of food scarcity. The overall abundance and diversity of food appears to have supported a substantial and dense population, according to early explorers, but this very concentration and the role of the Amazon as a major line of penetration into the interior meant that the *várzea* Indian groups were early victims of disruption and destruction by Europeans.

Elsewhere in the tropical forest culture there was a pattern of seasonality in the economy and mobility of the tribes, with the village being used during the crop season, and short and long distance movements of at least part of the tribe at other times, to exploit other resources by hunting and gathering.

The more diversified economies of the tropical forest tribes supported larger populations than those of the hunter-gatherers, sustaining village communities of up to 2000 people, though groupings of 50 to 60 appear to have been more common. Settlement forms varied considerably. A single large multi-family hut might constitute the village, making dwelling place and community synonymous, or the village might consist of a number of single or multi-family dwellings. The houses consisted of round or oval timber framed buildings thatched with leaves, grass and similar materials. Some rectangular forms were used, but these may have been early borrowings from Europeans. Village form also varied, from the single large dwelling to a series of family or multi-family dwellings arranged in a square, oval or semi-circle, providing a central space for communal activities. In the *várzea*, communities were aligned along the river banks.

The Amerindian appears to have lived in close and specialized association with the natural environment. There was a mutual interaction between man and environment, in which the Indian utilized the various and variable habitats existing within Brazil. The Indian made no distinction between man, nature and divine. He was an integral part of his environment, and this environment provided not only the means of subsistence, but was the source of myth and religion. The spiritual world of the Indian was one in which natural phenomena had an essential role – spirits were those of the stars, forest, water, animals and landscape features, and tribal myths were set in the real world which surrounded the Indian.

The Indians' knowledge of their environment was detailed and intimate. They had a well developed geographical sensitivity, in which awareness of the spatial distribution and seasonality of the means of subsistence were essential for survival. Knowledge of territory, both in terms of topographic features and of sources of food and raw materials, was profound. To the European the rain forest was merely a hostile environment – a collection of trees; to the Indian it consisted of a series of 'places', each with uses and values. The Indians seem to have had no developed sense of distance, which was measured in terms of travel time, and tribal territories *per se* do not seem to have been precisely defined. For most groups tribal territory seems to have been held and used in common, with the right to exploit its various resources. Where hunting and gathering maintained importance in the subsistence economy, short and longer term movement by individuals or groups took place to utilize such resources. Among the tropical forest cultivators, garden plots seem to have generally been individually worked, though land clearance might be a communal effort.

All of the groups appear to demonstrate a high level of adaptation to the physical aspects of the environment – terrain, rainfall, soils, vegetation, wildlife. Limited number, simple technology and subsistence economy meant that the Indian had limited impact on the structure and dynamics of the ecosystem within which he lived. The effects of their activities were limited in spatial scale and transient in time. The simple food-getting techniques of the hunter-gatherers supported small populations in unproductive (marginal) environments. Exploitation of natural products might lead to temporary exhaustion of fruit, fish and game sources, but nomadic migration permitted recovery. The slash and burn practices of the cultivators were in fact a close adjustment to the forest conditions, with few long-term effects on the vegetation. Garden plots were mere flecks in the forest cover, and techniques of clearance and cultivation limited the damage done to the soil, so that abandonment of the small plots, surrounded by virgin forest, facilitated recolonization.

In consequence, there are few direct survivals in the contemporary landscape of pre-contact Indian activities. The life-styles evolved by the Amerindians were adjusted to the environmental conditions of the humid tropics, and though they did not sustain large populations, they provided a solution to living in the tropics which was at least partially adopted by the Portuguese. At the time of contact with Europeans there were perhaps 1–1½ million Indians in Brazil. They were not a homogeneous group, consisting as they did of numerous small tribes, with many languages and diverse traditions. The discovery resulted in profound changes in their culture, numbers and spatial distribution.

The post-colonial period

The life-style of the Amerindians was substantially modified by their incorporation into the European world, in plantations, mines and missions; by their enforced retreat before the Portuguese into unfamiliar and more remote environments; and by the acquisition of European artifacts, primarily iron tools, and new crops such as bananas and sugar cane. Numbers declined in response to warfare, disease, enslavement and assimilation. As European penetration was primarily waterborne, the Indians of the coasts and Amazon banks were affected most rapidly and profoundly, but the sequent economic frontiers – into the pasture lands of the North-east in the seventeenth century, the goldfields of the South-east in the eighteenth, and the interior of the South and Amazonia in the nineteenth – resulted in modification, retreat or incorporation. Contacts in the twentieth century have further reduced the number of tribal Indians and the extent of the aboriginal landscape. Of an estimated 230 tribal groups existing in 1900, 87 had disappeared by 1957; and whereas more than half the groups existing in 1900 lived in isolation from Europeans, by 1957 only a quarter of the surviving groups were isolated. The estimated Indian population is below 100 000, and of the 143 surviving groups, 52 consist of less than 250 Indians.

Surviving Indian landscapes are at risk in the face of Brazil's recent renewed penetration of the last frontier of Amazonia, as highways, squatters, pastoralists and mining companies push into the last remaining refuge of traditional societies. Lack of previous interest has allowed these Indian lands to survive, but once resources utilizable by the developed world are identified, the Indian and his lands are at risk. Possession of land is crucial to the survival of the Indian, his life-style and his landscapes, and government policy has so far proved incapable of resolving the conflict between the Old and the New World. Land provides the basis of Indian subsistence and society; separated from it but unintegrated into the national economic system of modern Brazil, the Indian becomes dependent on a protectionist agency or reduced to misery on the margins of Brazilian society.

The influence of the Amerindian on the natural landscape of Brazil was never substantial, its extent was much diminished by the impact of Portuguese colonialism and is currently subject to further reduction and change. The contribution of the Indian to the landscape of today is therefore indirect rather than direct. The relationship between the Indian and the Portuguese was not entirely one way, for the Indians taught the Portuguese how to live in the New World, to eat strange foods and cultivate new crops, and they provided labour, women and souls for landowners, men and missionaries.

From the Indians the Portuguese learned to cultivate and process manioc, to use other crops and forest products, such as maize, palms, cashew and other nuts, and to sleep in hammocks. The adoption of slash and burn cultivation was a major borrowing, and one which has had profound effects on the Brazilian landscape, for instead of the temporary and careful use of land practised by the Indians, Brazilian use of slash and burn has tended to be followed until the land is exhausted, and on an extensive scale such that the possibility of recovery is reduced or prolonged.

A further important legacy is through language with the incorporation of Indian words into Portuguese, and the use of Indian place names. In the earliest contact period Tupi-speaking Indians were the major group in the coastlands and Tupi became the *lingua-geral* of Portuguese – Indian contact. Examples of this legacy include geographical, personal, botanical and zoological names, and diminutives. Thus Pernambuco, Niterói and Sergipe are geographical names of Indian origin; Iracema, an Indian personal name, has become a Cearense place name; *Cipó* (liana) and *capim*, as in Capim Branco (white grass), and Indian-derived suffixes such as *-açu* (large), *-mirim* (small) and *-piranga* (red) as in Itatiaiuçu, Sapucai-Mirim and Jacupiranga, have also been used to name places. Such remnants mark Indian perceptions of their landscapes.

For the tribal Indians who remain, opportunities to modify the Brazilian landscape are limited and diminishing. Contact with 'modern' Brazil must inevitably modify traditional life-style, or result in incorporation into that modernity. The advance of the new frontier into Amazonia further reduces the land available within which the Indian can pursue a life-style adjusted simply to the natural environment, while settlement on Indian Reserves provides, at best, a compromise between Indian and Brazilian values and practices, an adjustment to association with other tribal groups, and to an environment which is spatially constrained and may not be that within which the tribe has traditionally lived.

Part II

3

The colonial landscape

The discovery

The Age of Discovery established, for the first time, contact between the peoples and lands of the various parts of the Earth. The Portuguese discovery of Brazil was part of this experience in which the boundaries of the Eurasian land mass known, if vaguely, to Europeans, were extended by maritime exploration to include southern Africa, the Orient, Oceania and the New World.

The role of the Portuguese in this expansion is a seemingly paradoxical one for, in the mid-fifteenth century, Portugal was a small, poor country with about 1 million inhabitants. A number of factors are advanced to explain its extraordinary contribution to the discovery and conquest of new lands. It was one of Europe's first nation-states, securing what are essentially its present boundaries by the mid-thirteenth century. This status was achieved partly by crusading zeal against the Moors symbolized by the invasion of Cueta in 1415. Its coastal location gave it a maritime tradition of fishing and trading in European waters. Trade expansion to the east was checked by the Italian maritime states, so the Portuguese looked west to the Ocean Sea. A crucial figure in the fostering of exploration was Henry the Navigator (1394–1460), responsible for encouraging skills in navigation, cartography and shipbuilding.

The exploratory zeal of Henry and the Portuguese has been attributed to a combination of economic, religious and political motives, coupled with a basic curiosity about lands beyond the horizon. Major considerations were a desire for gold, spices and other wealth; crusading zeal against the Muslims; the search for Prestor John and for souls to save.

Under Henry's patronage, Portuguese seamen pushed into the Atlantic, discovering and colonizing the islands of Madeira, the Azores and Cape Verde, exploring the African coast, and leading to Dias' rounding of the Cape of Good Hope in 1488 and da Gama's voyage to India, 1497–99. The activity honed Portuguese sailing skills, and their occupation of the Atlantic islands fostered techniques of administration and utilization applied later in Brazil.

Contact with West Africa opened up the trade in negro slaves, an important element in the colonial economy of Portuguese Brazil.

Credit for the discovery of Brazil is usually given to Pedro Alvares Cabral, who made a landfall in southern Bahia in April 1500, on the second Portuguese voyage to India. The discovery is subject to speculation on two scores. Firstly, was Cabral's discovery pure chance, or did the Portuguese already know of or suspect new lands in the south Atlantic? Portuguese pressure for an adjustment westwards of the papal arbitration of 1493, which apportioned lands which might be discovered in the Atlantic by Spain and Portugal, and which resulted in the Treaty of Tordesillas of 1494, has been argued as supporting this opinion. Secondly, there is good evidence that Pinzon reached the north coast of Brazil some weeks before Cabral's landfall, while other evidence suggests contact with Amazonia in 1498–99.

Portugal's discovery, exploration and conquest of Brazil is one of the principal themes in the creation of the Brazilian landscape. Three centuries of Portuguese rule left the basic marks of language and culture. The activities of adventurer, colonist, bureaucrat and priest in settlement, economy, government and religion were crucial in the shaping of the pattern of Brazilian development. Amerindians and negroes made some contribution but their subordinate role in colonial Brazil limited their impact. During the colonial period Brazil was extensively explored and its present boundaries largely established; much of its territory was occupied and by independence in 1822 significant settlement had taken place.

First impressions

In coming to terms with Brazil the Portuguese were literally pioneers in a New World. Their approach was shaped by what Penrose (1963) has identified as three influences – theory, actuality and myth. Theory was the product of the attempts of scholars to explain the world on the basis of imperfect information; actuality was what men had actually seen; and myth was the product of generations of romance and fairy tale. Goodman (1972) has claimed that the period 1500–1800 saw a change from the age of wonder to the age of reality, and the Portuguese adventure in Brazil came early in this change. They were pioneers not only in space but in time, for not only did they extend knowledge of the world but contributed to a change in the nature of knowledge itself. J. H. Parry (1963) suggests that the Iberian exploration combined the courage and skill of Atlantic Reconnaissance with the curiosity, inventiveness and knowledge of the Mediterranean Renaissance. The discovery of Brazil took place at the beginning of the transition from the medieval period to the Renaissance, and transition, tension, conflict and contradiction are essential and recurrent themes in the development of Brazil, and find expression in its landscape.

In their initial contact with Brazil, Portuguese interpretations were shaped by their experiences and the prevailing beliefs of the period. For medieval man the west had been the *terra incognita* of myth – of Atlantis, St Brandon's Isle, Brasil Rock. Baudet (1965) has argued that the enduring myths of medieval man were mobile in space and time, so that the discovery of the New World provided a new locale for the earthly Paradise, for untold wealth and for the bizarre beasts and men of European fable. Here might be found giants, pygmies, Amazons, El Dorado and the Seven Cities.

The earliest records of Portuguese contact with Brazil are terse in the extreme. Indeed, many of the uncertainties about the discovery stem from Portuguese secrecy about their voyages. The record is incomplete. For a long period the New World was seen and described in terms of the Old, and the strange and unusual received attention over the commonplace. There were few systematic descriptions or analytic records. Reports were written in the contexts of a search for profit, rivalry with others, self aggrandisement and mere tale-telling.

The initial report on Brazil from Cabral's fleet, dated 1 May 1500, noted, 'a large mountain, very high and round, and other lower hills to the south of it, and flat land covered with large trees'. Perhaps significantly Cabral's first acts were to name the mountain Monte Pascoal (Easter Mountain) and the land Terra de Vera Cruz (Land of the True Cross), and to exchange gifts with the natives. The report concludes with observations on the scale and nature of what had been found. 'The entire shore is very flat and very beautiful. As for the interior, it appeared to us from the sea very large, for, as far as the eye could reach, we could see only land and forests, a land which seemed very extensive to us'. Noting that the climate was very good, cold and temperate, the chronicler continues, 'Its waters are quite endless . . . if one cares to profit by it, everything will grow in it because of its waters' (Greenlee 1937: 32–33).

The veracity of letters of Amerigo Vespucci, allegedly written about a voyage along the north coast of Brazil late in the fifteenth century, has been questioned, but if their reliability is uncertain, they nonetheless reflect what people expected to hear, combining elements of both terrestrial paradise and hell. He writes of a land which, if very pleasant and fertile, was also inhabited by cannibals, innumerable serpents, other horrible creatures and deformed beasts. There were extensive and dense forests, with great trees which grew 'without cultivation, of which many yield fruits pleasant to the taste and nourishing to the human body'. He noted that gold was the only metal found. His assessment was that 'if the earthly paradise is in some part of this land, it cannot be very far from the coast we visited' (Markham 1894: 48).

Views such as this predominate in the reports of explorers, early colonists and missionaries. The possibility of precious metals and spices, the characteristics of the natives and their life-style, the vastness and beauty of the land all colour the reports to Lisbon.

Yet, curiously, despite these eulogies, Portugal's interest in its new lands remained limited for the first three decades of the sixteenth century. Though the land of the True Cross might have mineral and other riches, and natives, these could not compare with the known riches and advanced civilizations of the Orient. Contact with Brazil during this period was limited and reports filtering back to Portugal tended to perpetuate the contrary themes of an earthly paradise and a homeland for the medieval bestiary of creatures of fable.

Early initial exploitation

One of the few obviously exploitable resources of the new land was a dyewood, *pau brasil*, from which the country took its name – a symbolic change from religious piety to practical economics. The wood was collected and traded by the Indians in return for simple European artifacts. The settlement associated with this first economic activity was essentially transitory. The trading factories established by the Portuguese (and others) for the dyewood trade consisted of simple dwellings surrounded by stockades and sometimes a small clearing for food cultivation. The Indians also provided some food by hunting and gathering, taught the Portuguese to grow manioc and other crops, and acted as guides. The Portuguese introduced some plants and livestock from the Old World. Activity was essentially small scale and located near protected harbours and available brasil wood stands, moving on when these were exhausted.

This limited coastal contact provided the early images of Brazil in Europe, expressed in explorers' reports, travellers' tales, and early maps and pictures. The earliest known drawing from Brazil, of 1505, shows in some detail the Indians and their cannibalistic predilictions. The very fine map of Lopo Homen of 1519 encapsulates the image and reality of early Brazil. It shows four splendidly costumed Indians, and four others preparing brasil wood using European tools. It also includes gaudy parrots, monkeys and the mandatory dragon. The extensiveness of the forest cover is also implied, though perhaps significantly for later interpretations of Portuguese and Brazilian attitudes to natural resources, over half the trees shown appear to have been felled.

Portuguese interest in the territory increased as the attractions of the Orient faded, and in the face of French activity in the dyewood trade. A small fleet was sent in 1530 to drive out the French, explore the coast and establish settlements. This resulted in the founding of the first settlement, at São Vicente.

In 1532 the crown's interest was strengthened, with the designation of captaincies, or land grants, which divided the coastal strip and, in theory at least, extended inland to the line of Tordesillas. This captaincy system had been used by the Portuguese in the Atlantic islands and combined elements of feudalism and capitalism. Land was granted to a donatory by the king, to whom allegiance and certain obligations were owed, but at the same time development of the captaincy required investment and was potentially a source of profit. The *donatarios* were generally not great nobles or wealthy merchants, but members of the gentry and lesser nobility. Few had the resources with which to develop their captaincies. Of the fifteen created, five were not colonized, eight were of limited success, mainly because of Indian harassment, and only two, those of São Vicente and Pernambuco, were successful. In addition to Indian hostility, the proximity of mountain terrain to the coast, the forest cover and the lack of easy river routes all checked penetration into the interior. The export orientation of the economy also required easy access to ocean transport. Despite its length the Brazilian coast has relatively few good harbours, and it is significant that four of these – the bays of Todos os Santos, Vitória, Guanabara and the Santos estuary – together with Recife protected by its reef, were settled before 1570, and provided small islands of settlement linked by sea.

The captaincies were of limited success but they created strategic settlements and saw some development. They formed the first substantial attempt to transplant Portuguese civilization and culture to Brazil, and they left a legacy in the political landscape, forming the basis for some present-day states, and giving names to six of them. However, as a result of the limited progress, a more centralized system of control under a governor-general was introduced in 1549, with Salvador de Bahia as capital. The crown provided greater financial support and encouraged colonization. A crucial element in late sixteenth century development was the cultivation of sugar. It had been introduced during the captaincy period, but was encouraged more positively after 1549.

Economic cycles

Although *pau-brasil* was the country's first important export, sugar is the first commodity associated with the 'economic cycles' which have dominated Brazil's economic history and contributed so much to its spatial development. In each of these 'cycles' Brazil provided a commodity for world markets and, for a period at least, dominated world output of that commodity. In each case, production and export tied Brazil firmly into external trade, both during the colonial period and after independence.

The principal economic cycles have a rough temporal sequence – brasilwood (1500–30), sugar (1530–1650), gold (1700–80) and coffee (1840–1930) – and there were lesser cycles producing rubber, cacao and oranges. The cycles had not only a history but a geography. Just as they succeeded each other in time they had an impact on the human geography of Brazil and were responsible for the creation of distinct landscape features. Each was responsible for the settlement and development of a particular area, and it is essentially to these cycles that the creation of the oikoumene of Brazil could be attributed.

The notion of the economic cycles has some limitations however. As expounded by Preston James (1969), the cycles were characterized by the spectacular rise of a commodity, its sale in an expanding market which generated substantial profit, and then its decline, usually in the face of more ordered production from competing areas abroad. The booms, according to James, led to the development of a specific region, an influx of population and its concentration about an urban nucleus. As the product began to decline in importance, people moved on to new frontiers, or remained in a decadent area. It is in this latter phase that the concept has some shortcomings however, for the decline of the product was normally relative rather than absolute. In the case of brasilwood and gold, the finite nature of the resource did lead to their exhaustion, but the sugar lands of the North-east and the coffee lands of the South-east remain in production to the present. Similarly, though the areas affected by the cycles may have experienced short-term stagnation, the demographic and economic impact of the boom period provided a foundation for later, alternative development. It is significant that three of Brazil's principal economic and demographic concentrations at the present time, Rio de Janeiro–São Paulo, Minas Gerais, and the North-east coastal strip, were the foci of the coffee, gold and sugar cycles, though their present economic importance is in reverse order to their significance in history. In these areas there exists in the landscape a combination of survivals from the heyday of their boom periods, with later accretions and modifications. It is probably only in the case of the late nineteenth century rubber boom in Amazonia that the boom and bust cycle in its extreme form was experienced and where, until recently, the boom landscape persisted in a relict form, where it had not been totally erased by the re-advance of the jungle.

Landscapes of cane

In the case of sugar, demand for it was rising on the European markets, and Portugal had experience of its cultivation and processing in the Atlantic islands. The coastal strip of North-east Brazil offered good soil, adequate rainfall and relative proximity to Europe. The Portuguese fleet provided the means of transporting the sugar. The crop was therefore responsible for settlement, development and considerable prosperity, and for the introduction of two major and persisting elements in the Brazilian landscape, the plantation and the negro. Some land had been given in smallholdings (*roças*), which provided food crops, but large units (*sesmarias*) were much more common and provided the basis for the continuing place of large land holdings in the tenurial pattern of Brazilian agriculture.

The plantation was probably the most important colonial legacy in coastal Brazil, and provided the mechanism for effective occupation and settlement. The Portuguese were pioneers in the introduction of the plantation system into the tropics, but it was closely tied to Europe, and not only Portugal, for its technology, capital and markets.

The sugar plantation created a distinctive pattern of land use and of landscape. Cane dominated the usage of the plantation lands, and the organization of cane production and processing created a pattern of dispersed settlement nuclei, clustering around the *engenho* or sugar mill. The settlement comprised, in addition to the mill itself and other processing sheds, the dwelling of the landowner (the *casa grande* or 'big house'), a chapel, slave quarters, workshop

Fig. 3.1 An old sugar engenho in the zona da mata, Pernambuco. Sugar cane covers the foreground and the slopes.

and storehouses. In the best areas cane was effectively a monoculture, with little land for food crops, but some pasture for oxen. The forest cover was quickly removed, not only to create canefields, but to provide fuel for the boilers. This was essentially a rural civilization, in which a sea of cane surrounded the processing plant and dwelling places. The *casa grande* was a simple but substantial building, with thick walls and an external veranda, and a sloping roof of tile or thatch. The slave dwellings were of mud and thatch. Most *engenhos* were located near a stream to provide water power and transport. By 1600 there were over 100 *engenhos*, and Brazil had become the world's principal sugar producer.

These large estates, dominated by patriarchal landowners and worked by slaves, producing a single crop for European markets, were largely self sufficient. This structure became characteristic of Brazilian agriculture and shaped much of the colony's social and economic life. Similar agrarian structures developed in association with cotton and cattle, but reached their epitome in the canelands of the North-east.

Exploration of the interior

Until the end of the sixteenth century the hostility of the environment and the Indians, and the need to be close to navigable rivers or the sea in order to export produce to Portugal kept the colonists close to the Atlantic seaboard. Only one significant settlement, São Paulo, founded in 1558, was located inland. Map 5 indicates the limited extent to which the Portuguese had explored and settled the land by 1600. The Portuguese controlled the coast from the Amazon to Paranaguá, though there was little settlement north-west of Cap São Roque, or in the interior.

During the seventeenth century this pattern was substantially changed as explorers and settlers pushed into the interior South-east, Amazonia, the north-eastern *sertão* and the South. A potential check to penetration was the Tordesillas delimitation and the uncertainty as to the whereabouts of the boundary between Portuguese and Spanish territories. This obstacle was reduced between 1580 and 1640 when the two kingdoms were united. Of particular importance in the advance into the interior were the *bandeirantes*, operating from São Paulo from about 1560 onwards. The origin of this term is somewhat uncertain. It relates to the Portuguese word for flag *(bandeira)* and it has been suggested that it refers to an expedition following the flag of a leader. It may also relate to a small group of troops. The term has come to be used to describe bands of men, usually of Portuguese origin, but also including Indians and half castes, who roved over lands that are now Brazilian, during the period from the mid-sixteenth to mid-eighteenth centuries. Their motivation combined persisting beliefs in mythical wonders in the interior with a brutally realistic concern for wealth.

The area around São Paulo was not a prosperous part of early colonial Brazil. It yielded no mineral resources and its plateau-top location isolated it somewhat from colonial commerce. Richard Morse (1965) has argued that it attracted the more restless migrants, those best able to survive the journey to Brazil and the plateau, and who were prepared to face its limited opportunities for profit. In a land short of European women São Paulo was even more deprived, so that there was a high degree of miscegenation with Indian women, giving rise to the half-caste *mamelucos*, who were an important element in the *bandeirante* groups.

These groups ranged widely, initially in search of Indians to enslave and then, in the late seventeenth century, precious metals and gems. The *bandeiras* were mobile and self sufficient, living off the land. Their significance is not in landscape creation for, in their essential mobility, they made little direct impact upon it. Instead they played a crucial role in defining the territory which was to become Brazil. Their expeditions took them into Paraguay and towards the Plate in search of Indians, northwards along the Tocantins towards the Amazon and to Piaui. A major *bandeira* was that of Antonio Raposo Tavares, beginning in 1648. Its route was close to what have become the frontiers of modern Brazil, following the courses of the Paraguay, Guapore, Madeira, Amazon and Tocantins rivers, encircling much of what are now the Centre-West and North regions of the country, and well beyond the theoretical line of Tordesillas.

Essentially nomadic, the *bandeirantes* established few settlements; a few of their stopping places later developed into small communities. Where they did settle, as pastoralists in the São Francisco or as miners in the gold fields of Minas Gerais, they abandoned their *bandeirante* role. In general they did not represent the westward spread of a frontier of settlement but provided the circumstances for the subsequent advance of that frontier. The reports of their journeys are terse and basic, telling us little of the lands they saw or their reactions to them. One such traveller for example noted that his hazardous experiences so disturbed him that he had no time to describe the country he traversed or name the physical features passed. Many of the reports are similarly restrained, recording river conditions, basic characteristics of topography, the availability or lack of food and of potential sources of wealth. Thus a report from a journey in western São Paulo in 1722 noted 'the relatively flat land has clumps of trees and is well watered'; and later, 'a dangerous river with plenty of fish, good pasture and wood nearby' (Burns 1966: 102–16).

The *bandeirantes* were pathfinders for others. Their activities defined a national space in which others might operate. Until recently however large areas traversed by them showed little sign of the passing of the *bandeiras* or of successors. It was only where their penetration revealed resources for development that they were followed by settlers – in the North-east, South-east and South. In the deep interior, significant penetration has been essentially a recent phenomenon.

Landscapes of conversion

The period of *bandeirante* activity overlapped with that of another group which was also active in the early penetration of Brazil, that of the religious missions. The legacy of the missions was perhaps even more ephemeral than that of the *bandeirantes*, partly because the two groups were competing, in different ways, for Indians. Priests had travelled with Cabral, and had been appointed to the captaincies. Brazil's first bishop arrived in 1552. It was, however, the Jesuit missions to the Indians which had particular impact. One of the motives of Iberian expansion was conversion of pagans to Christianity, and the priests set out to convert the Amerindians. They learned Tupi-Guarani and began to teach the Indians not only Christianity but also agricultural and handicraft skills.

Initial contact was adjacent to the European settlements, but the Jesuits also founded *colégios* at which to educate Indian youths. One of the earliest, and subsequently most important, of these was at Piratininga in 1553, which formed the nucleus of present-day São Paulo city. Other *colégios* and *aldeias* provided the nuclei for other Brazilian settlements. Contact with Europeans was felt, by the colonial powers, to be part of the process of acculturation of the Indians. However, a basic conflict emerged, for the Jesuits sought greater segregation in order to secure the conversion of their charges, the Indians were open to corruption by alcohol and prostitution, and, in a land deficient in labour, the nucleations of pacified Indians provided a tempting source of potential slaves.

In consequence the missions tended to operate away from the existing towns, often in advance of the effective frontier of Portuguese settlement. Gathered into the mission nucleations (*aldeias)* Indian life-style was profoundly changed. In addition to attempting their conversion, the Jesuits closely regulated the life-style of the Indians. Economic activity was changed from dependence on shifting cultivation, hunting and gathering, to more static production of crops for subsistence and trade. The traditional tribal long house was replaced by family huts, generally laid out in a regular pattern, with the church a dominating feature.

The missions were the most important attempt at co-existence between Europeans and Indians, and ultimately failed. Nucleation and contact with Europeans exposed the Indians to unfamiliar diseases, which greatly reduced their numbers. Most significantly, the *aldeias* became the focus of the conflict between the religious desire to save souls and the secular need to enslave bodies. Ultimately the latter triumphed. The potential slave source of the *aldeias* soon attracted the attentions of the *bandeirantes* and those close to São Paulo soon succumbed. In 1607 the province of Paraguay, incorporating parts of present-day Bolivia, Paraguay, Uruguay, Argentina and of the Centre West and South of Brazil, became a mission area for Spanish Jesuits. The missions they established in Brazil, in western Paraná, north and central Rio Grande do Sul and western Mato Grosso, soon became targets for the *bandeirantes.* By 1641 they were overrun and destroyed, and their Indians enslaved or put to flight.

In the late seventeenth century a new phase of missionary activitv began in the south, with the establishment of seven missions (the Sete Povos) in western Rio Grande do Sul, linked to a further 23 missions in Paraguay. Established between 1682 and 1706, these missions survived longer, protected by their relative isolation from the *bandeirantes*, and by the lesser desire for Indian slaves with the growth of the trade in African slaves. All of the missions were built on a grid plan, around a central square and the church, with the Indians living in one-room houses. They cultivated food crops for the mission, and cash crops such as cotton and maté for sale, and captured cattle from wild herds. The missions survived until 1750 when, under the Treaty of Madrid, the boundaries between Spain and Portugal were demarcated. These Spanish missions were to be transferred to the west bank of the Uruguai River. The Jesuits and Indians resisted, but were expelled in 1756, the villages destroyed, and only the mission churches remain.

The River-Sea and the forest

Conflict between missionaries and colonists over the Indians was also significant in the development of Amazonia in the colonial period. The Amazon was one of the earliest areas of European contact with Brazil – by Spaniards, and it clearly lay within Spanish territory as delimited by Tordesillas. It was neglected, however, because of the unattractive nature of the coastlands at its mouth, and the difficulty of access, for the Spaniards over the Andes and for the Portuguese because of adverse sailing conditions along the 'East-West' coast from the established settlements on the 'North-South' coast. The Spaniard Francisco de Orellana sailed down the river from the Andes in 1542, recording a substantial native population and abundant food resources. There were other voyages and explorations, but activity remained limited until Dutch, French and English interest around the delta rekindled Iberian interest, and in 1616 the Portuguese founded a fort at Belém to control the entrance to the river. As the joint kingdom of Spain and Portugal came to an end Spanish penetration of the upper river from the Andes prompted Portuguese concern there also, and the journey of Pedro Teixeira, 1637–39, from Belém to Quito not only pushed Portuguese territory well beyond the Tordesillas delimitation, but left a vivid description of the area. The Spanish Jesuit Cristobal de Acuna, who accompanied Teixeira on his return journey, comparing the River-Sea to the Ganges, Euphrates and Nile, wrote: 'the river of Amazons waters more extensive regions, fertilizes more plains, supports more people and augments by its floods a mightier ocean; it only wants, in order to surpass them in felicity, that its source should be in Paradise' (Markham 1859:61). De Acuna's report is a glorious catalogue of the size of the river, the richness of its fish and turtles, the fertility of the soils, the diversity of the fruits and the moderate nature of the climate. Timber, cocoa, tobacco and sugar were noted as 'four products which, if cultivated, would undoubtedly be sufficient to enrich not only one, but many kingdoms' (ibid. 76). For good measure, rivers, lakes and towns of gold were reported, as well as the existence of Amazon warrior-women.

Despite this apparent cornucopia, colonization and settlement of Amazonia was slow and difficult. Access from the early colonies of the North-east and South-east was impeded, on land by the forest and by sea by the adverse sailing conditions of the 'East-West' coast. Contact with Lisbon was easier than with Salvador, and from 1626 to 1775 the area was separately administered from São Luis and Belém, as the Estado do Maranhão e Grão Pará. Within the river system its sheer size facilitated navigation and penetration, so that water became, and largely remains, the principal means of communication. However, even the rivers gave access only to their margins; immediately beyond them the forest was a formidable barrier. Settlement was, therefore, confined to the river banks and junctions.

In the attempted exploitation of the area the Indian again was a source of contention between missionaries and settlers. Several missionary orders in addition to the Jesuits were active in Amazonia. They followed a similar pattern of drawing the Indians into nucleated *aldeias*, seeking to Christianize and Europeanize them, and changing their life-style. In 1750 there were 63 such *aldeias*. In addition to subsistence crops the Indians grew cotton, coffee, sugar and tobacco and collected the important spices – the *drogas do sertão* – from the forest. Such commodities as cinnamon, cloves, sarsparilla and cacao became increasingly important as Portuguese influence in the Orient declined. On Marajó island the Jesuits established cattle ranches.

In these activities the missions were in competition with the secular colonists, who sought Indian slaves with which to cultivate and to gather. The settlers of Maranhão-Pará claimed they were too poor to buy negro slaves and that the Indians were better suited to the local environment. Again the *aldeias* made easy targets. In addition, slaving was more organized and legitimized in Amazonia. In consequence enslavement, coupled with epidemic disease, rapidly reduced the dense population noted by Orellana. The slaving expeditions and other explorations were responsible for increasing knowledge of the tributaries of the Amazon, and, via the Tocantins, Tapajos and Madeira-Marmoré-Guaporé creating overland links to the South-east. This penetration took the Portuguese far into 'Spanish' territory, such that in 1750 these lands were identified as Portuguese and the present boundaries of Brazil largely established.

Hostility to the activities of the missions and their attempts to protect the Indians contributed to the expulsion of the Jesuits from Brazil in 1756. The principal legacy of the missions was their role as nuclei for a number of the region's towns. These included Altamira, Bragança, Cametá, Monte Alegre and Santarém. The controlling forts, of Belém, Manaus, Macapá, Óbidos and Boa Vista, were also points of urban growth.

The degree of development of Amazonia during the colonial period was very restricted. The obstacles posed by the physical environment were too great, given the very small population, both white and Indian, involved in trying to exploit the region. Cultivation was confined to the delta and a few areas along the river banks. Elsewhere there was only the gathering of forest products, whose scattered sources fostered dispersed, irregular and small settlements. The colonial economy in Amazonia was limited both in scale and impact. It was essentially exploitative, and provided no basis for more stable development. The gap between the perceived potential of this tropical paradise and actual achievement was substantial. Padre Acuna's notion that 'this great river, which excludes no one from its treasures, but rewards all who wish to take advantage of them' (Markham 1859: 133) was not speedily realized.

Cattle in the *sertão*

Physical obstacles of a different kind influenced the nature of early development in the interior *sertão* of the North-east. This extensive plainland, with low, seasonal rainfall, few perennial rivers, occasional drought and the poor scrubby seasonal *caatinga* vegetation, was initially unattractive to settlers. In the coastal sugar economy, cattle were an important adjunct, providing beasts of burden and sources of meat. As the sugar economy prospered and cane became more of a monoculture, cattle were pushed out of the sugar coast of

Pernambuco and Bahia, initially into Alagoas and Sergipe, but (as cane spread there also) into the interior, where cane could not compete.

Cattle raisers pushed into the *sertão*, particularly along the water lines. The poverty of the vegetation demanded little in the way of clearance, but its low carrying capacity made large land holdings essential. The pattern of land use which evolved depended on extensive grazing of this poor vegetation by such low quality *mestiço* cattle as could survive in this harsh environment. These cattle ranged freely over the unenclosed *sertão*, tended by the *vaqueiros*, the cowboys of the North-east. There was little cultivation or improvement of pasture. Settlement was sparse, the focus of the pastoral unit being a simple ranch house and its associated corrals. A few small nucleations sprang up at water sources and salt licks, and at rest stops and fords along the cattle trails to the cattle fairs and coastal markets.

What emerged was a pastoral economy, with limited impact on the landscape, and which survives, at least partially, in land ownership and land use patterns, to the present day. This was cattle country *par excellence* and closely linked to a cattle culture. This legacy is reflected in surviving place name elements. In interior Ceará, Boa Agua (Good Water), Ôlho d'Água (spring), Riacho Verde (Green Brook) reflect a major concern of the cattlemen in this water-deprived land. Gado (Cattle) is even more explicit. Elsewhere in the North-east Kempton Webb (1974) has recorded Bezerros (Heifers), Currais Novos (New Corrals), Pastos Bons (Good Pastures) and Boi Morto (Dead Cow).

Cattle and colonies in the South

In the development of the South, in the colonial period, pastoralism also played a role, but of a rather different nature to that in the *sertão*. In this area, which now consists of the states of Paraná, Santa Catarina and Rio Grande do Sul, the process of settlement was more closely defined by the authorities. This was the one area of South America where there was overt rivalry between Spain and Portugal for territory, and much of Portuguese, and Brazilian, policy in the development of this area has been to secure and confirm its possession against the claims of Spain and its heirs.

The northern part of the region, immediately to the south of the Paranapanema river, had been the scene of Jesuit mission activities early in the seventeenth century, largely decimated by the *bandeirantes*. Occupation of these lands, however, was slow. They were the part of the colony most remote from Lisbon and, for most of the coast, the Serra do Mar runs close to the sea. It forms a formidable barrier, often a single scarp of up to 1000 m, cutting off the narrow coastal strip from the interior plateaux. Some settlement pushed south along the coast, founding Paranaguá in 1640, São Francisco do Sul in 1658, Florianópolis in 1675 and Laguna in 1676, but penetration into the interior was negligible, and movement south stopped. Beyond Laguna the coast is associated with extensive dune areas and lagoons offering few possibilities for settlements which depended on coastal communications.

The Portuguese leapfrogged this area, and sought control of the more attractive open grasslands of the far south, and of the north bank of the Plate estuary, by founding the colony of Sacramento in 1680. This was the only significant Portuguese advance from which there was a later retreat, ending in the creation of independent Uruguay in 1828. The colony changed hands four times between 1680 and 1716 and to secure the lands to the north the Portuguese encouraged colonization, with penetration along the coast from Laguna and overland from São Paulo.

At about 30 °S the Serra do Mar turns sharply westward. To the south are open grassland plains. They have abundant water, a mild climate and there were feral cattle derived from runaways from the missions and the pampas. These encouraged the development of a pastoral economy, initially for hides and later for dry meat or *charque*. In addition, other stock – horses, mules and sheep – were raised. The bases of this expansion were Pôrto Alegre and Rio Grande (1737), but the pattern of settlement was again one of large holdings, the *estancia*, with the cattle ranging freely over the extensive unimproved grasslands. An important factor in this pastoral economy was the creation, in 1733, of an overland trail from the grasslands to Sorocaba, in São Paulo. Along this trail were driven not only beef cattle for slaughter, but horses and especially mules, the essential beasts of burden in the colonial economy. These animals were traded at the great stock fair at Sorocaba held in April and May. Because of the poverty of harbour sites along the southern coast, this route also served as a line of penetration for colonists from São Paulo, and facilitated the occupation of the territory by the Portuguese.

Because of the geo-political importance of the South, the colonial administration was active in the deliberate settlement of the area, and during the mid-eighteenth century pioneered a distinctive pattern of colonization, which was to have profound effects on the landscape and to be of even greater significance in the nineteenth century. Elsewhere in Brazil much of the earlier colonial settlement was spontaneous and based mainly on large land grants. The new process began with the desire to settle the fertile and strategically important island of Santa Catarina. The colonists were brought from the Azores and Madeira where there were problems of over-population. The basis of migration was to encourage young married couples. Considerable care was taken to ensure that they were properly equipped for the voyage. On the island and adjacent coast land was to be cleared, houses created and settlement layout designed before the arrival of the colonists. They were to receive supplies of animals and seed, domestic and farm equipment and initial foodstuffs. Settlements were to consist of about 60 families, with each family receiving a small plot of land. The scheme, designed to secure the occupation of the whole coast of Santa Catarina and Rio Grande do Sul, was not fully realized. However, it introduced a distinct form of colonization, a smaller scale of agricultural activity and pioneered a settlement form to be of greater significance a century later. Moreover, because it was dependent on the labour of the colonist, rather than the exploitation of slaves, it initiated a pattern of almost exclusively white settlement. The European rural, small farm, settlement of this coastal strip was a distinct feature in eighteenth century Brazil.

Landscapes of gold

In contrast to these attempts at ordered development in the South, the development of the interior of the South-east and the Centre-West was rapid, unplanned and uncontrolled. The area above the Serra da Mantiqueira was explored by the *bandeirantes* in search of Indians and mineral riches. The latter eluded them until the last decade of the seventeenth century, when they found gold in the area which became known as the 'General Mines', which forms the centre of the present-day state of Minas Gerais. The discovery precipitated a 'gold rush' with repercussions not only for the local area and Brazil, but for Portugal and Europe. The prospect of wealth drew in migrants and their slaves from other parts of Brazil and from Portugal. It resulted in the first substantial concentration of European settlement in interior Brazil. The wealth generated flowed into Portugal and diffused into the rest of Europe.

The gold boom in Minas Gerais lasted until the mid-eighteenth century. The gold was initially obtained by panning in the streams and rivers, and later by working the hillsides and by a limited amount of mining. The direct impact of these activities on the landscape, other than a few scarred hillsides, was negligible. The indirect consequences however, in the creation of a very distinct urban landscape, were profound, for the wealth from gold sustained one of the most significant and beautiful contributions to the cultural landscape of Brazil, the baroque townscapes of the Minas Gerais goldfield.

The working of the river gravels was transitory and the miners mobile, living in crude dwellings in *arraiais* or mining camps. Once more complex working of the hillsides and shaft mining began, some settlements became more substantial and permanent. The mining economy, in contrast to other colonial economic activities, had an urban focus. As early as 1711 three mining camps, Mariana, Ouro Prêto and Sabará, were given *vila* (town) status. The location of the mining areas in the mountains, with an accidented topography, discouraged ordered and planned towns. This setting, however, provided the frame for the baroque townscapes which evolved, their wealth reflected in the romantic charm of their churches, palaces and public buildings. The *arraiais* coalesced into loose agglomerations, straggling along the valleys and over the hilltops, linked by long, winding streets and steep stairways. The key to their picturesque form is in the originality and homogeneity of their architecture. In settlements such as Ouro Prêto numerous fine baroque churches and public buildings dominated the hilltops, surrounded by low, red-tiled, white-walled houses, with doors and windows picked out in red or blue. Balconies, verandas and public fountains provided elements of

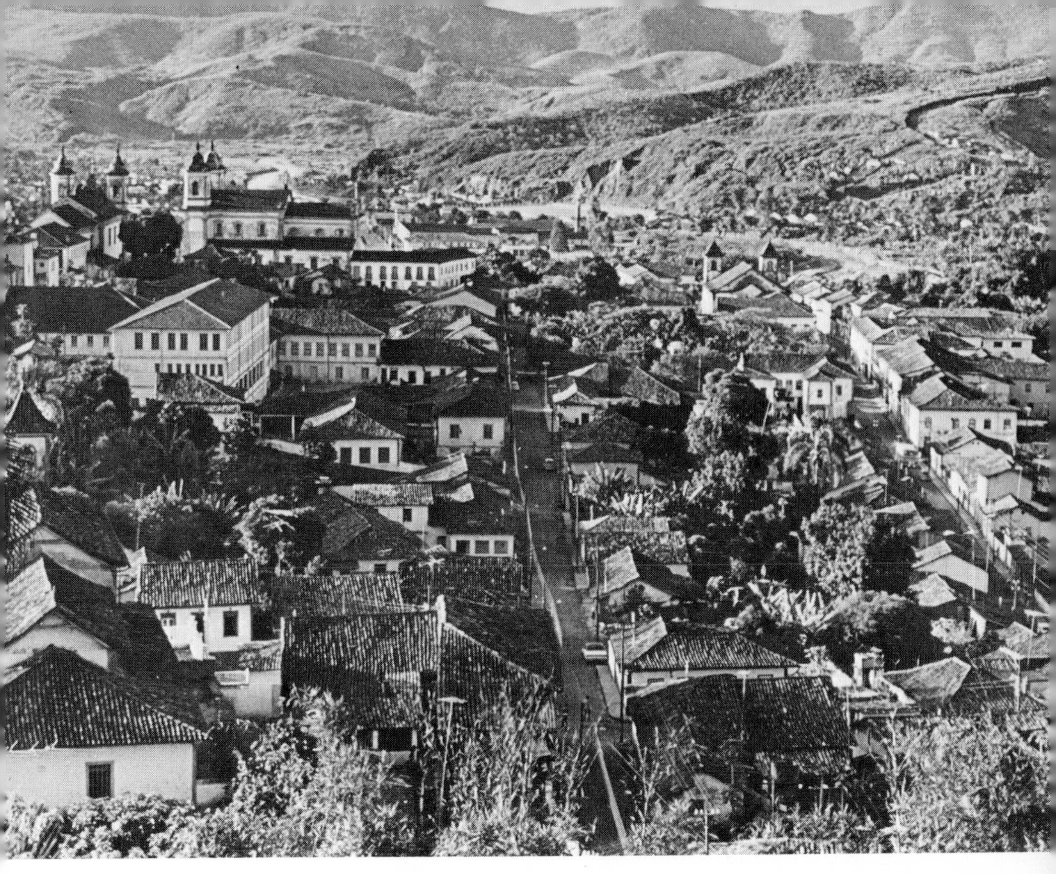

Fig. 3.2 Mariana, Minas Gerais, a baroque town of the gold boom. The hillsides behind are scarred by mining.

detail in these distinctive townscapes. Charles Boxer has identified Vila Rica de Ouro Prêto, the Rich Town of Black Gold, as the quintessence of this peculiar Mineiro civilization, but many other towns in the area – São João del Rei, Caeté, Pitangui, Tiradentes and Congonhas – contain striking elements of this florescence of an authentic Brazilian culture. These townscapes are distinctive not only in broad terms, but also in detail, with the embellishment of the baroque and rococo churches and public buildings by local craftsmen. The most noteworthy of the latter was the *mulatto* Antônio Francisco de Lisboa (Aleijadinho), whose work around the church of Nossa Senhora de Bom Jesus de Matosinhos in Congonhas is a masterpiece of urban landscape creation.

Mineral finds also stimulated similar landscapes, but on a smaller scale, elsewhere in the South-east and Centre-West. The discovery of gold in Bahia, Mato Grosso (1718) and Goiás (1725) provoked similar if short-lived gold rushes, and saw the creation of urban nodes with characteristic urban landscapes, in Cuiabá, Vila Bela (the town of Mato Grosso), Vila Boa (the town of Goiás), Jacobina and Rio das Contas. The discovery of diamonds in the Serro do Frio, in northern Minas Gerais, in the 1720s gave rise to mining towns such as Diamantina, though the exploration of the gems was much more tightly controlled by the Portuguese than was the case in gold mining.

The mining boom was sporadic in time, place and extent. It resulted in the rapid and substantial influx of population into the interior. By 1711 it was estimated that there were 30 000 people in the Minas goldfields. The gold-rush into Goiás and Mato Grosso pushed the frontier of the settlement in the Centre-West well beyond the line of Tordesillas. The profound shift in the economic focus of the colony, from the canefields of the North-east to the goldfields of the South-east resulted in the transfer of the capital in 1763 from Salvador to Rio de Janeiro, which had become the focus of the movement of migrants, supplies and gold between Minas Gerais and Portugal.

The ephemeral nature of the mining economy resulted in the stagnation of the mining towns as the gold was exhausted, but favoured the survival of these gems of colonial splendour, as museum cities little changed by later events, so that they persist to the present with little internal change or peripheral accretion. At the height of the mining boom demand for food supplies had resulted in some settlement and cultivation on the routes from Rio de Janeiro and along the São Francisco valley route from the North-east. The decay of mining saw some change in the activities of the towns, and they became centres of diffusion of population into pastoral activities in Minas Gerais.

The late colonial landscape

With the decline of mining the economy of Brazil in general stagnated somewhat in the latter half of the eighteenth century, though there were a few exceptions, again associated with boom products. Rising world demand created a market for cotton, and the territory of Maranhão became a major exporter. Previously a poor and little developed area it became, assisted by a cotton monopoly granted to the Cia. Geral do Comércio do Grão Pará e do Maranhão in 1756, a wealthy and prosperous state. The company provided credit, slaves and equipment for cotton growers and sustained a boom into the nineteenth century. In its preference for drier conditions cotton was grown inland in the North-east, away from the cane areas, in Maranhão, Ceará and Paraíba, but like cane was produced mainly on large estates.

Tobacco also became a crop of some significance, though the areas producing for export were limited, in Bahia, Sergipe and Minas Gerais. Tobacco was also distinctive in that it required more careful cultivation than cane and cotton; it needed less preparation; and was therefore often associated with smaller scale production and smaller farm units.

The Lisbon government attempted to stimulate the Brazilian economy in this period by improving the production and processing of established crops, particularly sugar, and by initiating and expanding the output of others, such as indigo and rice. Although such initiations gave some impetus to the economy, they did not significantly change its basic pattern.

Other European lands

Prior to 1800 the development of Brazil was almost entirely in Portuguese hands. Interest in the dyewood trade by other European powers provoked the creation of the captaincies in 1532. Forays around the mouth of the Amazon by the British, Dutch and French were the stimulus to the establishment of Belém and Portuguese penetration into the river.

The French and Dutch were also responsible for somewhat more substantial developments. After probing along the coast the French established a settlement in Guanabara Bay in 1555, the nucleus of La France Antarctique. They were largely confined to an island in the bay, and were finally expelled in 1567. They left no significant legacy, but the Portuguese confirmed their claim to the area and site with the foundation of the city of São Sebastião do Rio de Janeiro. The French persisted in their interest in Brazil, and occupied lands further north, particularly around São Luis de Maranhão, between 1612 and 1615. On their expulsion they again left little tangible evidence of their occupation in the landscape.

The Dutch occupation of lands in the North-east between 1630 and 1654, motivated by a desire to control the sugar industry, was of much greater significance. Their attempts to develop the sugar economy were disrupted by guerilla attacks, to the general detriment of the plantations during this period. Their attempts to introduce Dutch colonists had limited success and the principal imprint left was in the remodelling and expansion of Recife by Johan Maurits of Nassau, who was governor of Netherlands-Brazil between 1637 and 1644. The city's watergirt site provided the Dutch with a familiar environment. In addition to constructing new streets and bridges for the existing town, they laid out a new settlement, Mauritsstad, on an adjacent island. The layout transferred contemporary European urban forms to Brazil, with a regular layout, parks and palaces. Maurits was also responsible for organizing scientific surveys of the Dutch territories and for sponsoring some of the earliest landscape paintings of Brazil.

The urban scene

Society, economy and landscape in colonial Brazil were essentially rural. Economic activity was concentrated in the cane and other croplands, the grazing lands and the mining areas. The foci of these activities were the *engenhos*, *fazendas* and mining camps. Landowners provided the social élite and the politically powerful in Brazil, though ultimate political power resided in Lisbon. In consequence of these influences, towns played a lesser role in colonial Brazil. At the time of independence only 12 settlements had been given the status of *cidade* (city) and 213 that of *vila* (town) (Map 5).

Most early towns were located on the coast, the point of contact and trade, between the rural areas of production and metropolitan Portugal. Their function was essentially that of entrepots. Of the towns established before 1600 all, except São Paulo, were on the coast. Over the next century urban development took place mainly along the coast from these initial nuclei. Only in the eighteenth century was there more significant urban development inland, in the mining areas of Minas Gerais, Goiás, Mato Grosso and Bahia, along the Amazon, and to a lesser degree in the north-eastern *sertão*.

Of the 12 settlements with city status in 1822, five were in the North-east (Salvador, João Pessoa, São Luis, Olinda and Oeiras), four in the South-east (Rio de Janeiro, Cabo Frio, São Paulo and Mariana), with Cuiabá and Goiás in the Centre-West and Belém in Amazonia. Early urban nuclei were good port sites, defensive points and missions. After the first phase of colonial contact, as the economy developed, urban service centres within the various areas of activity emerged, at *fazendas,* halts on cattle trails, mining camps and agricultural colonies. The origin of such settlements is betrayed in their place names – Fortaleza (fortress), Ouro Branco (white gold), Minas Novas (new mines), Missão Velha (old mission), Currais Novos (new corrals) and Pouso Alto (high resting place). In many cases, in areas with dispersed populations, the establishment of a chapel served as a focus for the agglomeration of basic service functions, operating on Sundays and religious festivals. Such nucleations had few residents, and consisted of simple dwellings, a small chapel and shops and often only a single street.

The form of Portuguese towns in Brazil is often compared with those of Spanish America, in which the carefully planned regular layout of the latter is contrasted with the picturesque confusion of the Brazilian towns. One source suggests that city streets in Brazil wound their way through the accidents of topography, and that urbanism was marked by tropical abandon, with the towns being not the product of premeditated planning, but conforming to the framework of nature, and merging with the landscape. Early settlements, such as those of Salvador, Olinda and Rio de Janeiro were on defensible hilltop sites, and descriptions of them emphasize the dominating hilltop locations of churches, convents and public buildings, surrounded by small winding streets and a disordered mass of simple dwellings. Such towns have been described as typically Portuguese, medieval in their haphazard growth and lack of planning, and resembling metropolitan Lisbon. Recent work (Delson 1979) has suggested that in some areas of Brazil, however, town foundation was a more deliberate facet of Portuguese colonial policy, and that some of these towns were similar in layout to the geometrical Renaissance forms of Spanish American towns, with attempts to predetermine street layout, the location of principal buildings and use of particular building materials.

At the end of the eighteenth century, as the period of Portuguese colonial rule drew to an end, the territory of Brazil had been broadly defined, much of the land had been explored and in some areas significant occupation and settlement had taken place. Overall, though, the human impact on the natural landscape was limited. Much of the exploration had left few permanent marks. In some areas – the Amazon forest, and the pastoral lands of the *sertão* and the far south – exploitation was extensive in character and limited in im-

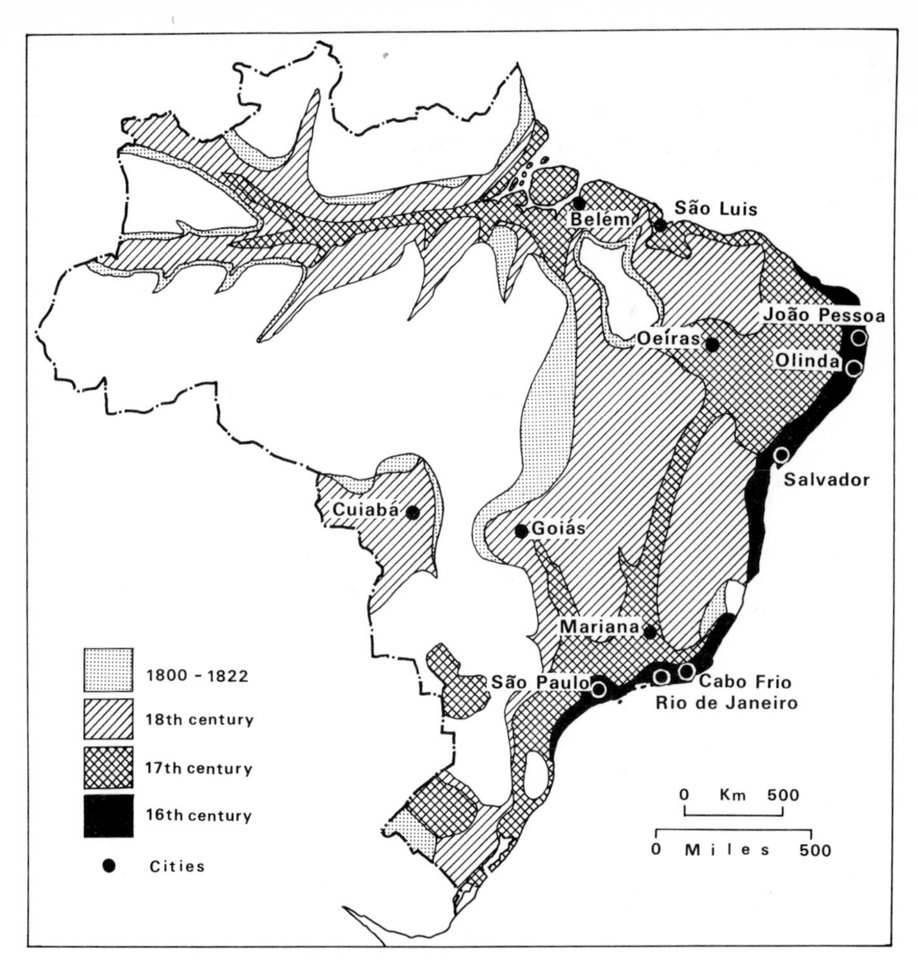

Map 5 Brazil: the advance of settlement during the colonial period.

pact, merely exploiting the natural environment. Substantial settlement, except in the mining areas, remained close to the coast. Only in the coastal lands and mining zones had distinctive man-made landscapes – of cultivation, rural settlement and towns – begun to emerge. Outside these areas the spaces remaining to be settled were immense. The period of Portuguese colonial rule in Brazil was an important one in determining the extent of the territory and the character of its development, but its significance lay perhaps more in shadow than substance, providing the groundwork for later more comprehensive and profound transformation of the landscape.

4

The African landscape

Africans made a major but essentially involuntary contribution to the shaping of the Brazilian landscape. Between the mid-sixteenth century and 1888 the African as slave was an essential instrument in the making of the Portuguese colonial landscape. Once the Portuguese had decided to exploit the abundant natural resources of their new territory to supply European markets, a means to carry out that exploitation had to be found. The population of Portugal was small and uninterested in manual labour in the tropics. The Amerindians were also few in number, had been further reduced by early colonial contact and were reluctant to provide labour for the Portuguese. In consequence the latter turned to an alternative labour source, a black population enslaved in Africa and transported to Brazil.

The precise numbers of slaves imported is uncertain. Estimates range from 3 million to 18 million, but the most careful estimates suggest about 3 600 000, of whom 80 per cent were brought between 1700 and 1870. They came from various parts of Africa, but particularly the Guinea Coast, Angola and Mozambique. They were derived from West African and Bantu racial groups, a variety of tribes, and from diverse cultural and economic traditions. In the course of shipment to Brazil, sale and slavery, these various groups and traditions were intermixed, erasing distinctive inheritances and creating a more uniform Afro-Brazilian culture.

The independent contribution of blacks to the Brazilian landscape has not been in keeping with their numbers, either before or since emancipation. Both Portuguese and Africans found themselves in a new land, but while the Portuguese were free to adjust to this new ecological environment and to shape it in their own interests, the Africans, torn from their homelands and brought to Brazil in slavery, were forced to adjust as economic and social inferiors. As slaves they were merely agents of change in an economic pattern moulded by the dominant society and culture. The institution of slavery provided the framework within which the African lived. He was forced to adopt new language and culture, such that much of his traditional society was shattered and his own cultural heritage submerged. His role was to labour, providing the common denominator in the task of building and shaping the colonial Brazilian landscape. Without slaves the development of the colonial economy and landscape would have been impossible, but the blacks were not free agents in the transformation of the landscape; the landscapes they created were at the behest of and in the interests of Portuguese landowners and European markets.

The principal points of entry for slaves were Rio de Janeiro, Salvador and Recife but their distribution was intimately linked to the evolution and pattern of the colonial and early post-colonial economic cycles. It was black labour which cleared the virgin tropical forest, planted, harvested and processed crops, provided labour in the mineral workings, and artisan skills and domestic service in the towns. The distribution of slaves and their contribution to landscape change were most potent therefore in the canefields of the coastal strip of the North-east and Rio de Janeiro, the tobacco and cacao lands of Bahia, the mining areas of Minas Gerais, Goiás and Mato Grosso, the early coffee *fazendas* in Rio de Janeiro and São Paulo, and in the coastal cities.

The greatest impact of blacks on the Brazilian landscape was probably in the coastlands of the North-east, where the combination of cane monoculture, large landholdings and slave labour created landscapes which persist to the present. It has been suggested that this combination of land and slaves made possible the transformation of Brazil from a possession of limited utility to a profitable agricultural colony. The slaves were involved in clearance of the forest, cultivation of the cane and its processing, on the integrated sugar plantations. The numbers of slaves involved varied. A plantation might employ as many as 1400 slaves, but 60 to 80 appears to have been more common. The principal cane landscapes were, and remain, in the coastlands from Paraíba to Sergipe, the Recôncavo of Bahia and in the Baixada and Paraíba valley of Rio de Janeiro.

The discovery of gold in Minas Gerais generated a new activity which made extensive use of slave labour. Gold working was undertaken both by individual prospectors and by men controlling small groups of slaves, generally less than a dozen. Some mining techniques appear to have been derived from West Africa, for some slaves had a greater knowledge of mining than did the Portuguese, and were highly prized. In general the simplicity of the techniques and the mobility of the mining zone left limited direct impact on the landscape.

The mining boom and its demand for slaves was succeeded by the coffee cycle, developing in Rio de Janeiro, southern Minas Gerais and São Paulo. As in the case of sugar, early coffee production combined large landholdings, monoculture and slavery, and again slaves were the agents of deforestation and cultivation. Slaves in Brazil were a mobile resource, transportable to areas where they were to be used, either direct from Africa, or from a declining region to a developing one. This mobility was particularly significant in the case of coffee, for the effective end of the slave trade in the 1850s came just as the coffee boom gathered momentum, and slave labour was crucial in the creation and maintenance of the coffee economy and landscape. A contemporary comment had it that 'Brazil is coffee and coffee is the negro'. In consequence slaves were moved from the declining or stagnant areas of the cane and gold fields to the new frontier of the coffee lands. There was a marked shift in the distribution of the slave population to Rio de Janeiro, southern Minas Gerais and São Paulo, such that in 1884, shortly before emancipation, almost 60 per cent of the remaining enslaved population was in these three provinces.

The ending of slavery in Brazil was a slow process. The slave trade was banned in 1831, but did not effectively cease until 1852. In 1871 children born of slaves were declared free and in 1885 slaves over 60 years of age, with freedom for all slaves being secured in 1888.

The independent impact of the African on the Brazilian landscape during the first 350 years of the country's existence was limited. During the period of slavery some sought to escape its burdens by suicide, rebellion, purchasing their freedom or running away. Escapees did create a more positive, if temporary, element in the colonial landscape, for runaway slaves sometimes banded together to form African communities. These were mainly small, consisting of between five and 20 people, but others, for example in Minas Gerais, had several hundred inhabitants, and the most famous, Palmares in Alagoas, contained up to 11 000 people. Most of these settlements, known as *mocambos* and *quilombos*, were shortlived, being destroyed by the Portuguese, but Palmares survived for most of the seventeenth century, despite several efforts to subdue it. It has been suggested that the *quilombos* came closest to recreating African society in the new environment of Brazil. Although the larger communities do appear to have recreated African social structures, their life-style, from various descriptions, appears to have blended African practices with borrowings from both Amerindians and Europeans. *Quilombo* dwellers seem to have derived the use of hammocks and the processing of manioc from the Indians, and in some cases practised shifting cultivation of manioc, yams, rice and other crops. Although they sought isolation from the Europeans, there was also some raiding and trading with plantations.

Location of the *quilombos* was, of necessity, defensive. Most chose inhospitable and defensible sites distant from established settlements, though some maintained contact with the Portuguese. *Quilombos* around Salvador and Rio de Janeiro for example were at sites which are now suburbs of those cities. The form of the *quilombos* seems to have varied from a simple cluster of huts to well organised territories containing several communities. One of the Palmares settlements consisted of over 200 buildings, including church, smithies and meeting hall. Others had a rectilinear pattern which may have derived from the form of the plantation slave quarters rather than any African origin. They were usually well fortified.

Records of the *quilombos* are scanty, mainly written by their Portuguese destroyers. With no oral or documentary record deriving from their inhabitants, and because they were sacked by the Portuguese, little evidence of their existence survives. The principal legacy is in the survival of Quilombo as a place and topographic name. In Minas Gerais alone more than 20 settlements retain the name, along with the Serra and Morro do Quilombo.

Some slaves secured their freedom by purchase or manumission, and it is estimated that by the end of the eighteenth century freedmen constituted possibly one-fifth of the coloured population. However, few social and economic opportunities were available to the free coloureds, so that their role in landscape change was limited. The majority were involved in retailing or artisan work, as wage employees in agriculture or mining, or as small farmers. Others drifted into casual labour or impoverishment.

During the colonial period the African made a major contribution to the human landscape. Despite the rigours of the Middle Passage and of slavery, in 1817 blacks contributed 1.9 of an estimated population of 3.8 million people. Whites provided 1 million and a further 0.5 million were *mulattoes*. The latter represent a further aspect of the African contribution to the human landscape for, as the product of miscegenation between black and white, they came to constitute a significant element, of mixed blood, in the population. The ratio of black to white was even higher in some areas, such as the cane and gold fields, and in the towns. In 1775 two-thirds of the population of Salvador was black or *mulatto*, and the population of Rio de Janeiro in the early nineteenth century was estimated to be of similar proportions.

At emancipation over 700 000 slaves were given their freedom, but since 1888, with higher mortality rates than other segments of the population, the influx of European immigrants and miscegenation, the proportion of coloured people in Brazilian society has tended to decrease. At the time of Brazil's first census, in 1872, 63 per cent of the population were recorded as black or brown; by 1950, the last occasion on which questions on colour were asked in the census, the proportion had fallen to 37 per cent.

On emancipation many rural slaves had left the plantations for the towns, but found few opportunities for employment, given their lack of education and skills, and competition from European immigrants. Some returned to the plantation areas where, because they had no land and were unable to acquire new skills, they were forced back into commercial agriculture as wage labourers or sharecroppers. Even here they faced competition from European labour, especially in São Paulo. In consequence many blacks and *mulattoes* found themselves with only marginal roles in the rural economy, and renewed exodus to the cities did little to improve their status. Lacking land, capital, skill and education many coloureds became, and remain, trapped in a culture of poverty. In 1969 blacks and *mulattoes* constituted about one-third of the population of Rio de Janeiro, but probably two-thirds of the *favela* population. Emancipation did little to improve the economic, social, cultural or political position of the Brazilian black, and in consequence the contribution of his heirs to landscape change has remained limited, and concentrated in the negative landscapes of marginality, poverty and the rural and urban slum.

African labour was responsible for the transformation of much of coastal Brazil from a natural to a man-made landscape, but the slave had no choice in the form of landscape which was created. Given the nature of the institution, there are few indications of the African slaves' perception of the Brazilian landscape, either in its pristine or in its transformed state. Even as a free agent over the past century, the bulk of the population of African origin has exerted little substantial influence on the evolving landscape. Continuing deprivation has meant that in the articulation of landscape taste and in the creation of landscape the role of the man of colour has been restricted. The contribution has been essentially indirect, as a tool of the change process, as a significant contributor to the human landscape of population mix, and in the infusion of African elements into Brazilian life-style. There is a significant African contribution to the cultural landscape, in survivals of dress, cuisine, music, dance and folklore. Samba, capoeira and berimbau are contributions to music and dance, the costume of the Bahiana is an African legacy, and there are important contributions to cuisine, particularly in the North-east. The survival of African religious cults and their blending with Roman Catholicism is also significant. The contribution of a number of these elements – dress, dance, music and religion – has a particular and major expression in carnival.

African traditions have also survived in the arts, such as woodcarving and painting. Some of this legacy is associated with particular artists, notably in the colonial baroque of the North-east and Minas Gerais. One of the most distinctive legacies is that of the crippled *mulatto* Aleijadinho. He was probably Brazil's first great artist in architecture and sculpture, and the focus of a school of colonial art which finds its greatest expression in the baroque churches and townscapes of the eighteenth century mining towns of Minas Gerais. In Bahia the mulatto Francisco Chagas provided a similar legacy, while in Rio de Janeiro, Valentim Fonseca e Silva created not only some of the religious architecture, but also some of the public artifacts in the city's parks and open spaces.

There is also an African contribution to the Portuguese language, which has some survival in place names. These include not only those related to *quilombos* but also for example Caxambu (drum), Macaia (leaves) and Marimbondo (wasp).

These legacies aside, however, the population of African origin has not made a positive contribution to the Brazilian landscape commensurate with its numerical size. For over 300 years the contribution was largely involuntary, and despite a century as a free agent, social and economic deprivation have muted the potential impact. In the twentieth century the proportion of blacks in the population has fallen, and also shown an absolute decrease. At the last date for which there was comprehensive evidence, 1950, the black population was most significant in those areas where slavery was most important – Bahia, Rio de Janeiro, the North-east and Minas Gerais. In absolute terms the ranking was slightly different, with Minas Gerais, Bahia, São Paulo and Rio de Janeiro containing the major concentrations, with some evidence of an urbanward shift. These four states (including the former Federal District of Rio de Janeiro) contained over 60 per cent of the black population and 40 per cent of the brown population in 1950. For the majority of this population, its principal alternatives are in working someone else's land in the countryside or in migrating to the limited opportunities of the cities.

Part III

5

The neo-colonial landscape

In the first century of Brazilian independence there were two elements in the evolution of the landscape, of continuity and change. The landscapes of continuity were those of the survival of colonial activities – the persistence of gathering activities in Amazonia, of extensive pastoralism and of large-scale cash cropping of sugar cane and cotton. Into this same pattern of continuity fall landscapes created by new export products, geared to external markets and characterized by boom and bust conditions. Two products, coffee and rubber, perhaps exemplify most clearly the essential character and landscape-creating role of Brazil's economic cycles. Such boom commodities created landscapes which were distinct in form and detail from those of cane, cotton and cattle, but which were similar in character and structure.

Their role as export products however points to the other element in the nineteenth century landscape, that of change. Although Brazil secured political independence from Portugal in 1822 she did not secure total independence from Europe for other, non-Iberian, countries exerted considerable influence on the shaping of the post-colonial landscape. Rising demand for tropical produce and the search for markets for products of the Industrial Revolution drew Brazil into new trading links, with consequences for the development of the economy and its spatial expression. In part this simply perpetuated the landscapes of continuity, in creating new areas of boom exploitation, but it also led to the introduction of new innovations from Europe and North America, which had both direct and indirect impact upon the landscape.

Brazil was not merely passive in this role. Many Brazilian politicians saw the country's right and proper place in the world economy as a supplier of raw materials, to be exchanged for imported manufactures. Moreover the élite sought to ape many of the changes taking place in Europe, not only in the economy, but in society and the arts. If close Portuguese control of Brazilian development was shaken off, it was not immediately superseded by indigenous and autonomous actions, for the shaping of the landscape and of landscape tastes in the nineteenth century were profoundly influenced by external factors.

The late colonial legacy

The first two decades of the nineteenth century were of crucial significance for the evolution of the post-colonial landscape, for they saw the initiation of several trends, sometimes contradictory, which were to have lasting consequences. The flight of the Portuguese court from Lisbon to Rio de Janeiro in 1808, to escape the Napoleonic invasion of Portugal, was the catalyst for many of these changes. The transfer of the court was a unique event in European colonialism, and perhaps the most significant single event in Brazilian history. For 300 years Brazil had been closely controlled by Portugal. Development was by and in the interests of Portugal. All major decision-making had taken place in Lisbon. The diffusion of ideas was inhibited by the absence of universities and printing presses. The landscape which existed in 1808, where it had been modified by man, was essentially a Portuguese creation. The arrival of the court loosened colonial control and set in train a series of changes which had impacts at varying spatial scales. It initiated a period of intensive change in the society, economy and culture of Brazil.

The arrival of the King together with a court variously estimated as containing between 8000 and 15 000 people had an immediate impact on the backward and essentially provincial city of Rio de Janeiro. The sophisticated manners and tastes of the metropolitan court had a substantial demonstration effect upon the colonial population. Considerable urban improvement took place, with the paving of streets, careful regulation of the layout of new streets and squares, and the building of residences for members of the court. Rio de Janeiro became not only the functioning capital of Brazil but of the Portuguese empire. Provision for imperial administration meant new public buildings and the growth of a bureaucracy. Between 1800 and 1821, when the court returned to Lisbon, the city's population had grown from 40 000 to 110 000. Other urban improvements included the opening of theatres, libraries, colleges and a botanical garden. The city began to spread away from its colonial core, reclaiming marshland and seashore, and creating affluent suburbs along Guanabara Bay, in Laranjeiras and Botafogo.

The city became a focus on which converged men, capital and initiative. Prosperous landowners began to establish town houses in order to be near the court. Control of the nation became more firmly centralized in Rio de Janeiro and a clearer dichotomy between 'city' and 'country' and between 'capital' and 'interior' began to emerge. The court and the capital began to dictate fashions and attitudes to the rural interior.

The King also took steps to foster the advance of the colony. Economic and cultural reforms relaxed old colonial controls. Encouragement was given to advances in agriculture, industry, transport and commerce. Increase in the planting of cotton was fostered, support was given to the incipient coffee industry and the planting of wheat in the southern provinces was begun. In 1808 the ban on manufacturing activity in Brazil was lifted, with the declared objective of 'increasing national wealth, improving the value of agricultural production, and creating employment'. This allowed the growth of a textile industry, an iron industry flourished briefly, and steam engines began to be used, particularly in the sugar mills of the North-east. Transport links to the dispersed settlement nuclei were improved. Colleges and libraries were established and the country's first printing press permitted. In 1815 Brazil was elevated to become part of the 'United Kingdom of Portugal, the Algarves and Brazil', this elevation acknowledging 'the copiousness and variety of the precious elements of wealth' it contained.

Between 1808 and 1814 the King enacted a series of measures which had profound effects on the external relations of Brazil and exposed the country to foreign influences. Trade was permitted with all friendly countries and not just Portugal. Trade goods could be carried in foreign ships. Foreigners could obtain land grants and establish factories. Such measures effectively ended three centuries of Portuguese mercantilism and released Brazil into the emerging pattern of European-dominated free trade.

These concessions encouraged foreigners to come to Brazil, as merchants seeking trade, as scientists seeking to explore and catalogue the richness of the tropical environment, as artists to record this exotic land and as craftsmen to sustain and stimulate the European tastes of the court. Foreign scientists and technologists, 'English mechanics and shipbuilders, Swedish iron workers, German engineers, French artists and manufacturers' were invited to Brazil to introduce the innovations of industrializing Europe. Foreign travellers, scientists and naturalists left a substantial record of observations of the Brazil within which they found themselves.

The court, educational improvements and foreign visitors brought greater awareness of European progress and achievement, which Brazil sought to emulate. Cultural life and the cultural landscape were particularly subject to European influences. Of special significance was the arrival of a French artistic mission in 1816 to establish an Academy of Fine Arts. The mission included architects, sculptors, painters and craftsmen. They introduced what became effectively an official art, and established neo-classicism as the dominant architectural style. The architect Grandjean de Montigny was a decisive influence. Not only was he the architect of official buildings and private houses, but he was also a town planner and landscape painter, and thus very influential in shaping urban landscapes and landscape tastes. He and his disciples were responsible for many major public buildings – palaces, theatres, hospitals, the custom house and Academy of Fine Arts in Rio, as well as buildings in Recife, Belém and other cities between 1816 and 1870s. Their style was copied elsewhere in town houses and coffee fazendas. In addition to this stylistic dependence, limited industrial development made Brazil depend on imported building materials from Europe, such as construction and decorative ironwork, cement, marble and roofing materials.

Such trends of course exemplified a profound dichotomy, between the tastes of officialdom and the urban élite on the one hand, and the persistence of much simpler styles and aspirations in the countryside. The immediate impact of these urban-based changes was limited in the rural areas. While the rural masters might adopt new fashions, the life-style of the bulk of the rural free and slave populations was scarcely touched, though new components were introduced.

Settlement by foreigners was encouraged. The King was anxious to introduce farmers from northern Europe who, it was hoped, would bring more advanced agricultural techniques. The first organized foreign colony was established at Nova Fribourgo, in the mountains behind Rio de Janeiro, in 1819 when some 1700 Swiss Catholic immigrants were settled. This pioneer immigration was followed by other Swiss and German groups to colonies in Rio de Janeiro and the southern provinces during the 1820s.

In 1821 the court returned to Lisbon, but its 13 years of exile had both immediate and long-term consequences. Brazil declared its independence in September 1822. However, though it had claimed political independence from Portugal, the period of transition in the early nineteenth century had enmeshed Brazil firmly into economic, social and cultural dependence on Europe, which was to have profound influences on the nature and pattern of development. Independence moreover did not provide a sudden break with earlier traditions. The colonial style economy was not easily thrown off. The opening of the ports had merely widened the market for tropical products previously shipped to Lisbon. Brazil remained heavily dependent on the sale of a few primary products to limited markets in Europe. In the 1820s sugar and coffee provided over half of exports, which also included cotton, hides, indigo, cocoa, wood, gold and gems. In return Brazil imported European iron, metal goods, textiles, clothing, pottery and other manufactures. The brief flurry of industrialization was shortlived, for the British, in return for their role in safeguarding the court's flight to Brazil, secured favourable tariff concessions which exposed infant industries to the full force of competition from British industrialization, until 1844 when stronger tariffs were imposed. The British were also soon active in seeking to end the slave trade on which much of Brazil's economic activity depended.

Freedom from Portugal was thus replaced by European, and particularly British, economic influences. Portuguese colonialism was replaced by European neo-colonialism. Early progress in newly independent Brazil was thus affected as much by external influences as by internal actions. External demands were instrumental in perpetuating the role of economic cycles, by stimulating the production of new export commodities, which affected new areas of the national territory and created distinctive landscapes.

Landscapes of coffee

Coffee is one of the most crucial elements in the transformation of the Brazilian landscape. Its impact was profound, both in its direct rôle in the creation of the landscapes of coffee cultivation, and in its indirect effects in generating other social and economic changes which had expression in the landscape. It resulted in the conversion of extensive natural landscapes in South-east Brazil into man-made landscapes of cultivation. It generated population, rural settlements, towns, transport lines and factories. It shifted firmly the economic and demographic focus of the country from the North-east to the South-east. For much of the first century of independence it was possible to claim that 'Brazil is coffee'. It dominated not only the economic structure but also society and politics. From 1830 to 1964 coffee was the principal export, reaching its apogee in 1924 when it provided three quarters of export earnings. Coffee was intimately linked to the history and geography of Brazil, from independence until well into the twentieth century and has left an indelible mark upon the landscape.

The crop was introduced into Amazonia in 1727 and over the next 40 years spread slowly, grown on a small scale for local consumption. By the 1770s it was being cultivated around Rio de Janeiro, and it was from there that the coffee 'boom' began. This was a period when the earlier mineral boom in Minas Gerais was in decline and markets for coffee were expanding in the United States. From its initial focus in the hills and lowlands around Rio de Janeiro, coffee spread over the Serra do Mar and into the Paraíba valley. It was from this area that coffee first became a significant Brazilian export and Brazil an important coffee supplier on the world market.

Development in the valley took the form of the clearance of the rich forest cover by the axe and fire, and the planting of the coffee bushes. It was in the Paraíba that the destruction often associated with the spread of coffee was most acute. The bushes were planted in rows up the valley slopes for greater ease of access for cultivation, weeding and harvesting, but such a practice also fostered soil erosion. In addition to misuse of the hillsides, other aspects of cultivation were careless. The bushes began to yield after three years, and continued to do so for 10 to 20 years. With care they might yield for up to 40 years. Without care yields began to decline sooner and, with the loss of soil fertility, there was little incentive to replant. Instead the abundant virgin forest available encouraged mobility, so coffee shifted north into Minas Gerais and Espírito Santo, west along the Paraíba and over the Serra da Mantiqueira and on to the plateaux of São Paulo, where it found ideal conditions for its growth and expansion.

The landscape of coffee was in essence nomadic, established on virgin lands after the destruction of their tree cover, depleting the soil, and moving inexorably onwards, until finally checked by its climatic limits. The duration of cultivation depended on the fertility of the soils, topographic conditions and climate. The influence of man once the bushes were established was negligible, for few efforts were made to improve cultivation techniques; as yields declined the coffee frontier moved on. Sustained by the advance of the railway and availability of labour, forests were cleared, bushes planted, rural settlements appeared and towns sprang up. Much of the landscape of southern Minas Gerais, Rio de Janeiro and of São Paulo was shaped by the restless cycle of transient coffee.

Fig. 5.1 The former coffee lands of the Paraíba valley, Rio de Janeiro. Small areas of woodland remain on the hills, but the coffee plantations have become pastureland, and the *casa grande* the centre of a cattle farm.

In the Paraíba the essential features were, as in the sugar cycle of the North-east, large land holdings, monoculture and the use of slave labour. On the coffee *fazenda* the natural forest was replaced by a forest of coffee, which surrounded the small nucleation of dwellings, processing plants and ancillary buildings. The patterns created were essentially those of uniformity, in the patterns of plantation layout, the methods of clearance and cultivation, the seasonal rhythm of the farm year and the dwelling houses of the *fazendeiros*. Such dwellings were initially simple buildings of wattle and daub, but as coffee prospered and generated both wealth and a rural aristocracy, houses became more substantial and pretentious. These *sobrados* became larger and more ornate. European architects and craftsmen were employed in their design, and their fittings were often European in origin or inspiration. These lavish houses contrasted with the rude dwellings of the slave labour force.

The coffee beans were moved by mule train over the Serra do Mar to Rio de Janeiro and a series of small ports on coves and bays to the west of the capital. Ports such as Parati, Ubatuba, Caraguatuba and São Sebãstiao shared the prosperity of the Paraíba but as this declined and the locomotive replaced

Fig. 5.2 A former coffee port to the west of Rio de Janeiro. Formerly served by mule trains bringing coffee for export, such towns declined when the railways penetrated the coffee lands.

the mule, they were cut off from their hinterland, stagnated and remained fossilized for a century, until the coastal Santos – Rio de Janeiro highway reawakened them as attractions for tourists and second-home owners from São Paulo and Rio de Janeiro.

The building of railways into the Paraíba in the 1870s focused the coffee boom more firmly on the cities of Rio de Janeiro and São Paulo. However, the Rio de Janeiro section of the valley was already in decline, as the virgin forests were used up and soil fertility diminished. In addition the abolition of slavery deprived the Paraíba *fazendeiros* of their cheap labour source, and they were less able to attract European immigrant labour. Left behind in the Paraíba were the cultural landscapes of the passing of the coffee bushes, the holes and grooves of erosion scarring the hillsides, the substantial mansions and the remnants of coffee-drying floors and other buildings.

Once over the Serra da Mantiqueira and on to the *planalto* of São Paulo coffee found large areas of virgin land and fertile soil, ideally suited to its cultivation and to an increase in the cultivated area. In its initial phase in São Paulo coffee moved into lands which had previously been settled and which were partly in cultivation, so that here its impact was to modify an existing human landscape, rather than creating an entirely new one by replacing the natural landscape. Beyond this area, however, the undulating plateau, which was less accidented than the Paraíba valley, less prone to erosion and more suited to the development of a railnet, offered substantial scope for the rapid advance of a new frontier of coffee. The construction of the Santos – São Paulo railway over the obstacle of the Serra do Mar in 1867 and the modernization of the port of Santos provided an outlet channel for coffee, and other railways permitted the coffee frontier to be pushed deep into the interior. Campinas was the first importance focus of the coffee boom in São Paulo in the period 1860–85 but the advance of the Paulista, Mogiana and Sorocabana railways in the 1860s and 1870s provided axes of advance in the symbiotic relationship between coffee and the railway. Recognition of the fertility of the *terra roxa* soils made Ribeirão Prêto a new focus of the industry, but even on these soils careless cultivation led to soil depletion so that coffee moved on to the poorer soils of western São Paulo, reaching its maximum extent by 1930. Subsequently over-production, the Great Depression and the loss of markets in the Second World War saw a decline in the area cultivated, and also substitution of São Paulo by Paraná as the location of the coffee frontier.

Crucial factors in the spread of coffee were suitable environmental conditions of climate, topography and soil. Climatic checks are excessive heat and humidity, and the risk of frost, which set limits to its altitudinal range and to its latitudinal spread north and south. The principal zone of cultivation in São Paulo was between 500 and 800 m. The main producing states have been São Paulo, Rio de Janeiro, Paraná, Minas Gerais and Espírito Santo, with some small areas, generally at higher altitude, in the North-east. Certain soils, particularly the *massape* in Rio de Janeiro and the *terra roxa* in São Paulo and Paraná, have been most sought after because of their high fertility, but the spread of coffee was almost irrespective of soil. The principal consequence of the use of poorer soils was a more rapid decline in soil fertility and a consequent greater rapidity in the advance of the frontier.

The pattern of land ownership and land use on the Paulista frontier differed little from that of the Paraíba valley, with large holdings dominated by the cultivation of coffee. A major element of distinction though was the replacement of African slaves by free European immigrant labourers. These '*colonos*', imported from Italy, Spain, Portugal and later Japan, cleared a plot of the *fazenda's* virgin forest, planted coffee bushes and cared for them. In return they usually received a wage and the right to cultivate food crops such as maize, beans and rice between the coffee bushes. They were often migratory, moving on when the bushes matured, to the latest frontier, often aspiring to become small landowners in their own right. Over a longer period, as coffee yields declined, the *fazendeiros* and the coffee bushes also moved on.

The pattern of settlement on the *fazenda paulista* was one of nucleation, often adjacent to a stream to provide drinking water and power. The settlement consisted of the house of the *fazendeiro*, offices and the simple houses of the *colonos*, successors to the slave *senzalas*, and often in the form of a row or rows of dwellings. Buildings necessary for the cleaning, drying, husking and storing of the coffee beans formed part of this cluster. This hamlet was surrounded by the chessboard layout of the plantation and its coffee bushes. Spacing of the bushes varied, but was essentially regular, with an interval of about 3.5 m between bushes being most common, giving a highly regimented layout.

There are two images which have come to be closely associated with the landscapes of coffee, the notions of a 'sea of coffee' and of a 'hollow frontier'. In the case of the former, a view across the hill crests of São Paulo might give a vision of an unbroken ocean of dark green bushes stretching to the horizon. This was, however, something of an illusion, for despite their apparent contempt for nature the *fazendeiros* did not show some appreciation of the sublteties of climate, so that coffee planting was confined to the interfluve crests and upper valley slopes, leaving the valley bottoms to other uses. On the *terra roxa* soils up to 80 per cent of the land might be under coffee, but elsewhere it might be only 20 per cent.

The notion of a hollow frontier is widely held and has been demonstrated, in which the advance of coffee left behind a hollow frontier of depleted and eroded soils and declining population. However, while it can be shown that coffee advanced like a wave across the plateau, and was associated with a parallel swell of settlement, its legacy is less clearcut. Map 6 shows the advance of coffee in a series of stages from its beginnings in the Paraíba valley until 1950. The movement of the frontier west along the Paraíba, northwards into eastern São Paulo, westwards, and then southwards into Paraná is apparent, but the pattern of decline is less obvious. Land remaining in coffee in 1950 included areas which were originally planted before 1886. Even where coffee moved on, it did not leave behind a vacuum of destroyed lands bereft of people. Some former coffee lands were tired and impoverished but they were put to other uses. The abandoned lands of the Paraíba were resettled by cattlemen from Minas Gerais, who used the grasslands left behind to develop pastoral activities to supply the burgeoning urban markets of Rio de Janeiro and São

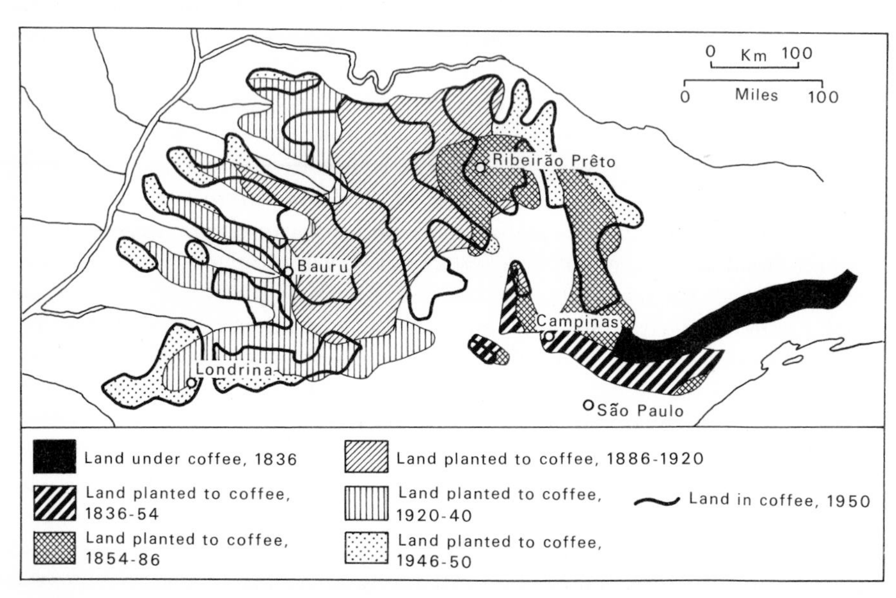

Map 6 South-east Brazil: the spread of coffee.

Paulo. On the Paulista plateau the large coffee *fazendas* were broken up and sold off as small lots, often to former coffee *colonos*. Around the towns these smallholdings became *chacaras*, supplying market garden produce, poultry and eggs. Further away, as rural *sítios*, they became producers of food and cash crops such as maize, beans, manioc, fruit and sugar. The lands left behind by the mobile coffee frontier were not therefore landscapes of devastation, but of alternative agricultural use. They have become poly-cultural farm landscapes and are important contributors to Brazil's agricultural output. The transformation from *fazenda* to smallholding also modified the landscape of rural settlement, as the nucleations associated with coffee cultivation and processing became redundant, and were succeeded by patterns of dispersed settlement on individual holdings. Coffee may have moved on but it left behind, not an empty 'hollow' frontier, but people and land engaged in other activities, and giving a more diverse and stable landscape.

In addition to the consequence of declining yields the coffee boom also, towards the end of the nineteenth century, began to suffer the consequences of production in excess of world demand, by Brazil and foreign competitors. The government sought to maintain prices by keeping Brazilian coffee off the market. While this had some effect in the short term, it encouraged foreign and domestic producers to keep their land under coffee, and it was not until the inter-war period that the government tried to encourage a reduction in output. This resulted in land being taken out of coffee and being converted to other uses, and for production to be derived from more intensive rather than extensive use of land. Between 1960 and 1976 the area under coffee fell by more than half, and the national coffee 'forest' was reduced from 4300 million to 2600 million bushes. Output, subject to climatic vagaries, has shown a less consistent downward trend from 40 million 60 kg sacks in 1960 to 22 million in 1975. Severe frost in 1975 destroyed the crop in Paraná and led to a northwards retreat of coffee cultivation, with the re-establishment of a new, more rational, coffee frontier in older coffee lands in Minas Gerais less at risk from frost.

In addition to its important role in the economy and its impact on the rural landscape, coffee has had other effects on the country which have helped to shape other present-day landscapes. The coffee barons of Rio de Janeiro and São Paulo replaced the sugar plantation owners of the North-east as the major social, political and economic force in Brazil. The government began to act in their interest, for example in the ending of slavery and its substitution by European immigration, and in the sustenance of coffee production in the crises of the late nineteeth and early twentieth centuries.

Coffee was also important in stimulating economic change. More than in any of the previous economic cycles, coffee engendered diversification. The wealth it created provided investment in other agricultural activities, in infrastructure and in industry. Its free labour force provided a market for goods and services, and its associated railnet opened up other resources and provided wider and more accessible markets than had existed previously. It also stimulated urban growth, not only in its major commercial foci of Rio de Janeiro and São Paulo and the port of Santos, but in the expansion of existing towns and the creation of new ones, which sprang up at railheads and junctions, and as regional service centres, as in the cases of Campinas, Ribeirão Prêto, Bauru and Araraquara. The map of the urban geography of western São Paulo still shows clearly the lines of penetration of the railroads.

The coffee landscape was essentially a mobile, dynamic one. The migratory wave of coffee spread across the South-east, clearing the ancient, natural forest and substituting an ephemeral, planted one. As yields declined, the frontier moved forward. In 150 years it had swept from Rio de Janeiro, over most of São Paulo, to its limits in northern Paraná.

Its influence was profound and dynamic. It was responsible for extending the frontier of settlement and for the peopling of large areas of territory. Though coffee passed on, the settlement it generated remained, and new, more stable, activities emerged. Coffee represented a 'civilization' in Brazil; it was responsible for an important phase in the country's history, and one which created and leaves a significant legacy on the landscape.

Landscape of rubber

Almost contemporaneous with the coffee cycle was the boom associated with rubber. Though it operated in a much larger territory than coffee, its impact on the landscape was much less profound, with little permanent imprint. Rubber exemplifies most clearly the boom and bust nature of the economic cycles, with the identification of a resource over which Brazil had substantial control, a 'rush' to exploit it, the generation of wealth and then collapse. Although known to the Indians, rubber did not become important until the mid-nineteenth century when the process of vulcanization made it more usable, and world demand began to rise, with its use in rainwear, insulation and tyres.

The Amazon jungle was a major source of rubber, particularly from the tree *Hevea brasiliensis*. As these trees existed in the forest and took 20 years to mature, there was no move to plant them when the wild product could simply be collected – and was claimed to be superior. Entrepreneurs secured large concessions of land which hopefully contained rubber trees. Two basic problems were that the rubber trees were scattered widely through the forest, rather than occurring in close stands, and that the collection of rubber required labour, which Amazonia lacked. Rumours of potential wealth combined with hardship in North-east Brazil, particularly the drought of 1877–79, generated a labour force. Between 1853 and 1910 the regional population increased from 250 000 to almost 1 million.

Rubber collecting was an extractive activity *par excellence*. The rubber tapper was required to collect the latex from the trees in his area, scattered along a trail of up to 10 km in length. Access to the rubber region was riverine, so that the tappers settled along the river banks, living in simple isolated huts and connected with the outside world by river boat which brought in supplies and took out the rubber crudely processed by the tapper. The best rubber sources were deep in Amazonia, particularly in the Madeira, Purus and Juruá rivers, so that immigration was particularly marked to this area, giving it slightly higher population densities even to the present day, and securing the territory of Acre from Bolivia in 1903.

Output of rubber, its price and its contribution to foreign earnings rose rapidly. In 1901 coffee accounted for 46 per cent of Brazil's exports and rubber for 28 per cent. Escalating demand, the extensive nature of the collecting economy, the shortage of labour, combined with Brazil's failure to plant rubber trees, eventually led to the creation of rubber plantations in Asia. World rubber prices fell rapidly after 1910 and the boom collapsed.

For much of Amazonia the boom and its collapse had negligible impact. The activity was crude and left little mark on the forests. The population had grown, but people now left the region, moved to the towns or lapsed into simple subsistence hunting and gathering activities. In contrast to the other cycles, the rubber boom left no foundation for alternative activities.

It did however leave some legacy in the regional landscape, possibly the most explicit symbols of the boom and bust cycles and their associated mentality. Rubber generated great wealth, which was dissipated in conspicuous consumption by a few rubber entrepreneurs. The foci of the rubber trade were the towns which grew up, particularly at the river junctions. These increased rapidly in size and prosperity. Between 1848 and 1900 the population of Belém increased from 15 000 to 50 000 and that of Óbidos from 1200 to 30 000. The most spectacular growth was that of Manaus, which increased from 5000 to 50 000 between 1879 and 1890. Mere numerical increase however was not the most striking consequence. Rubber wealth sustained urban improvements, so that the provision of urban services such as electric lighting, tramways and telephones made Manaus and Belém among the most 'modern' cities in Brazil at the turn of the century. Manaus in particular has been described as a rich man's folly, as wealth was spent not only in financing urban services, but in buying in the current fashions from Europe in housing style, furniture, clothing and luxury goods. This conspicuous extravagance and its derivativeness reached its culmination in the Manaus opera house. Embellished by European artists, it incorporated Scottish iron, Alsatian tiles, Italian glass and marble, and French porcelain. It survives, along with the ostentatious houses of the rubber barons, as an enduring symbol of the rubber boom.

Amazonia was also the source of another boom product, cacao. The cacao bean was initially a collected product, obtained from trees native to the Amazon valley, and formed part of the 'drugs of the *sertão*', along with vanilla and cloves, collected during the colonial period. In contrast to rubber, however, it was developed as a plantation crop in the Ilhéus and Pôrto Seguro area of Bahia in the early nineteenth century. Output increased rapidly in the latter part of the century and by 1920 Brazil was the world's second largest producer. Although associated with a speculative boom, the impact of cacao cultivation on the landscape of southern Bahia was less apparent. As the cacao tree requires shade, the forest cover was not completely removed, and therefore the cacao plantations blend in with the native woodland, such that it has been claimed that there is no agricultural landscape of cacao; it is a landscape of cultivation which cannot be seen (Porto Domingues and Keller 1958: 53–54). Cacao processing requires some installations adjacent to the *fazenda*, but the general impact of settlement is limited, for cacao cultivation demands limited labour except in the harvest season when migrant labour is drawn in from other parts of the North-east. The boom did however stimulate, and sustains, the expansion of two urban centres, Ilhéus and Itabuna.

Immigrant landscapes

During the colonial period modification of the natural landscape was carried out by the Portuguese and their African slaves, but in the nineteenth century Brazilian governments began to admit and encourage free immigrants from elsewhere. These migrants came primarily from Europe, though after 1908 there was some significant immigration from Japan. Migrants were sought to increase the population and to occupy and secure territory. It was hoped that they would help to increase agricultural output to meet domestic and export demands and that European labour would encourage modernization. Immigration was also a counter to the inevitable end of slavery, and would serve to increase the white element in the population.

The numbers involved in this migration lack precision, for though there is general agreement about the numbers of arriving migrants, figures relating to return migration or movement on to other parts of Latin America are less certain. Before 1870 immigration was of limited significance, though it began to increase after 1850 as it became increasingly obvious that the institution of slavery could not survive. Between 1820 and 1870 there were about 250 000 immigrants. The rate then quickened, particularly after slavery was abolished. Between 1871 and 1890 there were some 750 000 immigrants. The largest single entry was in excess of 200 000 in 1891, and between 1891 and 1920 over 2.5 million immigrants arrived. The rate then began to slow, with 1 million arrivals between 1921 and 1940, and 700 000 between 1941 and 1960. The national composition of this influx varied over time, but over the period 1820–1960 Portuguese immigrants provided 32 per cent of the total, Italians 30, Spanish 13, Germans and Japanese 4 per cent each, with the balance from a range of other countries.

Although the Portuguese were understandably a principal source, in the late nineteenth century Italy became important, providing almost two-thirds of the total. After 1910 the Portuguese regained their pre-eminence, and have since contributed almost one-third of the diminishing flow of immigrants. Foreigners never contributed more than one-tenth of the total population. However, they tended to concentrate in the southern part of the country where their impact was consequently much greater. Furthermore their contribution to development and change in Brazil was greatly in excess of their numerical contribution. They were a crucial factor in a major period of change, which saw the abolition of slavery, the rise of the coffee boom and the growth of cities and factories.

Initially there were two major areas requiring new alternative labour sources, with very different demands in terms of the type of labour sought and with different consequences upon the landscape. One sphere was in the process of agricultural colonization, where the immigrants were agents of innovation and modernization. The other was in the perpetuation of the traditional practices of the economic cycles, in fostering large-scale coffee monoculture. The latter was the greater absorber of immigrant labour.

Extension of the coffee landscape

Foreign migrants on the coffee *fazendas* simply provided a substitute for slave labour. They effectively maintained an existing pattern of land use and, in the short term at least, did little to create new landscapes. Instead, in combination with rising demand for coffee and the access to new lands provided by the railway, they facilitated the extension of the coffee landscape. In its initial expansion coffee drew in slave labour from the decadent areas of earlier economic cycles, but with the end of the slave trade, slave labour became a diminishing resource. As the coffee barons became more influential in Brazil, they became involved in both the abolition of slavery and its substitution by free labour. The recruitment of such labour began in the 1840s, with migrants receiving their transport costs, initial subsistence and a plot for crops. They were responsible for looking after a number of coffee trees, and received a share of the profits of coffee sales. Abuse of this sharecropping system and other difficulties led some European governments, at various times, to prohibit migration to Brazil. Interest in free labour intensified as abolition approached in the 1880s, and led to a substantial influx of migrants. In 1886 the São Paulo plantation owners formed an organization to promote subsidized European immigration, which rose from less than 5000 a year, to over 90 000 in 1888. São Paulo became a major recipient of immigrants. Before 1885 the state had taken less than one-fifth of immigrants; in the 1890s over two-thirds went to São Paulo.

A very high proportion of these were subsidized, coming as agricultural labourers to work on the coffee *fazendas*. They took over the role of the slaves, clearing the forest as the coffee frontier spread across São Paulo, planting coffee, cultivating subsistence crops and caring for the coffee bushes. The form of land clearance and usage did not change with the substitution of African slaves by European immigrants, nor did the settlement pattern, as the nucleation of *fazenda* dwellings and processing plants persisted.

In the late nineteenth century most of the migrants to the coffee fields were Italians, mainly tenant farmers and labourers from northern Italy, but in the early twentieth century southern Italians began to make a larger contribution. Migrants came initially to secure employment as rural labourers rather than to gain access to land, though it is evident that they were encouraged to migrate in the expectation that they might eventually obtain some land. The labour system which evolved facilitated this, for sharecropping was replaced by wage labour and payment for harvest work. The immigrants also were provided with housing and the right to use a plot to produce subsistence crops. They could thus hope to save enough capital to buy land on the coffee frontier. Alternatively, as the frontier moved on or the coffee boom eased and land went out of coffee, the selling off of the large *fazendas* enabled the immigrants to buy smallholdings. This had the consequence of changing the pattern of landholding to one of smaller units, of diversifying the cropping pattern from one of large-scale monoculture to small-scale polyculture, and of modifying the settlement pattern from one of dispersed nucleations on the *fazendas* to the dispersal of individual dwellings on the small farms. The longer term consequence therefore of foreign immigration into São Paulo was to sustain a substantial change in the rural landscape.

Migrant expectations

For some migrants the attraction of Brazil was the opportunity for employment provided by the coffee boom; for others it was the possibility of securing land. The motivations of migrants from both northern and southern Europe were the same as those which impelled the flight of millions of others to North America, Argentina and Australia. They were pushed out by political disturbance and warfare, and by diminishing opportunities in rural areas. There was increasing land hunger in consequence of population growth, in a situation where land ownership was monopolized by relatively few large landowners, and there was little or no access to land for a large rural labour force. In areas such as northern Italy this was exacerbated by the disastrous impact of cheap American grain on local agriculture.

Brazil never attracted labour on the scale of North America, nor did she offer the same incentives; there was, for example, no equivalent of the Homestead Act. But the emigrants were fleeing adverse conditions, and if Brazil did not offer free land, the availability of a free passage provided an attractive escape to an impoverished peasant, irrespective of destination. Indeed, in the case of the coffee *fazendeiros*, this was the ideal pattern, for migrants with money for fares and the purchase of land were unlikely to find employment as wage labourers attractive. Conversely the need to work off the passage price provided an indebted labour force. Subsidized fares made São Paulo attractive, and the only line of escape for the poorest rural emigrants. A crucial element in emigration was therefore to escape to better opportunities. It was not a response to a vision of paradise in the New World, but to the pressure of the adverse conditions in which the rural labour force of late nineteenth century Europe found itself. Job opportunity on the coffee *fazenda* was therefore attractive. It is apparent though that for many emigrants the possibility of acquiring land was also a powerful motivating force, and some such possibilities did exist.

There were however some checks to migration to Brazil, in addition to the adverse impression created by the early sharecropping practices on the coffee *fazendas*. It was widely believed that the climate in Brazil was inimical to physical labour by Europeans. So long as slavery survived, it was a deterrent to would-be migrants, who would be competing with slaves. The predominance of Roman Catholicism in Brazil was a disincentive to Protestant migrants. Established patterns of landholding were particularly significant. Most settled areas were controlled by large landowners, so that access to land for immigrants was only possible in areas largely undeveloped, which were often isolated and remote.

The second branch of the migrant stream was, however, primarily concerned with access to land. Numerically less significant than migration to the São Paulo coffee lands, it nevertheless had a very profound effect in the areas in which it operated, creating new and very distinctive landscapes. It was particularly important in the three southern states of Paraná, Santa Catarina and Rio Grande do Sul, giving them cultural and human landscapes distinct in Brazil. There was a similar but smaller scale impact in Espírito Santo, Bahia and Amazonia, and there was some overlap of the two streams of labour immigration and agricultural colonization, in São Paulo.

Visions of a new land

It is evident that both migrants to the coffee *fazendas* or the agricultural colonies had only vague notions of what to expect in their new country. They had little knowledge of either place or conditions. For these rural dwellers knowledge of the world beyond their local community was limited. What attracted them was not the particular geographical charms of São Paulo or even Brazil, but the existence of jobs and land. Many of them were illiterate, and have left no written record of their expectations or impressions.

Their sources of information were the propaganda of government, shipping companies and colonizing agencies anxious to promote immigration, and letters from earlier migrants to relatives and friends at home. These came from the literate few, who might be untypical, and generally from those who were successful. The recruiting agencies inevitably portrayed the attractions of the new land in glowing colours. Promotional literature played down the obstacles such as climate and stressed the European-ness of the country. It assured potential migrants of the hospitality with which they would be received, the ease with which they would be able to repay the cost of their fares and the facility with which they would become established landowners in a fertile land with a mild and healthful climate. Letters home from pioneer migrants tended to emphasize the distinctiveness of the new-found land and its attractions, and to minimize the difficulties to be faced.

Landscapes of colonization

Organized agricultural colonization had begun before independence, with the foundation of Nova Friburgo, but the early use of foreign agricultural colonies was limited. The German colony of São Leopoldo in Rio Grande do Sul was established in 1824, and others were set up, primarily for strategic reasons, in Rio Grande do Sul, Santa Catarina and São Paulo. By 1840, though, there were fewer than 12 000 settlers in such colonies.

Government policy towards agricultural colonization was inconsistent. Interest was renewed in the 1840s with the establishment of colonies in Espírito Santo and Santa Catarina, as the government sought to encourage settlement in neglected areas of the country. This concern led to a focusing of colonization schemes in the southern area, to confirm Brazilian occupation of the region. A significant problem for the success of such schemes was that the government's concern was with the occupation and peopling of territory and less with their economic viability. Many were therefore located in remote and isolated areas and had limited opportunities to develop commercial agriculture until transport access improved.

Colonies were organized by the national and provincial governments and by private colonizing companies. Detailed arrangements varied but generally the colonists transport costs were subsidized, they received some form of support until they were established and they could obtain land in the colony on easy terms. By 1850 there were about 20 colonies in the South and over the next 25 years a further 30 were established, also mainly in the South. By 1875 the population of the colonies was about 50 000. In the early phase Germans were the principal migrants, but after 1875 Italian migration increased. In Rio Grande do Sul this gave rise to some spatial separation between the earlier areas of German colonization, along terraces of the Jacuí valley and the lower slopes of the serra, and the Italians on the plateau top. The other main areas of nineteenth century colonization were the Itajaí valley, which was predominantly an area of German settlement, and southern Santa Catarina in which Italians predominated. These concentrations provided substantial areas in which the landscape was shaped essentially by the colonization process. Elsewhere colonization schemes had less extensive impact and formed small foci of distinction created by the foreign immigrants. Included among these were a number of settlements in São Paulo, Paraná, Espírito Santo and Rio de Janeiro, and isolated examples in Minas Gerais and Bahia.

The colonists came into new geographical environments which they had to interpret, and which they changed. They tended to respond initially to the strange and the exotic but also, as farmers, to the potential of their new land. A group of Italians travelling to the settlement zone of Rio Grande do Sul in 1878 noted the beautiful panoramas, the exuberant vegetation, the variety of birds and the productive citrus groves they saw. Their reaction to the colony on which they were to be settled was one of lyrical approval of the salubrious climate, crystal waters and the fertile land, which was good for familiar crops

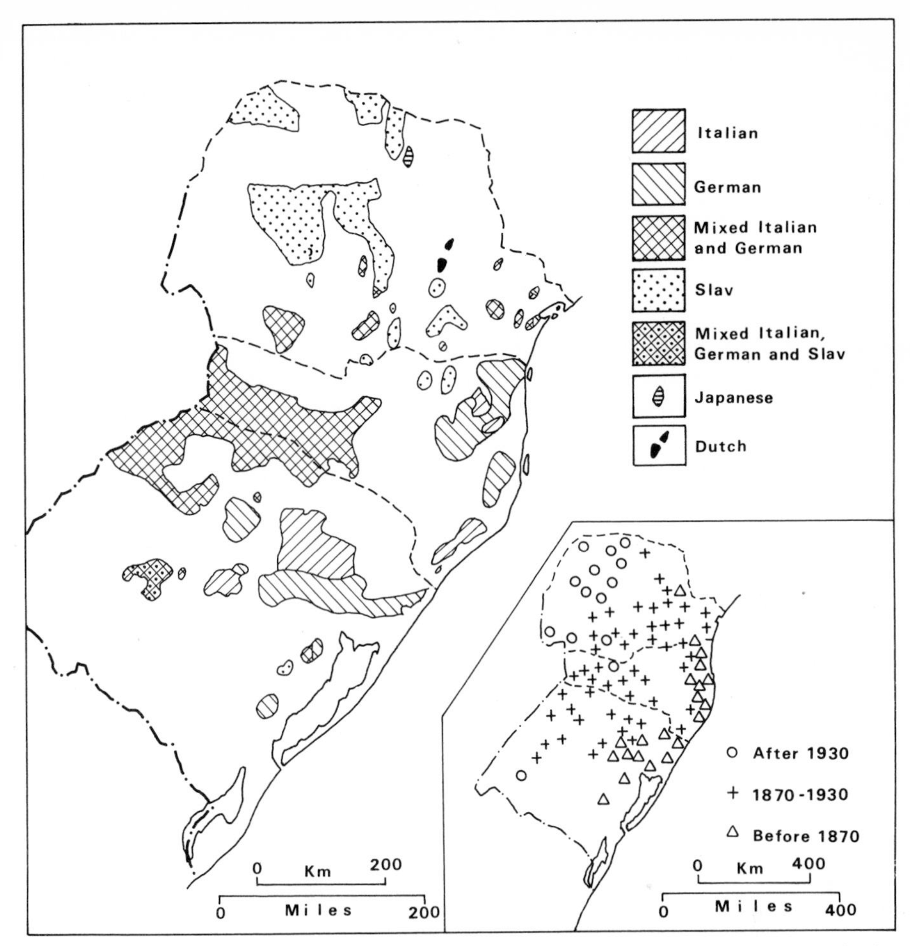

Map 7 South Brazil: the principal areas of European colonization. Inset: the date of establishment of colonies.

of wheat and maize and where the vine grew rapidly (Lorenzoni 1975). Later, Polish immigrants reacted similarly (Stawinski 1976), noting the fertility of the soil and its suitability for their cereal crops. Regarding the alleged climatic deterrent, all the migrant groups, whether from northern or southern Europe, commented on the warmer climate, but it proved no check to their labours.

The colonists commented on a number of features of their new environment. They reacted to the isolation and the silence. Most of the colonies were pioneer settlements in unoccupied areas. The colonists, coming from long-established, well-settled and generally heavily populated areas, found their isolation in the forest a strange experience. In the pattern of settlement which evolved, their dwellings were dispersed, and they were often isolated from established communities by distance and poor routeways.

Many of them remarked on the lack of diversity in their environment, again a contrast with their homelands. Pierre Monbeig (1952) observed that in Brazil the same geographical characteristics, of rocks, soils and topography, extend over hundreds of kilometres. In contrast to the variety to which he was accustomed, the European in Brazil found that uniformity was the dominant trait over vast distances. In the same way the forest cover of the southern pine forests lacked the diversity and tonal variety of familiar European vegetation.

The colonists however soon set out to modify the natural environment within which they were deposited. Generally, in contrast to what they had been led to expect, they found themselves having to establish their colony from scratch.

In the colonization zone in Rio Grande do Sul the colonies consisted of large blocks of land pierced by trails cut into the forest. Along these trails individual lots were distributed, with a frontage of between 200 and 250 m, running back to a depth of 3 km, where they abutted on to similar lots on a parallel trail. This gave lots of about 75 ha, but later colonies had lots of 40 to 60 ha, with the trails consequently closer together. The lots had access to water and usually a simple dwelling was provided. The colonist began to clear his lot, using, like his Amerindian and Portuguese predecessors, fire as an agricultural tool. Trees were felled, the vegetation burned off and crops planted between the stumps. Over time the land was properly cleared, but usually the lot was divided into different uses, with cropland, pasture and some woodland. The colonists grew a combination of familiar crops brought from Europe and new ones acquired in Brazil. Their initial concern was subsistence, with sale of any surplus, but once access to outside markets improved, they began to specialize in producing vegetables, fruit, pigs, dairy cattle and chickens. There was some specialization by different national groups. Italian colonists for example were largely responsible for a major expansion in viticulture, and the Italian colonization zone remains Brazil's principal wine-producing region.

The colonists created a landscape distinct from that produced by the Portuguese and the economic cycles. It was a landscape of poly-culture, smallholdings and family labour. They introduced new crops and farm practices. Land use tended to be more intensive and careful, and made use of crop rotation, fertilizers and machinery. Initial dwellings were rudimentary, but once land had been cleared and planted, they were improved, generally using styles familiar from their homelands. In consequence areas of colonization were made distinctive not only as areas of German or Italian settlement but also by variants and details reflecting home building features of the communities and regions in which the migrants originated.

The colonists in the South transformed the virgin forest into a cultivated land. An Italian colonist of 1883 has left an illuminating record of his initial impression of the natural landscape of Rio Grande do Sul, and the likely consequences of colonization upon it. 'On the top of the serra was revealed a marvellous panorama. The virgin forest extended as far as the eye could see, like waves of the ocean, the valleys of dark green, and with vast areas of *araucaria* pine which, in the distance, decorated the horizon with its crowns, like giant sunshades. Above our heads a clear and limpid sky and majestic sun reflected the strong and austere forest which, unfortunately, in less than 40 years, will be devastated and felled by the strong arm of the Italian colonist' (Lorenzoni 1975: 111).

Clearance of the forest provided the colonist with the land he prized so highly. In contrast to the Luso-Brazilian, for whom land was a source of wealth and prestige, the colonists' aspiration was for a piece of land for his own use, which could be worked by his own labour, and which would provide sustenance for his family. Possession of land gave him freedom. The colonists felt that their condition had improved. They were better off in Brazil than in Italy, Germany or Poland. There was, for whoever wanted it, sufficient work, food and drink, without too much effort – and as for landlords, they were left in Europe! (de Boni 1977: 41).

In occupying the land the colonists made their mark not only physically, but in the names they gave to the places and areas they settled. Many recorded nostalgia for their homelands, as in Nova Italia, Nova Roma, Nova Veneza, Nôvo Hamburgo and Nova Teutônia. Examination of current place names in the South reveals many such transposed names, together with those derived from immigrant personal names – Alfredo Wagner, Anita Garibaldi, Felipe Schmidt and Frederico Westphalen.

The colonists usually formed complete communities and were distinct in their ethno-linguistic origins. The colonies were located in remote areas, away from native Brazilians, so they retained their European traditions, creating replicas of the communities from which they had come, and reinforcing this by encouraging other migrants from their homelands to join them. The colonies were initially almost closed worlds, cut off by distance and poor communications, but this was modified over time as roads and railways penetrated inland. Some groups, such as those from southern Europe, found it relatively easy to integrate, but Germans, Slavs and other northern Europeans and the later Japanese immigrants were more distinct and preserved their distinctiveness longer. In some cases distinctiveness was deliberately fostered. In the late nineteenth century German colonizing societies operating in Santa Catarina encouraged migration of people willing to retain their German traditions, language and customs. In the twentieth century the Brazilian government took action against this exclusiveness and began to encourage integration into a national society by insisting that education be in Portuguese. Immigration was also more closely controlled by the imposition of a quota system in 1934, by which annual immigration from a single country in any one year was set at 2 per cent of the immigration into Brazil between 1884 and 1933.

In spite of these controls, the colony areas retain something of their distinctiveness in population composition, tradition, land use and language. Map 8 illustrates the survival of language, in which 90 per cent of the population which did not habitually speak Portuguese were to be found in São Paulo and the three southern states. Almost two-thirds of the total were Brazilian-born German and Italian speakers.

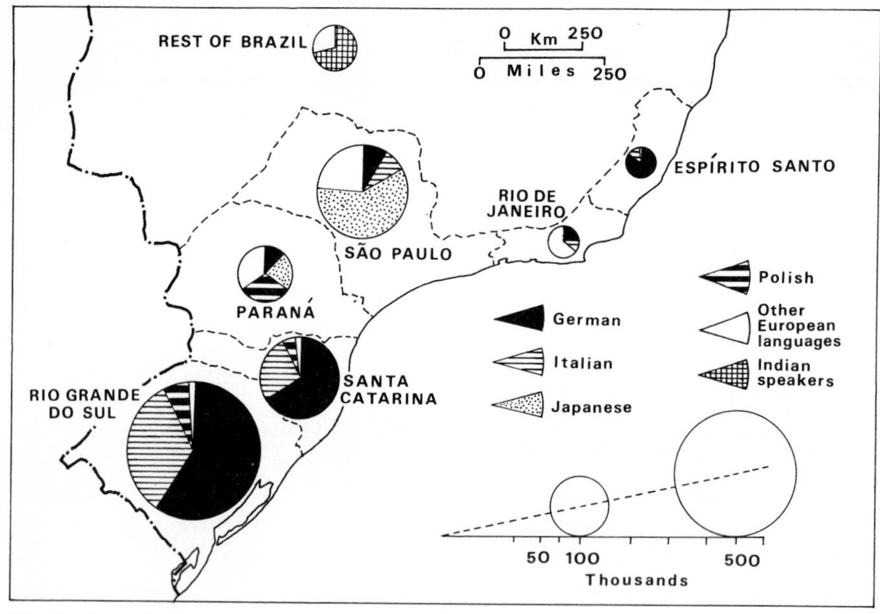

Map 8 South Brazil: the distribution of people whose first language was not Portuguese, 1950.

Although they never contributed a high proportion of total population, the colonists made a major impact in the limited areas in which they settled. In addition, their higher standard of health and sanitation facilitated higher rates of population increase, so that second and third generation immigrant stock made a substantial contribution in excess of original numbers. As a result of the influx of immigrants and these high rates of natural increase, the principal migrant recipient states of São Paulo, Rio Grande do Sul, Santa Catarina, Paraná, Rio de Janeiro and Espírito Santo increased their share of the national population from one-fifth to about one-third between 1872 and 1920. In detail these legacies are even more marked. It was estimated that in 1934 over half the population of São Paulo state consisted of immigrants or their Brazilian-born children. In 1950 in some regions in the state over one-fifth of the population was still Italian, and in 1970 people of Polish origin constituted 96 per cent of the population of the district of Carlos Gomes in the Rio Grande do Sul.

In their early history the colonies created very distinctive 'foreign' landscapes. In the last quarter of the nineteenth century it was claimed that Italian colonization in Espírito Santo gave the impression one was visiting a foreign country (Cavati 1973). It was suggested that in 1910 the Itajaí valley could make one believe one was visiting Switzerland or Germany (Ramos 1975). The post-war colony of Pedrinhas in São Paulo was described as 'a piece of beautiful Italy' (Borges Pereira 1974: 160).

Over time some of the distinctiveness has broken down, as the colonists have been assimilated. Population growth, pressure on land, and the attraction

Fig. 5.3 Germanic elements in the townscape of Blumenau, Santa Catarina. Although the town has many original features introduced by German colonists, its rise as an ethnic tourist centre has led to the construction of pseudo-Germanic façades.

of the cities has lead to outmigration to other areas. In consequence, on the more recent agricultural frontiers and in the towns, the national groups have begun to mingle with each other and with the Luso-Brazilian population. Even so, in the core areas of colonization, there is still a clear legacy in their landscapes which distinguishes them from the rest of the country. In the case of the Itajaí valley, its persisting qualities are admirably captured in Alexander Lenard's '*Valley of the Latin bear*'. In fact the German character of the area is now being exploited as a tourist attraction, with its original features being supplemented by the operation of ethnic restaurants, folk museums and ersatz building façades. Indeed, the whole coastal strip of Santa Catarina is being portrayed as a living heritage of European colonization.

Although the main phase of colonization was in the nineteenth century, some colonies have been established subsequently, and because of their recence retain strong elements of their natural origins. John Augelli (1958a) has described the Latvian colony of Varpa in São Paulo. Established in 1923, this group developed particular agricultural specialties, and retained its linguistic and religious distinctiveness. Its landscape was marked by physical appearance of its inhabitants, the particular pattern of their farm practice and by the Baltic style of their buildings. Dutch colonies established in Paraná, São Paulo and Rio Grande do Sul have similar distinctiveness (Augelli 1958b).

Japanese immigration has also been significant. It is recent, well documented and, because of the non-European origin of the migrants, has introduced a most distinctive element into their areas of settlement. The pattern of Japanese migration closely matches that of earlier European migrants. Japanese were recruited initially to replace European labour on the coffee *fazendas* after Italy had prohibited migration of its nationals to Brazil in 1902. Later they came as organized agricultural colonists and independent farmers.

Initial migration reflected the *fazendeiros* desire for labour and Japan's anxiety to decant surplus population. Between 1908 and 1924 about 35 000 Japanese entered Brazil, subsidized by the São Paulo government. They worked on the *fazendas* under similar conditions to earlier Europeans, receiving housing, a food plot and wages for work on the coffee lands. Like their predecessors, when they had accumulated some capital they became sharecroppers or tenant farmers before acquiring their own land.

After 1920 the *fazendeiros* became less interested in recruiting Japanese labour but the Japanese government was anxious to maintain an outlet for surplus population, and began to subsidize emigration to Brazil via the Japanese emigration company Kaigai Kogyo Kabushiki Kaisha (K.K.K.K.). The company recruited and transported migrants, provided them with loans to establish themselves, and invested in agricultural colonies. The peak year of migration was 1933, when almost 25 000 Japanese arrived, but subsequently the number declined, and only recommenced on a small scale, after 1950.

Most of the immigrants became independent farmers, either on arrival or after a period on the *fazendas*. Their settlement followed the penetration of the Noroeste, Alta Paulista and Sorocabana railways into western São Paulo. In addition, some agricultural colonies were established in the same area, in the south-west coastlands of São Paulo, in north Paraná and in Amazonia.

The Japanese were highly successful as farmers. By the late 1930s, although they contributed less than 2 per cent of São Paulo's population, they provided over one-tenth of its agricultural output. They have adopted traditional Brazilian crops such as coffee, cotton, beans and sugar cane, and also introduced specializations such as tea, jute, raw silk and black pepper. Similarly they have maintained some intensive farming methods brought from Japan, particularly where they have engaged in horticulture near the major cities, but on the frontier they have borrowed slash and burn clearance and more extensive land use practices from native Brazilians.

In their settlement pattern the colonies do not appear to have transported traditional village forms. Instead of the characteristic Japanese compact agricultural village, they have established dispersed dwellings on their farm lots, with only a small administrative nucleation. As independent farmers their settlement pattern is indistinguishable from that of the isolated farmstead of the Paulista small farmer. Attempts to introduce traditional Japanese house styles met with difficulties, so that their rural dwellings resemble those of native Brazilians with a few Japanese embellishments.

In the post-war period there has been some movement of the Japanese from the agricultural frontiers to the periphery of the cities, and to the area east of São Paulo city, where they have become very important intensive horticulturalists. There has also been some movement into cities, and in cities such as São Paulo, distinctive Japanese ethnic districts have emerged, marked by specialty shops, restaurants and the use of Japanese signs. Estimates suggest that by 1978 there were 750 000 Japanese-Brazilians.

Movement to the cities has been characteristic of all the migrant groups. Some nineteenth century migrants moved directly to the towns from Europe. This was particularly the case with late nineteenth century Portuguese immigrants, but other groups moved to the cities after a period in the countryside. In the city they contributed workers, craftsmen, merchants and entrepreneurs. Immigrant Germans and Italians for example appear to have been major industrial innovators. In what are now two of Brazil's major industrial areas, immigrant innovation was significant. In 1935 over 70 per cent of São Paulo's industrial enterprises were owned by people of non-Portuguese origin. In Rio Grande do Sul Germans founded most of the state's early industrial plants, and in 1916 dominated the textile, furniture, brewing and leather industries (Roche 1959).

By the early part of the twentieth century immigrants formed an important element in the population of the major cities. In 1920 one-third of the population of São Paulo and one-fifth of that of Rio de Janeiro was of immigrant origin, and in these cities immigrant quarters, of Italians and Japanese for example, began to emerge. In Pôrto Alegre an industrial zone created by German immigrants developed, there were German residential areas and the central area and its public buildings showed the imprint of German architects.

Some of the original colonies grew to be urban centres in their own right, and retain some of their immigrant features, as in Blumenau, São Leopoldo and Nôvo Hamburgo.

Foreign immigrants, though relatively few in number, had a profound and persisting impact on the society, economy and landscape of Brazil. They contributed to a substantial increase in the population, especially in the South-east and South, and significantly modified the racial structure. They facilitated the spread of the coffee landscape and introduced the very distinctive pattern of small farm poly-culture, and contributed significantly to the urban and industrial growth of the late nineteenth and twentieth centuries.

Foreign capital and investment

External demands sustained and extended the influence of economic cycles; foreign immigrants created new rural landscapes. A third extraneous influence on the nineteenth century landscape was the impact of foreign investment and innovation. In fact these three elements were not separate one from the other, but closely intertwined. For example, external demand, immigrant labour and the railway were essential factors in the advance of the coffee economy.

Foreign innovations represented primarily the diffusion from Europe and North America of the technological advances of economic revolution. In Brazil these might be broadly categorized into five groups, affecting mining, agriculture, industrialization, transport and other infrastructure.

During the colonial period mining activities had been largely confined to the extraction of gold and gemstones by simple techniques and mainly at surface workings. The Portuguese crown had sought to regulate these activities, but after independence foreign companies were permitted to operate mining activities in Brazil and a number of gold mining companies were set up, primarily with British capital, to seek bedrock gold in Minas Gerais and a number of other states. During the nineteenth century at least 20 such English companies were created (Leonardos 1970: 320), but the success of Morro Velho and Gongo Sôco prompted more speculative adventures. Such companies introduced deep mining techniques, working to several hundred metres and using substantial labour forces, which initially included European overseers and negro slaves. Few of these companies survived into the twentieth century, but they did create settlement nucleations in Minas Gerais, some of them, as in the case of Nova Lima, with a distinctly English cast to their townscape (Burton 1869/1969: vol. I).

Brazil also identified coal as a necessary ingredient for economic progress and the government tried to encourage the search for and production of coal. Coal of generally poor grade was found in the three southern states and there were spasmodic and small-scale attempts to exploit it during the nineteenth century. These efforts involved particularly English and German engineers and capitalists. In two cases, the Arroio dos Ratos coalfield in Rio Grande do Sul and that of southern Santa Catarina, English companies opened up mines and built railways to transport the coal to the coast. These ventures were of limited success, but formed the nuclei for more substantial mining operations in the twentieth century. In the case of both gold and coal the creation of mining landscapes was spatially very concentrated. In many cases the legacy has largely disappeared, though Nova Lima, Criciúma and São Jeronimo are still identifiably 'mining towns'.

During the nineteenth century much of Brazilian agriculture remained traditional, using slash and burn techniques to clear the forest, few tools and depending primarily on manual or animal power. There was change in some sectors though. The sugar industry had lost its pre-eminence on a world scale, partly because production techniques had remained unchanged since the early colonial period, using low-yielding cane varieties, poor methods of cultivation, animal power and crude processing techniques. In the early nineteenth century new cane varieties were introduced from other sugar-producing countries. Steam-powered sugar mills began to replace water – or animal-driven mills. Increasing use was made of cane-trash (*bagasse*) as a fuel. This reflected one impact of sugar production on the landscape, for the use of wood as fuel had cleared extensive areas of woodland and timber shortage was posing difficulties for the industry.

The most significant change derived from the introduction of more modern equipment which gave higher yields of sugar from cane. The original colonial land grants had formed the basis of the *engenhos*, but to the efficient the new mills needed larger inputs of cane. This resulted in the amalgamation of *engenho* holdings into larger units, or forced independent cane growers to sell cane to these new mills – the *usinas*. The increased size of holding and the need to move the cane rapidly for processing resulted in the construction of a network of narrow gauge railways through the cane lands. The replacement of animals by steam power reduced the need for pasture and increased the area available for cane cultivation. Such rationalization amplified the scale of operations in the cane fields. The colonial pattern of cane monoculture focused on the *engenho* and its nucleated settlement was magnified, with the industrial plant of the *usina* providing the focus. The disappearance of the *engenho* was a prolonged one, but the process of concentration has continued up to the present, with the role of large units of production becoming even more marked. In the *zona da mata* of the North-east holdings of more than 100 ha control four-fifths of the farm area, and sugar plantations account for over four-fifths of the cultivated land. The introduction of newer processing techniques has thus prompted a continuing process of increases in scale. Cane monoculture has persisted, focusing upon the sugar factories, and their processing and storage facilities, offices, *usineiro's* mansion and factory workers housing. Small nucleations in the cane fields are the dwellings of the cane workers and often mark the sites of former *engenhos* now absorbed in the process of expansion. Similar processes also occurred in other sugar areas, such as those of São Paulo. In other sectors of agriculture too, the introduction of new machinery, for the de-husking of coffee or the ginning of cotton, contributed to the modernization and expansion of the agricultural activities.

The introduction of agricultural machinery was also a contributing factor in the early modern industrialization of Brazil. Simple industries processing food and export materials, and producing cloth and other necessities had begun on a very limited scale during the colonial period, though often restricted by Portugal. The trade concessions made to Britain in 1808 were further inhibitions until 1844, but subsequently some manufacturing activities began to grow. The increased use of agricultural machinery required maintenance, and repair shops provided the basis for early engineering works. Although much of this activity was on a very small scale, it did contribute to the transformation of a society and economy which was dominated by agriculture and primarily rural in character, to one in which urban and industrial activities had a growing place. Small-scale industrial landscapes began to evolve.

The example of industrialization in Europe prompted some Brazilians to seek to encourage the process in Brazil. This resulted in the establishment of iron foundries, shipyards, textile mills and other factories. Such activities tended to be established in the major towns of the North-east and South-east. European immigrants, with some prior experience in industrial activities, were also industrial innovators, establishing workshops and small factories in São Paulo and the southern states. In the case of Nôvo Hamburgo in Rio Grande do Sul, for example, the early activities of German colonists as cobblers provided the basis for a workshop and later factory scale footwear industry. In Rio Grande do Sul much of the early industrialization was begun by immigrants and located in the areas of German and Italian settlement (Roche 1959.)

In the incipient industrialization process the foreign contribution was primarily in the provision of machinery and know-how; in contrast to some other sectors of the economy, direct foreign investment was limited. Nevertheless foreign capitalists did make some contribution. British capital, for example, invested in textile mills in São Paulo, Petrópolis, Taubaté and Rio de Janeiro, iron foundries in Recife and Salvador and flour mills in Rio de Janeiro.

The impact of nineteenth century industrialization was limited. By 1907 there were about 3000 industrial establishments, the majority of them small scale. By that time three-quarters of industrial activity was to be found in Rio de Janeiro, São Paulo, Minas Gerais and Rio Grande do Sul. Its significance is two-fold – the modification of the economic structure, thereby introducing an element of diversity into the landscape; and the initiation of a spatial pattern, in which states of the South-east and South emerged as the more industrialized parts of the country.

Foreign investment was much more significant in the improvement of Brazil's transport system. During the colonial period mules and ox carts had been the main means of overland transport, with shipping providing the external and much of the inter-regional transport. The development of steamships increased the speed and scale at which trade goods could be moved, and linked Brazil firmly into the pattern of international trade, increasing demand for the country's tropical produce. Of much greater impact on the landscape was the development of the railway. In the first half of the century Brazil had begun to improve its road system, culminating in the opening of the 144 km macadamized road between Petrópolis and Juiz de Fora in 1861 (Momsen 1964: 73–76). This development was virtually contemporaneous with the arrival of the railroad in Brazil, and for the next 60 years the railway rather than the road was the main focus of transport improvement.

Brazil's first railway law was passed in 1835 but the first railroad, from Guanabara Bay to the Serra do Mar, was not opened until 1854. The concentration of population close to the coast meant that railways were lines of penetration, being constructed in advance of traffic. Their construction therefore required direct government involvement or government guarantees of a return on private capital. Most early railroads were built under the latter terms. The original five concessions were for lines into the interior from Recife, Salvador, Rio de Janeiro, Pôrto de Caxias and Santos, which later formed parts of more extensive systems. Railway construction posed considerable problems, for along the eastern seaboard the serras formed a barrier between the narrow coastal plain and the interior, an obstacle graphically described as a 'wall without gates'. Heavy seasonal rain on the mountains hindered both construction and maintenance of the track. Crossing the serra involved major construction work, particularly for the lines from Rio de Janeiro, Santos and Paranaguá, but once over the scarp the terrain was more amenable to railway building so that dendritic nets spread out, particularly in the coffee lands behind Santos and Rio de Janeiro.

The pace of construction was initially rather slow. About 750 km of railway was opened before 1870. Over the next 20 years over 9000 km were opened, and a further 11 000 between 1890 and 1910. The early concessions were granted on a piecemeal fashion and it wasn't until the 1870s that a more organized strategy of railway development in the national interest began to emerge. Even so, lack of careful control produced a system with a variety of gauges. Guaranteed interest payments were partly related to length of line, so many routes were circuitous rather than direct and once over the scarp major construction works of cuttings and embankments were uncommon. The pattern which emerged was one with fairly complex networks in the South-east, and lines of penetration from coastal ports and a few isolated lines in the interior in other regions. When the system reached its maximum extent, of some 38 000 km in 1960, over half the track was concentrated in Minas Gerais, São Paulo and Rio de Janeiro.

The development of the dense railway net in those states was closely linked to the spread of coffee. According to Richard Graham coffee and rails spread together, forming a partnership in the conquest of a new frontier (Graham 1968 : 51). The relationship was symbiotic – the railway permitted the advance of the frontier, coffee provided a profitable freight, particularly for the San-

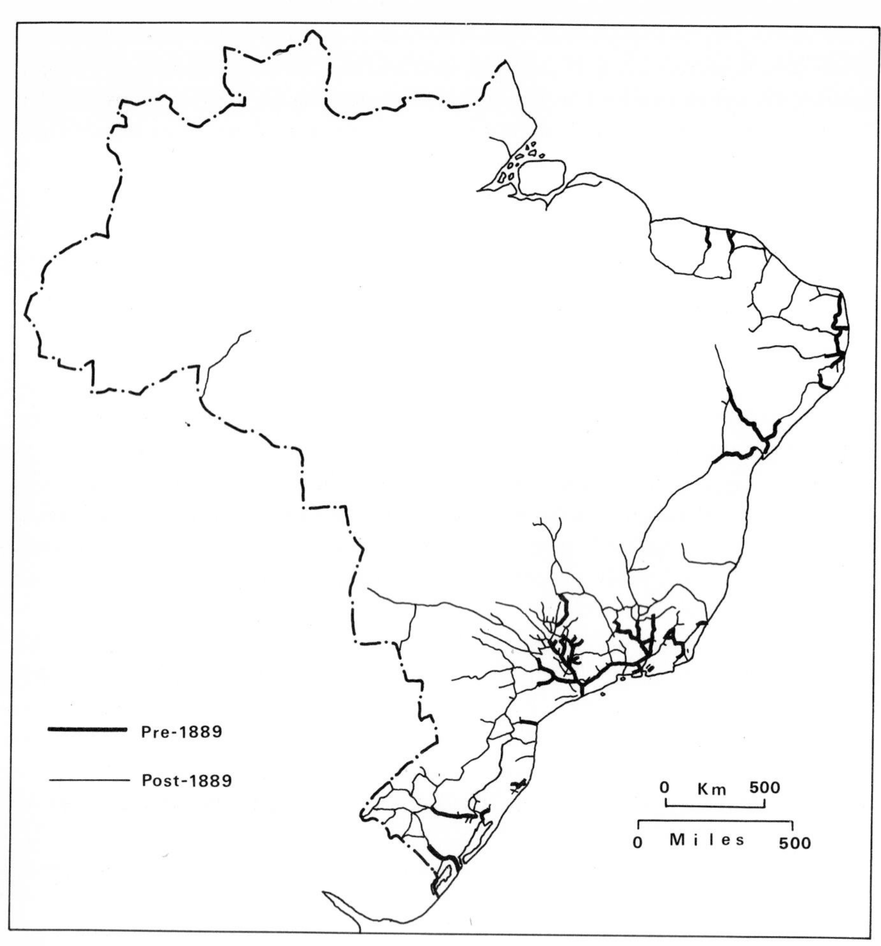

Map 9 Brazil: the spread of the railway.

tos – Jundiaí railway which funnelled Paulista coffee through São Paulo and Santos.

The railway therefore made economic advance and change possible. It was also a stimulus to urban growth. Some railways linked existing settlements; other lines opened up new areas so that towns grew up at stations, junctions and railheads. The penetration of the Dom Pedro II railway from Rio de Janeiro into the Paraíba valley fostered the growth of Barra do Piraí as the transhipment point between the railway, and river and road traffic along the valley and into Minas Gerais (Momsen 1964: 77–81). The advance of this railway, as the Estrada de Ferro Central do Brasil, into Minas Gerais prompted new urban growth. Lafayette, the station for the town of Queluz, quickly became the nucleus of a large colony of houses, inns and stores (Dent 1886 : 179). The Central was also responsible for making the rich iron ore deposits of central Minas Gerais accessible, encouraging both mining and iron working

(Dickenson 1967). In São Paulo the advance of the railways northwards and westwards permitted the advance of coffee and a concomitant rise of urban settlements. Although railway equipment was originally imported from Europe and the U.S.A. the need for maintenance and repair prompted the establishment of repair shops which became both settlement foci and nodes of engineering skills. The use of steam locomotives in a country deficient in coal demanded the import of coal or the use of other fuels, primarily wood. The railways were therefore important contributors to the process of deforestation, both in fostering the advance of the frontier of cultivation and in their demands for wood for their own use. Wood and charcoal continued to be a major fuel source for locomotives into the twentieth century and as late as 1957 accounted for one-third of the railway fuel bill. Timber shortages did encourage some railway companies, particularly in São Paulo, to undertake reafforestation projects.

Other transport advances were also significant. Coupled with the growth of steam navigation and the expansion of external trade, several of the principal ports were improved. Such improvements were an integral and essential part of the export-orientated nature of Brazilian development. In a number of cases foreign companies or engineers were involved in schemes for port modernization, including Rio de Janeiro, Salvador, Recife and Fortaleza. In the case of Manaus the Booth Steamship Company, through its subsidiary Manaos Harbour Ltd, built a complex floating harbour to cope with the tidal range of the Amazon. The work included a Customs House imported from England. One of the most important improvements was that at Santos. The opening of the Santos–Jundiaí railway and the rise in coffee exports placed great pressure on the inadequate facilities of this, São Paulo's only deep sea port. It was described at the time as being in a deplorable state, lacking quays, cranes and storehouses. Between 1888 and 1909 it was substantially improved, by a Brazilian company, with the building of extensive quayside and storage facilities. As a result of these improvements and the expansion of the Paulista economy, freight handled by the port rose from 125 000 tons in 1892 to over 1 million in 1901, with profound consequences on the prosperity and population of the town.

The development of urban public transport systems, initially horse-drawn vehicles and later electric streetcars, had significant impact on the larger towns. Such systems facilitated their spatial spread and greater internal differentiation in residential patterns. In Rio de Janeiro the tramways encouraged the growth of fashionable residential districts south along Guanabara Bay and on to the Atlantic beaches, and working class areas northwards along the docks and railway lines.

Other facets of urban life were improved. The élite sought to encourage progress in Brazil, by borrowing from European and North American models. One dimension of these aspirations was to foster urban improvement, by introducing city-serving facilities of water, drainage, gas and electricity. Again the know-how was imported and in many cases was provided by foreign companies. Thus before 1890 British capital was involved in the provision of water and drainage systems for Rio de Janeiro, São Paulo, Santos and Recife, and gas companies for these cities and for Salvador, Fortaleza and Belém. Such advances were not without their incongruities; Hadfield (1869: 36) noted the curious effect of 'gas lamps peeping out from the thick foliage of tropical plants, as if in competition with the fire flies dancing about'!

Later in the century electricity came into use. The first power station began to operate in 1883. Foreign companies again played a role in this provision. In Rio de Janeiro and São Paulo the Canadian-based company which became known as 'Light' was responsible for the electrification of the city tramway systems and the supply of electricity to streets and houses. Provision of power to these cities involved innovative use of the potential of the Serra do Mar, by diverting west-flowing streams over the escarpment. The exploitation of this substantial resource provided ample power capacity for industry, important in a country short of solid fuels. The early provision of electricity in São Paulo and Rio de Janeiro gave further impetus to their emerging pre-eminence in the urban hierarchy of Brazil, and to the evolution of factory districts within the urban pattern.

In addition to these infrastructural improvements the élite sought to remodel the urban scene, preferably to resemble the desired cityscapes of

Fig. 5.4 Foreign elements in the townscape of São Paulo: a British-built railway, a building of the formerly Canadian-owned 'Light' electric power company, and the Brazilian-made products of foreign automobile companies.

Europe. The model of Haussmann's redesigning of Paris was particularly influential in the case of Rio de Janeiro. New broad thoroughfares, open spaces and monumental public buildings were constructed. A major axis, the Avenida Central, was driven through the central business district, linking the port in the north with a landscaped boulevard in the south. Along it were located, in French Second Empire architecture, the National Academy of Fine Arts, the National Library, the Supreme Court and the Senate. The Municipal Theatre was closely modelled on the Paris Opera House. Much of the old, crowded inner city was cleared, and new avenues constructed. Land was reclaimed from the bay and waterfront gardens and boulevards laid out.

In 1911 Pierre Denis could suggest that Rio was still dominated by its physical setting, hemmed in by the forest and constrained by steep slopes on which building was not possible (Denis 1911: 95). If the broader physical context remained unchallenged man had begun to modify the detail, not only by extending and remodelling the built environment, but by restructuring the physical base. The process, which still continues, began during this turn-of-the-century urban renewal. The small hills, which had provided appropriate defensive sites during the colonial period, were obstacles to the renovated and

Fig. 5.5 The Avenida Rio Branco (formerly the Avenida Central) in Rio de Janeiro. In the centre the Teatro Municipal and to the right the National Library and Academy of Fine Arts. These early twentieth century buildings are now overshadowed by skyscraper office blocks. To the left is Cinelândia, the down-town cinema area.

modern downtown area. The solution was therefore to remove them, regardless of the historical legacy expressed in the buildings which covered them. Removal of the hills would provide further space for new building in the central business district and fill material with which to reclaim land from marshes and the seashore.

The architectural detail of these urban changes was also heavily derivative. Although French 'gingerbread' or 'wedding cake' styles were common, this period in Brazilian architectural history is designated as one of Eclecticism, in which borrowings incorporated 'the modest Tuscan', 'the imposing Gothic', 'the handsome Moorish', or 'the elegant chalet' (Mindlin 1956: 3). Authorities in the national and state capitals competed in the construction of public buildings – government offices, court houses, theatres, markets and so on. An extreme form of this borrowing was the importation of metal structures, given the lack of a metallurgical industry in Brazil. Examples of this metallic architecture includes markets in Belém and Recife, the Alencar theatre in Fortaleza, the Chá viaduct in São Paulo and the Palácio de Cristal in Petrópolis. Business and domestic architecture also drew diverse inspirations from abroad.

Although élite tastes for innovation and change clearly formed their most marked expression in the capital and other major cities, such transformations were not confined to them. Müller, writing of the towns in the São Paulo section of the Paraíba valley in the second half of the nineteenth century, notes their preoccupation with the beautification of the urban scene. Streets were paved, street signs erected and houses numbered. Trees were planted and small gardens laid out, and street lighting provided (Müller 1969: 59–63). This process of modernization and embellishment created urban landscapes more akin to those of Europe. Yet not all urban dwellers benefited from these advances. Services of water, gas and electricity supply, and transport provision did not extend throughout the built-up area. Even more significantly urban dwellers constituted only a small proportion of the total population. The rural aristocracy might acquire a town house and experience some of the benefits of urban civilization; for the bulk of the rural population neither life-style or landscape had changed significantly.

Foreign views of Brazilian landscapes

The removal of constraints on the access of foreigners to Brazil facilitated the arrival of Europeans and North Americans as scientists, merchants, missionaries and travellers. Many of these visitors left published records of their Brazilian impressions. Such books provide us with useful sources as to the landscapes of nineteenth century Brazil, for a variety of reasons. Although the foreigners included Germans, Austrians, Frenchmen and Danes, many were English or American, so that their views are easily accessible. They record the impressions of strangers to a far place. In a period before easy and rapid travel, and the advent of film and television, prose portraits provided the principal source of information about strange lands. These writings were aimed at readers in Europe and North America, and thus helped to shape the views of Brazil held in those areas; they also provided information for would-be investors interested in the possibilities of Brazilian development.

Hugh Prince (1971) has indicated the value of examining the reaction of people from differing cultural backgrounds to scenery, resources and lifestyles which they encountered for the first time. As in the case of the sixteenth century contact of the Portuguese, visitors from Europe and North America in the nineteenth century reacted to this new world in terms of both observed facts and of value judgements shaped by their source society. Many of these views were hostile. The writers viewed Brazil from a critical standpoint, whether it was contempt, open or veiled, for 'Latins', hostility to Roman Catholicism or opposition to slavery. In the case of English visitors, their attitudes were often the product of Victorian self-righteousness, in which the prosperity generated by the Industrial Revolution gave the English traveller an innate superiority over all 'foreigners'. A general conclusion about much of this literature is that it is generally, though not always, enchanted by the wonders of nature, but more critical of Brazilian society.

Some commentators have categorized this literature in purely chronological terms (Hamilton 1960; Naylor 1969). This approach has the virtue of using it to record landscape change over time. Goodman (1972) categorizes those who came explicitly to explore into four groups, the great naturalists, government and privately sponsored explorers and independent explorers. Such visitors were bona fide explorers, whose writings contain scientific observations of places and phenomena. The majority were not pioneers in unknown lands but observers and interpreters of it. One of them, Louis Agassiz (1869/1969) saw their role as exploring worlds whose existence was already known; to investigate, not to discover.

Other visitors were not qualified scientists, but were interested travellers who recorded their reactions, tending to stress the extraordinary rather than the commonplace, in what are in essence diaries of their journeys. A number of early visitors were attached to diplomatic missions, and took the opportunity to travel in Brazil, recording not only immediate impressions but also opinions as to the potentiality and problems of the exploitation and development of the country. Such an approach also colours the records of merchants and businessmen, many of whom resided in Brazil for a number of years.

The coverage provided by this material is uneven. Rio de Janeiro was the point of entry for many visitors, and a point of contact for others *en route* to and from other parts of the continent, so that there are many comments on the 'Marvellous City'. A number of visitors travelled inland from Rio, to Minas Gerais, especially to the gold and diamond fields, to the São Franciso, and to southern Goiás. Interest in the Amazon is almost obsessive and many scientists and travellers voyaged down the river system or searched the forest for flora and fauna. Records of the North-east and far south are less extensive.

The foreign view of Brazil in the nineteenth century, and one which is still not entirely defunct, is well captured by the missionaries Fletcher and Kidder in the preamble to their *Brazil and the Brazilians* (1866), where they suggest that the popular notion of Brazil consisted of mighty rivers and virgin forests, palm trees and jaguars, anacondas and alligators, howling monkeys and screaming parrots, diamond mining, revolutions and earthquakes. These, they claimed, were the component parts of the picture of Brazil formed in the mind's eye.

Certainly such images of the natural wonderland of Brazil are recurring themes in the writings of many of the nineteenth century visitors. It was the natural landscape and the natural environment which attracted and inspired them. Probably the most distinguished scientific visitor was Charles Darwin, who, on the voyage of the *Beagle*, visited Salvador and Rio de Janeiro. He reacted ecstatically to the Brazilian forest, with 'the elegance of the grasses, the novelty of the parasitical plants, the beauty of the flowers, the glossy green of the foliage, but above all the general luxuriance of the vegetation' (Darwin 1839/1958: 10). He noted the gaudy scenery of the Bahia de Todos os Santos, the beauty of that of Guanabara Bay, and the striking effect of the huge rounded masses of naked rock rising out of the luxuriant vegetation around Rio de Janeiro. It is the splendour of the physical environment which captures his imagination and dominates his writing – the colours of the sea and sky, the brilliance of butterflies, the fantastic forms of plants, the beauty and delicious fragrance of the flowers. For Darwin, as for others, this was a tropical paradise. On his return journey to England he recorded his inability to capture the essence of this environment. Having attempted to convey an impression of the landscape around Salvador, he claimed that though he had described the elements of the scenery, it was hopeless to attempt to paint the general effect. 'Epithet after epithet was found too weak to convey to those who have not visited the intertropical regions, the sensations of delight which the mind experiences' (ibid. 430). The land of Brazil was 'one great wild, untidy, luxuriant hothouse, made by Nature for herself, but taken possession of by man, who has studded it with gay houses and formal gardens'. He felt he would be able to retain individual elements in this landscape, 'but the thousand beauties which unite these into one perfect scene must fade away; yet they will leave, like a tale heard in childhood, a picture full of indistinct, but most beautiful figures' (ibid. 431).

Such eulogistic paeans about the wonderland of this tropical paradise recur in the writings of many of the foreign naturalists. Darwin, in common with his near contemporaries, and some twentieth century successors, interpreted this natural profusion as a symbol of great potential. Man's impact upon this vast resource was negligible – 'only a very small piece had been cleared, yet almost every acre was capable of yielding all the various rich productions of a tropical land. Considering the enormous area of Brazil, the proportion of cultivated ground can scarcely be considered as anything, compared to that which is left in the state of nature: at some future age, how vast a population it will support' (ibid. 20). Unsurprisingly perhaps, for such scientist-visitors, Nature was a magnificent obsession; man's role was negligible. His mark upon the landscape was limited; it was probably ephemeral before the aggressive forests. Furthermore, not only was man's impact upon the natural environment limited but frequently, by the standards of 'civilized' Europeans, much of what had been accomplished left much to be desired. For Darwin, Recife in 1836 was 'in all parts disgusting, the streets being narrow, illpaved, and filthy; the houses, tall and gloomy' (ibid. 431).

Impressions such as these are recurrent in the writings of the naturalists who visited Brazil. During the first half of the century a number of British naturalists, W. H. Edwards, H. W. Bates, A. R. Wallace and R. Spruce, spent considerable periods in Amazonia. Their writings again are dominated by detailed recording of their scientific activities and by their reactions to the magnificent luxury of the natural environment, against which man's activities are puny, threatened and certainly inferior in comparison to those of England. Bates, arriving at Bélem in 1848, was 'about to see and examine the beauties of a tropical country for the first time' (Bates 1863/1975: 1). The great primaeval forest contained, for him, so many wonders. The city of Belém was hemmed in by the perpetual forest, its suburban houses half buried in luxuriant foliage. His first impressions of the city are a negative catalogue of gloomy buildings, unpaved and narrow streets, irregular and mean houses, weed-grown gardens, ill-fed livestock and idle, sad-looking people; all offset and compensated for by 'the overpowering beauty of the vegetation' and 'the teeming profusion of nature' (ibid. 3). The record of his 11 year sojourn in the Amazon forest provides a wealth of detail about the natural landscape, and the limited amount of settlement and economic development which had taken place. Both Bates and Wallace saw this as a land of great potential. Bates noted soils 'of marvellous fertility, even for Brazil' (ibid. 255), and Wallace claimed that the virgin forest could easily by converted into an earthly paradise of rich pasture and meadow land, cultivated fields, gardens and orchards, containing every variety of produce (Wallace 1853 / 1972: 230–1).

One element of importance from these writings arises where their authors made long or return visits to Brazil, so that they record landscape change. Although Bates's view of the man-made landscape tended to be unfavourable, he does give some impression of the type of change taking place in Amazonia at mid-century. Thus Belém had been improved from the weedy, ruinous, village-looking place he encountered in 1848; by 1859 streets had been paved, handsome new buildings had replaced dilapidated ones and there had been general urban improvement, with the draining of swamps and the planting of trees along major avenues. The population had increased with the influx of Portuguese, Madeiran and German immigrants. Health conditions had improved, and there was greater awareness of European fashions and customs. For Bates, though, this growth and improvement had its adverse side. The forest which surrounded the town had been forced back by felling and 'ugly muddy roads' penetrated the once clean and lonely woods (Bates 1863 / 1975:

387). Houses, fields and food-processing mills had advanced against the once glorious forest scenery.

The conflict between man and nature is a recurring theme in these writings, as indeed it has been in the creation of the Brazilian landscape. This is particularly the case in description of Rio de Janeiro, where the extraordinary beauty of the natural landscape is contrasted with the poverty of the man-made one. Many authors deprecate their ability to describe the beauties of Guanabara Bay, though most make the attempt!

For D. P. Kidder 'the first entrance of an individual into such a harbour as that of Rio de Janeiro deserves to form an era in his existence' (Kidder 1845: I,20). For Mathison (1825: 7) the bay encompassed all possible combinations of picturesque scenery in one magnificent perspective. Gardner (1849: 3) felt the scenery was perhaps unequalled on the face of the earth, and described lovely little verdant and palm-clad islands rising from the bosom of the bay, with the surrounding hills and lofty mountains, gilded by the setting sun, forming a befitting frame for such a picture. For those less willing to wax lyrical, and for the benefit of readers at home, the bay was compared to more familiar, European scenes, though these varied from the Bay of Naples, to the Corniche at Menton, the Trossachs and Clovelly! Having expressed their approbation of the natural scenery of Guanabara Bay, many travellers counterposed the setting and the city of Rio de Janeiro – 'standing as it does on one of the most beautiful sites in the whole world, and with perhaps the finest harbour of any sea; everything, and more or less every person about it, is ugly, uninteresting, shabby and mean' (Burke and Staples 1886: 44). If its site was magnificent, nineteenth century Rio was, for most visitors, characterized by narrow, unpaved and dirty streets, with poor housing and an absence of striking public buildings. Adverse comments on the city colour the opinions of many foreign visitors in the nineteenth century, from John Mawe (1812) to W. R. Kennedy (1892).

In fact most Brazilian cities and towns appear to have failed to meet the exacting standards of metropolitan Europeans. Gardner described Conceição de Mato Dentro in Minas Gerais, as 'one of the most miserable places I have ever seen' (Gardner 1849: 367), while the lower town in Salvador consisted of 'one long street, which is both narrow, badly paved and dirty' (ibid. 56), and Santos was characterized by decayed landing places and dilapidated warehouses (Codman 1867: 55). D. P. Kidder (1845: II, 300) summarized the Brazilian urban scene: 'All the Brazilian towns have two peculiarities which add to their external appearance – first, the buildings have a uniform colour, white; second, every eminence or prominent point within them is adorned with a temple of antique structure'.

Visitors to Rio frequently travelled into its environs in the nearby serras and the Paraíba valley. Darwin recorded the simple form of a Rio *fazenda*, its design well suited to the climate, surrounded by its storehouses, stables and slave dwellings, and the patch of cleared ground producing coffee, manioc, rice and beans but hemmed in by the wall of the dark green luxuriant forest

(1839/1958: 19). Other visitors penetrated this area during the beginning of the coffee boom, and provide evidence of its dynamism. Mansfield (1856/ 1971: 101) visited a *fazenda* where, in a mere 11 years, the virgin forest had been transformed into miles of coffee and beautiful pasture. Walsh contrasted the new landscape of the dark shining foliage of a coffee plantation with that of the vivid transparent green of the canefields (Walsh 1830 II: 14).

Walsh was a relatively early visitor to Brazil and his travels in the South-east provide a nice portrait of the varying spatial pattern of the landscapes produced by man, from the rich plains around Rio into the Minas goldfields. By the late 1820s the fertile area around Rio de Janeiro was covered with *fazendas* and generally well cultivated, with the original forest largely replaced by bananas, mangoes and other fruit trees, contrasting with the more difficult environment of the serras, where the principal modifications were derived from mining rather than agriculture.

Walsh records the destructive impact of mining on the landscape, with the river banks bearing the scars of the extensive search for gold 'furrowed out in a most extraordinary manner' (Walsh 1830: 105). This destruction provided a poor setting for the once Rich Town of Black Gold (Ouro Prêto), set 'in the midst of bare, sterile mountains, whose naked flanks are ruptured and torn open in search of gold, leaving no objects but unsightly quarries above, and an irksome, sandy muddy plain below' (ibid. 194). The once golden city presented a decayed, repulsive and disagreeable look. Caldcleugh (1825: 248) was similarly unimpressed, commenting on the decayed state of the town, its lack of noteworthy buildings, and its undistinguished churches. Burton (1869 / 1969: 140) was even more dismissive: the baroque churches of the mining towns were 'primitive, tawdry and grotesque'.

Burton's journey from Rio, through the goldfields and down the São Francisco river, provides an interesting, if generally critical, portrait of mid-century Brazil. His comment on the lands around Entre Rios, 'cleaned out' for coffee by farming malpractice, is terse: 'every stream is a sewer of liquid manure, coursing to the Atlantic, and the superficial soil is that of a brickfield' (ibid. 42). Elsewhere he notes roads 'converted into rock ladders, rut-systems and quagmire holes' (ibid. 58), and stresses the necessity of transport improvement for the country's development, indicating that improved communications would bring civilization, prosperity and progress.

Like other travellers, he could admire the physical landscape. In the Serra da Mantiqueira – 'there was the usual beautiful Brazilian perspective, tier after tier of mountain, hill, hillock, rise and wavy horizon; the colours of the forest were black-green, light green, brown-green, blue-green, blue and azure' (ibid. 65). At the end of his journey the falls of Paulo Afonso were a dashing, dazzling, whirling, churning surfaceless mass – 'a wondrous study of fluid in motion'! (ibid. II, 444).

There are relatively few descriptions of the North-east, particularly the interior *sertão*. Numerous travellers left comments on the ports, especially Recife and Salvador, but few penetrated inland. Exceptions are Gardner, who travelled across Ceará, Piauí and Goiás to Minas Gerais, and Koster, who made several overland journeys in the region. For Gardner (1849: 138) the interior of Ceará, in the dry season was little better than a desert. Koster (1816/1966: 39) travelled in the interior during a drought year, noting that 'the grass was all gone, and even the hardy trees, the *acaju* and *mangaba*, seemed to feel the want of water'. He observed the response to drought which persists to the present day for, on one estate where the cattle were all dying, he found the people 'intending, if there was no rain very soon, to leave their houses' (ibid. 41). With considerable perspicacity he suggested that the land near Natal, in Rio Grande do Norte, could never 'in any state of civilization, or from any increase of population be rendered a fertile tract', but that improvement might be possible if wells were sunk, storage reservoirs built, and trees planted (ibid. 44).

The South also received few foreign visitors, though Bigg-Wither (1878/1968: 111) provides some portraits of the little developed parts of Paraná. His writings for example contrast the 'golden coloured prairie extending to the extreme bounds of vision, rolling away in giant billows' in southern Paraná, with the great forests of the remote interior, which comprised 'wild scenes of savage nature' (ibid. vii). He also provides descriptions of colonization schemes in the area, and particularly comments on the misleading publicity which had ensnared people to migrate in the belief they would become landed proprietors. Propaganda maps showed roads and railways which did not exist, small villages were shown in the same type as large towns; literature described noble rivers, broad expanses of green waving grass and belts of well-grown timber which recalled the woodlands of England. When the colonists arrived they found that reality 'proved so much harsher than the picture they had drawn in their own minds' (ibid. 184). Earlier Fletcher and Kidder (1866: 332–3) had commented on the emerging colonist landscapes of northern Santa Catarina, describing Joinville as 'the beginning of a new town in the wilderness, houses stuck down in the woods, and plenty of mud and children', and recording the smallness and newness of the houses, the deadened trees and the muddy streets.

It is perhaps unsurprising that many foreign visitors finding and often being overwhelmed by the super abundance of Nature, and observing the limited and, to their 'enlightened' eyes, inferior impact of man in tapping the wealth of this wonderland, felt that things could be much improved by European initiative and innovation. Burton noted the absence of European chemical science and modern machinery on the sugar plantations. Caldcleugh (1825: I, 53) felt that the country had been deprived of 'many of those beautiful articles of English manufacture'. An extreme view is that of Mansfield, who claimed 'what a paradise is, or at least might be, this country if it were possessed by the English'! (Mansfield 1856/1971: 20).

In the latter part of the century visitors commented on the landscape changes wrought by European activities. Mulhall's Anglocentric view noted 'the colossal works of improvement already completed or in course of construction, under English engineers' (Mulhall 1878: 519). These activities were particularly in the fields of resource development, infrastructural provision and urban improvement, where British capital was 'called upon to perform the wonders of a magician' (ibid. 600). The railways were a crucial element in landscape change. Codman praised the combination of English capital and American engineering in the construction of the Dom Pedro II railway, climbing precipices, bridging chasms and tunnelling solid mountains (Codman 1867: 61). Hadfield stressed the importance of railway development, for 'it is only when a railway penetrates the primeval forests and goes into the heart of a country, that an adequate idea can be formed of what it is capable of being made' (Hadfield 1869: 86). With uncanny prescience he identified the then newly opened Santos – São Paulo railway as 'one of the grandest works yet made by English capital in Brazil, and one destined to play a very important part in the future development of the fine province of São Paulo' (ibid. 58). He foresaw the profound consequences of the railway, claiming that 'Santos is not to be judged by its present status, but by what the railway must make it' (ibid. 241), and identifying its effects in extending the area within which coffee could be cultivated (1877: 161).

The writings of Hadfield are of particular utility in considering landscape change in Brazil, for he produced three studies spanning the mid-nineteenth century (Hadfield 1854, 1869,1877). These provide us, either from his own comments on change or by comparison of the three studies, with considerable insight into the process and pattern of social and economic change. These include modernization in the sugar industry in Pernambuco, the advance of the Paulista coffee frontier, the impact of steamships and railways on economic development and urban improvements in cities such as Rio, Recife and Salvador.

Towards the end of the century these sources diminish in significance. More practical volumes, as guides for investors, and more academic geographies began to appear. The traveller's tale genre began to concentrate on the continuing obsession with the mysterious interior of Amazonia, which lured in explorer-travellers such as Roosevelt (1914) and Savage-Landor (1913). Savage-Landor even in 1911 could interpret Brazil as scarcely developed. In his view all the wonderful riches of the country were still dormant. The coast was highly civilized; so, more or less, was the immediate hinterland of the large cities, but away from them or a narrow zone along the railways one relapsed, he claimed, into the Middle Ages (op. cit. 6). He also claimed that it was the Brazilians who least knew their own country, caring little about developing their beautiful land.

Twentieth century heirs to the traveller's tale tellers have tended to concentrate on Amazonian exotica – jungle, Indians, snakes, piranha fish, the abandoned relics of the rubber boom, themes beloved of popular literature on Brazil, and more recently of television producers. 'Exploration Fawcett' (Fawcett 1953) is a striking example of this form, with its concern for lost cities, snakes, fever and flies. Such works have created and perpetuate overseas a particular image of Brazil, a land and landscape of wildness and wilderness.

The neo-colonial period, in which Brazilian development was closely enmeshed with the rise of North Atlantic capitalism, can be traced into the twentieth century, and experienced a significant break at the time of the Great Depression, with its profound impact on Brazil's primary product export economy. By 1920 the population had grown to more than 30 million, as opposed to an estimated 4 million at independence. This population remained close to the coast, with over 90 per cent of the inhabitants living in the North-east, South-east and South regions. In Amazonia and the Centre-West population density was below 0.5 persons per km^2; in the North-east and South it was below 10 persons, and in the South-east close to 15 persons. Thus although the population had grown rapidly over the century, by natural increase and immigration, it remained spatially concentrated. Man's impact on substantial areas of the national territory remained minimal. Even in the relatively more settled coastal areas his impact was uneven, and some areas remained little changed.

The country was still essentially rural and agricultural in character. Nine-tenths of the population lived in settlements of less than 20 000 people, and two-thirds of the workforce were employed in agriculture. The late nineteenth and early twentieth century period was the apogée of Brazil's primary product export economy. Coffee had come to pre-eminence, and over the period 1890–1920 provided over half of the country's export earnings in all but four years. Coffee was supported by rubber in Amazonia, cacao in Bahia and sugar in the North-east, all creating distinctive landscapes and contributing to the modification of the natural landscape. The established pastoral economies persisted with little modification in the north-eastern *sertão* and the far south. These commercial activities were underlain by subsistence activities, largely dependent on traditional slash and burn cultivation.

Into these patterns created by the economic cycles had been intruded some new elements. Immigration had introduced new patterns of land holding, land use and distinct cultural landscapes in the southern states and, after the abolition of slavery, had contributed to changes in the balance of the racial structure of the population. New innovations, derived from the more advanced economies and societies of Europe and North America, in the form of new means of transport, urban services and changing fashions in architecture, dress and life-style had contributed to the modernization of the urban landscape. The beginnings of the growth of factory-based industries had contributed to urban growth, as had the influx of population by internal and international migration. The form of the cities was also in process of change, as they began to spread, and to develop greater internal specialization of both economic activity and social structure.

Even so it could be argued that neither the 'traditional' landscape of the economic cycles nor the 'new' landscapes imported, with or without modification, from Europe and the U.S.A. made more than limited impact on the totality of the Brazilian environment. In 1911 Pierre Denis could still interpret Brazil as essentially a monotonous natural landscape. The works of man in this landscape were insignificant. In contrast to Europe, where generations of men had worked to tame, discipline and diversify nature, in Brazil the recent and dispersed population was still struggling against natural forces stronger than itself; the human landscape remained unfinished. (op. cit. 88).

Part IV

6
The modern landscape

In the twentieth century Brazil has become less dependent on an export economy dominated by primary products. The two world wars and the inter-war depression revealed the vulnerability of such dependency, particularly when dominated by a single commodity, coffee. Throughout the late 1920s coffee provided over 70 per cent of export earnings. Subsequently that proportion has shown a generally downward trend, returning briefly to high levels in the early 1950s. By 1975 it contributed only 10 per cent, but rose slightly in 1976 largely in response to world price increases brought about by frost destruction of the Paraná crop. This changing structure has been encouraged by the Brazilian government, which has sought to reduce coffee output and to encourage the export of other commodities. In addition, attempts have been made to create a more diverse and self-sufficient internal economy.

This process of economic growth and diversification has, of course, had substantial consequences for the landscape. In addition, although the country has followed an avowedly capitalist path of development, the State has come to play an increasing role in the economy, both in shaping its direction and by direct participation. The State has also been increasingly involved in non-economic spheres, such as social welfare, housing and conservation. Thus, some of the trends in landscape evolution have been overtly shaped by the State.

If, in the process of development and diversification, the country has become somewhat less dependent in its relations with Europe and North America, it has still continued to borrow heavily, both for the technology used in the development process, and in the desired life-style sought by its population. In this two major trends have become apparent. One is an increasing move towards the towns and cities. Brazilian society has become increasingly urban in character. In 1940 less than one-third of the population of 41 millions lived in towns; during the 1960s the urban dwellers became a majority and in 1970, 56 per cent of the population was classed as urban. It has been predicted that during the 1980s there will be a fall in the absolute number of rural dwellers. Thus, for the bulk of the population, their everyday landscape is an urban one.

In common with the inhabitants of most developed and developing countries Brazilian citizens have shared in the so-called 'revolution of rising expectations', seeking a better standard of living and life-style, expressed in the consumer-good dominated affluence of Western capitalism, in which material possessions of radios, televisions, automobiles and household gadgetry are seen as symbols of a 'good life'. Such aspirations have become common in Brazil, partly fostered by the substantial participation of multi-national corporations in the country's 'economic miracle', contributing both directly to the 'miracle' and shaping the tastes of its beneficiaries. To some extent therefore there has been a trend towards the increasing universal uniformity identified by J. H. Plumb (1969). He suggests that ancient and distinctive patterns of living are crumbling, and being replaced by others, in which places in various parts of the world have more in common than they have in difference. That may well be, certainly for the Third World, an extreme or premature view. Nonetheless there are, in the Brazil of the 1980s, elements of such 'universal' landscapes. At the same time the benefits of economic progress, and their expression in the landscape, have not been equally shared. There are 'richer' and 'poorer' segments of society, districts of cities and regions of the country. Pronounced contrasts between town and country exist. 'Modern' and 'traditional' elements are juxtaposed. Moreover, as the trends of urbanization grow, there are growing contrasts between the relatively constrained urban landscapes experienced by the rising majority of urban dwellers, and those of the enormous and less-developed rural and natural landscapes inhabited by a diminishing minority.

Landscapes of development

1930 marks an important watershed in the process of Brazilian development, with profound consequences for the nature and pattern of economic progress, and with significant impact on the landscape. Throughout the colonial period, the Empire, and the Old Republic, Brazil had been essentially a rural country, in which the products of its land formed the basis of its export-orientated economy, which was underlain by simple subsistence activities. A high proportion of the population lived in the countryside, and effective political power was in the hands of large landowners and exercised in their interests. During the late nineteenth and early twentieth centuries, some stimulus had been given to industrial development and the towns had begun to grow, but in 1920 two-thirds of the active population were still employed in agriculture.

The world depression of the inter-war years revealed the risks of Brazil's dependency on a single vulnerable commodity, coffee, and prompted concern for both the diversification of the export sector and the creation of a more diversified and autonomous economy. The Revolution of 1930, which brought Getúlio Vargas to power, marked an effective end to the political power of the landed oligarchy of São Paulo and Minas Gerais. Vargas's strategy, particularly under the Estado Novo (1937–45), aimed at a nationalistic pattern of economic development and diversification. The State moved from its traditional economic liberalism to intervene directly in the economy, and in particular to foster an industrial sector.

In the nineteenth century Brazilian governments had fulfilled their basic roles of providing defence, law and order, and basic public works. From the early twentieth century there had been involvement in the economy, particularly to protect or stimulate the production of commodities such as coffee, sugar,rubber and maté. Since 1930 this involvement has been more comprehensive and explicit and the State has taken a major role in shaping the broad nature of the country's development path. Initially this was in terms of specific projects or the provision of infrastructure, but in the post-war period there has been a virtually continuous sequence of development plans which have markedly influenced the nature and pattern of Brazilian development.

In this context three major themes need to be noted. Firstly, although State-promoted projects may, of themselves, have very limited direct impact on the landscape, they may have profound symbolic or indirect consequences. While a power line, a highway or a factory may be a mere line or dot on the map and landscape, their wider implications may be substantial. Since 1930, as a statement of both intent and achievement, Brazil has been a 'developing country', seeking to achieve economic advance. Specific projects therefore have had great significance for Brazilians, in symbolizing the economic progress and transformation of their country. Such projects also bring other changes, as stimuli of growth, prompting migration, urbanization, other economic activities and so on.

Secondly, in the nature of Brazilian politics before 1964, and to some extent subsequently, development programmes and projects have been associated with particular political administrations. Especially in the period 1930–64 there was a tendency to foster large, prestigious projects, which became the symbolic achievements of a particular presidency and which might even perpetuate the president's name – the Presidente Vargas steelworks, the Dutra highway, the Presidente Castelo Branco dam. Such a pattern operated at all levels of Brazilian politics, from the parochial to the national. This Clochemerle-esque process has left its mark on the landscape, from public urinals and local bus stations to multi-lane highways, new towns or major industrial complexes. Such legacies may also document the career of a politician. A classic example is that of Juscelino Kubitschek, who rose from the prefecture of a town in interior Minas Gerais to the presidency. As mayor of Belo Horizonte he was responsible for the development of the suburb of Pampulha and its *avant-garde* buildings; the platform of his governorship of Minas Gerais was 'energy and transport', and resulted directly in substantial provision of electric power and paved roads and indirectly in substantial industrialization. The slogan of his campaign for the presidency, '50 years progress in 5', admirably captures the spirit and nature of recent Brazilian development; his administration (1956–61) saw very considerable and diverse economic advance, and the building of Brasília. Since the Revolution of 1964 the cult of personality in Brazilian

Fig. 6.1 Soccer is an essential part of the Brazilian scene, and the building of sports stadia is an integral part of government development programmes. The Estádio Magalhães Pinto, in Belo Horizonte, is named after a former state governor.

politics has been less overt, but successive administrations have continued to sponsor development strategies and projects.

Thirdly, although the State has taken a growing place in the development process, the Brazilian model of development has remained avowedly capitalist, so that the structure which has evolved has involved the participation of the State, domestic capitalists and multi-national corporations. Consequently the landscapes created by the 'economic miracle' which has taken place in recent years contain the influence of these three elements. Over the past half century Brazil has sought to 'develop'. The process of development has been shaped by the State, which has set a broad strategy to be achieved by a combination of public, private and foreign investment. That strategy has been dominated by two considerations. The first has been the need to provide an infrastructure on which productive development might take place, and thus requiring the improvement or provision of energy, transport, education and health facilities, housing and urban services. Secondly, the underlying premise of the development strategy was that the traditional economy, based on primary production and export, was vulnerable and therefore there should be economic diversification by the development of a manufacturing sector, to substitute imports and provide alternative exports.

Early State action was essentially nationalistic, and concerned primarily with the control of resources. Codes of mining and water use (for power generation) were promulgated, giving the State oversight of their exploitation. In 1939 the supply of petroleum was declared to be of national concern, and placed under the oversight of a Conselho Nacional de Petróleo. During the 1920s highways began to supersede the railways as a major means of transport, federal funds were made available for highway construction and in 1945 a Departmento Nacional de Estradas de Rodagem to coordinate a federal highway plan was established.

The Second World War had several effects on the pattern of Brazilian development. It revealed the inadequacies of the energy and transport systems, it prompted the production of raw materials for the Allied cause and it stimulated domestic industrialization in consequence of reduced imports. During the war several economic commissions examined ways of promoting Brazilian development, tending to focus on a 'bottle neck' approach, which favoured modernization and expansion of the infrastructure of power and transport as providing a base for development. During the war four specific projects were sponsored by the State, the Volta Redonda steelworks, Duque de Caxias lorry factory, Cabo Frio alkali plant and the Rio Doce iron mines, all but the latter located in Rio de Janeiro state.

The Volta Redonda steelworks was of particular significance in the changing direction of Brazilian development. It was seen as symbolizing the arrival of the Industrial Revolution in Brazil and as epitomizing 'in its long concrete walls, its towering stacks, and its complex machines the culmination of . . . hopes for changing Brazil from a predominantly agrarian nation to a modern industrial society' (Soares e Silva 1943). It was regarded not only as a symbol of Brazilian achievement but refuting the opinion that heavy industry could never come to the tropics. It was also, at the time, probably the largest single construction project undertaken in Brazil.

Since the war Brazil has utilized a series of development plans, of increasing complexity and comprehensiveness. The first, Plan SALTE (1949–53), was concerned with basic provision of improved health, food supply, transport and energy. The second, Programma de Metas (1956–60),was more broadly based, involving not only the infrastructure, but the productive sector, and promoted major industrial advance. It set 30 targets to be achieved by State, private and foreign investment. Described as the most comprehensive effort by a Western underdeveloped country to foster economic development (Jaguaribe 1968: 150), it resulted in progress in many spheres. Between 1956 and 1961 installed power capacity increased from 3.5 m kw to 5.2 m kw, oil refining capacity was virtually tripled, the extent of federal highways was increased from 22 500 km to 35 400 km and of paved highway from 2376 km to 9591 km. Progress in the industrial sector was particularly marked. Steel output was increased from 1.36 million tons to 2.28 million tons, with the construction of two major steelworks and the expansion or construction of others. Cement output increased from 2.7 million tons to 4.4 million tons, again from new and expanded factories. A substantial car industry, developed by multinational auto firms, was established, as well as two major shipyards. There was also expansion in the engineering, electrical goods and metal industries.

Such developments had two effects. Directly they introduced substantial new elements into the landscape – major factories and industrial concentrations, new highways, electricity grids and so on. Such developments are, of themselves, visually striking; they form major elements in the landscape, and often stand in marked contrast to the persisting elements of traditional Brazil. At the same time their total areal extent, relative to the totality of Brazil, is limited. Clusters of factories, major projects at virgin sites or the thin lines of roads and power cable are, in that context, insignificant (Map 10). Yet such developments also have indirect effects. Factories depend on labour concentrations and thus prompt urban growth, and attract migrants; highways and power lines are elements of modernization, diffusing the phenomena of change. The highways served to integrate existing regional economies and demographic concentrations, and provide the means of penetration into the interior. All of these developments have promoted changes in the landscape, introducing the paraphernalia of modern developed world technology into landscapes of underdevelopment.

Fig. 6.2 Economic progress. The industrial estate of Contagem, near Belo Horizonte, Minas Gerais. The foreground suggests the important role of road transport.

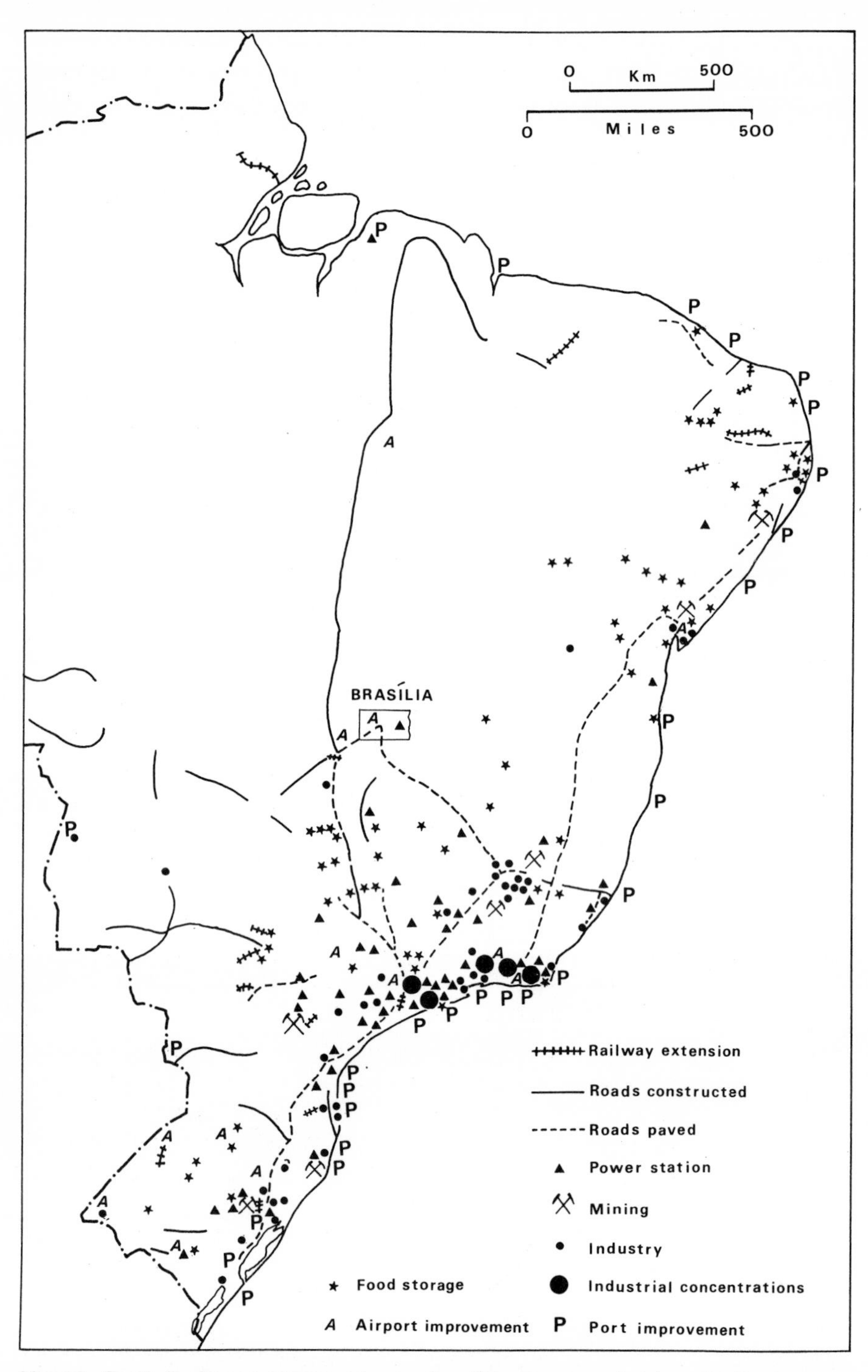

Map 10 Brazil: the impact of economic planning. This map, compiled from the Programa de Metas (1956–60), attempts to indicate the spatial impact of development planning. It suggests the spatial concentration of industrialization and power provision, and the thin lines of development provided by transport projects.

The early 1960s were a period of economic and political difficulty in Brazil, but the period between 1968 and 1974 saw a new spurt of economic advance, the period of Brazil's 'economic miracle'. This saw high rates of economic growth and economic progress, again within the framework of national economic plans and with principal stress on infrastructural advance and industrialization. Such strategies aimed at substantial expansion in industrial output, in areas such as steel and cement production, chemicals, cellulose and paper, engineering, shipbuilding and tractor manufacture, and in the provision of electricity and highways. In recent years, federal planning has given greater attention to the agricultural sector, attempting to increase output of food and export crops, and improve inputs of machinery, fertilizers, insecticides and better seeds. Investment in housing and basic urban services has also increased. During the period of the Second National Development Plan (1975–79) the balance of planned federal investment gave the largest proportion (25 per cent) to infrastructure, 14.6 per cent to industry and 6 per cent to agriculture. Social provision for health, education, housing, and urban services received 21.6 per cent, and the balance went to social security, scientific research and regional development. After 1973 the rate of economic growth slowed somewhat and the pattern of development was modified. Much of the earlier development strategy had been premised on the continued availability of cheap oil imports, and the rapid escalation of world oil prices by OPEC placed substantial burdens on Brazil's balance of payments, and forced some reappraisal of the energy and transport sector. Subsequently attention has been given to greater output of hydro-electric power, the development of nuclear power, a more intensive search for domestic petroleum sources and the exploitation of alternative energy sources such as oil shale and industrial alcohol. The latter has had a major impact on the production of sugar cane, from which the alcohol is distilled. More attention has also been given to rail and sea transport and the development of urban mass transit systems.

A major consequence of this planned development is that the State has come to play a major role in the shaping of Brazilian society and economy. Between 1947 and the early 1970s government expenditure as a proportion of gross national product virtually doubled, to 30 per cent, and State investment in the economic and social infrastructure, and in manufacturing, contributed a substantial proportion of total investment. In addition State-owned companies are among the country's largest. At least half of the top 30 firms in Brazil have substantial federal investment, and include the Petrobrás oil monopoly, the Cia. Vale do Rio Doce mining company, and the Cia. Siderúrgica Nacional steel company.

The State then has come to play a major role in the structure of the Brazilian economy, and this participation has spatial expression and landscape consequences. However, for a considerable period, although the State encouraged the growth and diversification of the economy, it did not seek to influence where that change took place. In consequence, before 1960 much of this modernization tended to concentrate in the economically most attractive area, the

South-east. Thus the states of São Paulo, Rio de Janeiro and Minas Gerais were the principal beneficiaries of infrastructural provision and industrialization, and the direct and indirect consequences of this progress were most apparent in the landscapes of this region; change elsewhere was much less marked.

Such processes perpetuated and intensified regional imbalances and inequalities, beween the more developed and modernized South-east, the less developed North-east and South and the largely undeveloped interior Centre-West and North. Concern for such inequality was expressed in the 1963–65 Plano Trienal, and regional development policy has become an explicit part of the three National Development Plans, 1972–74, 1975–79 and 1980–85. In these, attempts have been made to strike a balance between maintaining the growth impetus of the dynamic South-east, and fostering progress elsewhere. The 1972–74 plan incorporated programmes for national integration, the Programa de Integração Nacional (PIN), and land redistribution and stimulation of agro-industries, the Programa de Redistribuição de Terras e de Estimulo á Agro-Indústria do Norte e do Nordeste (PROTERRA). These incorporated the highway and colonization schemes for Amazonia and irrigation projects in the North-east. The 1975–79 and 1980–85 plans also identified some of the problems emerging from the very success of planned growth, with its concentration in the South-east and especially in the major cities which began to experience increasing congestion, pollution and overpopulation. In consequence efforts have been made to control and diffuse some of this growth in recent planning.

Although concern for regional inequality has only become an integral part of national planning in the last two decades, the State has shown concern for its impoverished areas for over a century. In the North-east periodic drought has prompted relief programmes and various strategies designed to improve conditions in the region. Between 1877 and 1945 the principal strategy was to build dams, initially as sources for irrigation, but more commonly to provide reservoirs for cattle and men in the dry season and drought years. These dams or *açudes*, have become a common feature of the *sertão* landscape. By 1976 there were over 1000 of these reservoirs in the North-east, with a storage capacity of 12 billion m^3 of water. Recent government policy has promoted greater use of this stored water and the exploitation of other sources to develop irrigated agriculture in the *sertão*. Public works schemes using refugees from the droughts have also given the region a good basic road net. Since 1959 regional development policy for the North-east has been broadened to include rationalization of the sugar economy – a strategy which met with little success – the introduction of drought-resistant crops in the interior and industrialization. The latter policy contributed to industrial growth and diversification, but development tended to concentrate in the principal cities of Recife, Salvador and Fortaleza (Dickenson 1980).

In Amazonia regional development programmes since 1946 have sought to improve basic conditions for the population and to secure more rational exploitation of the region's resources. As in the case of the North-east much of the growth and change tended to concentrate in the principal cities.

In addition to federal strategies to secure national and regional development, many of the states of the federation have formulated development programmes, seeking to promote economic advance. Such strategies tend to mirror those of the central government, providing improved infrastructure, agricultural change and industrialization.

In consequence then of the activities of government at national, regional and state level new elements of modernization are being introduced into the Brazilian landscape. Such changes include the creation of massive dams and storage reservoirs, major industrial projects, industrial concentrations and planned industrial estates, new farm equipment and farming techniques. These serve to introduce into the man-made landscape which has evolved over 450 years elements of developed world technology and landscape. The concentration of much of this modernization into the South-east, and particularly into the triangle formed by the cities of São Paulo, Rio de Janeiro and Belo Horizonte, has tended to polarize the contrasts between the economic 'core' of the South-east and surrounding 'periphery', and between the major cities and the less dynamic countryside.

Although the State has been a major agent in determining the nature of Brazil's development process, its commitment to a capitalist system has also meant the involvement of the private sector, and a good deal of the industrialization has been in the hands of multinational corporations. During the nineteenth century foreign investment concentrated particularly in the provision of infrastructure, but in the inter-war and post-war period investment in the manufacturing sector increased. This was particularly encouraged in the late 1950s, when it accounted for one-tenth of industrial investment. Such investment has been particularly important in 'growth' industries such as automobiles, engineering and electrical goods. The pharmaceutical, rubber and tobacco industries are also important areas of foreign investment. In consequence multinational firms such as Mercedes, Ford, Volkswagen, Mannesmann, Alcan, General Electric, Goodyear and Nestlé rank among Brazil's principal firms. In their location such firms have tended to concentrate in the South-east, particularly in Greater São Paulo, contributing to the evolution of industrial landscapes resembling in scale and structure those of the developed world.

The encouragement of economic advance in Brazil has prompted considerable change. The structure of the economy has been diversified, Brazil has become a major economic power, ranking as the eighth largest market in the Western world, and levels of development, as measured by *per capita* income, have risen. High rates of economic growth have been achieved particularly in the period 1956–61 and 1968–74, when the country was characterized by considerable dynamism and some areas at least were subject to rapid landscape change. The process has introduced into the landscape structures regarded as symbolic and characteristic of economic development, and has also prompted other changes, particularly expansion of the cities and of the urban population. Within the cities distinctive industrial areas have emerged, with concentration of factories, highways, railways, power lines and other features associated with industrialization. In consequence areas such as the Zona Norte of Rio de Janeiro, or São Bernardo in Greater São Paulo have industrial landscapes closely resembling those of Europe or North America. Elsewhere, in an effort to concentrate scarce resources for industrialization, industrial estates have been planned, forming distinctive and more regulated concentrations of industry, such as those of Contagem (Minas Gerais), Aratu (Bahia) and Paulista and Cabo (Pernambuco). The development of particular resources at previously unpopulated sites has prompted the growth of company towns dominated by a single factory.

Other elements of modernity are over 50 000 km of paved federal highway and over 25 000 MW of installed electric power capacity. As Brazil is seemingly deficient in fossil fuel, over 85 per cent of this power comes from hydroelectric sources. These sources include a number of major power stations, such as those at Furnas and Estreito in Minas Gerais, Ilha Solteira in São Paulo and Paulo Afonso in Bahia, and major projects at Tucurui in Pará, Itumbiara (Minas Gerais) and Itaipu (Brazil – Paraguay border). Increased electric capacity has made possible some provision of electricity in the countryside and although agriculture has tended to be rather neglected in federal planning policy, recent strategies have included extension of the area of land under irrigation, and expansion of the cultivation of wheat, rice, soya beans and other crops.

Townscapes

The 'drift to the towns' has been one of the most striking trends in twentieth century Brazil. Within 80 years there has been a profound transformation from a rural society and an agricultural economy to one in which towns and urban based activities have taken on a greater role. In 1970, 56 per cent of the population, or 52 million people, lived in places defined as urban. Some of these urban places have small populations and few urban functions, acquiring their urban status by virtue of being the seat of administration for a municipio, Brazil's basic political unit. If the figure of 20 000 inhabitants is taken as minimum size for defining a settlement as urban, then in 1970 such settlements contained almost 39 per cent of the national population, almost double their 1950 share of 21 per cent. What is even more striking in this urbanizing process is the growth of the larger cities. In 1970 over one-quarter of the population lived in cities with more than 250 000 inhabitants, as compared with 17 per cent in 1950. By 1980 the two major conurbations of São Paulo and Rio de Janeiro accounted for over 18 per cent of the national population and seven regional metropolises (Belém, Belo Horizonte, Curitiba, Fortaleza, Pôrto Alegre, Recife and Salvador) for a further 10 per cent.

The trends have thus been of rapid urban growth, due to natural increase and in-migration, and increasing concentration into the principal cities. Of the places defined as urban by the 1970 census, 303, with populations above 20 000, contained almost 34 million people. A further 13 million lived in 3640 smaller urban settlements. The level of urbanization also varies regionally. In 1970 over 70 per cent of the population of the South-east was defined as urban; in the other four macro-regions the proportion ranged from 41 to 49 per cent. Not only is the South-east more urbanized, but it has a larger share of its population in large cities. In 1980 over 46 per cent of the regional population lived in the three metropolitan areas of São Paulo, Rio de Janeiro and Belo Horizonte. In the North 17 per cent lived in Belém, in the North-east 16 per cent lived in Recife, Salvador, Fortaleza, and in the South 19 per cent lived in Pôrto Alegre and Curitiba. There is thus a contrast between the South-eastern core, dominated by the 'big cities', and the periphery, where most of the urban dwellers live in 'small towns'.

Although the urban scene has become increasingly the normal experience for a majority of Brazilians, the nature of that scene varies. Such variations are associated with many factors. Clearly the regional pattern of urbanization varies substantially. There are similarly profound contrasts between the urban experience and landscape of downtown São Paulo and that of a small town in the North-eastern *sertão* or the Amazon interior. There are variations

Fig. 6.3 Small town, Brazil. An urban scene in interior Ceará, with a lack of street paving or drainage. The mules distribute water in the absence of a piped supply.

with city size, with localization and with function. There are also variations within urban society; the urban perceptions and experiences of an established and affluent Paulista business executive are clearly very different from those of a newly arrived and impoverished rural migrant in Fortaleza or Recife.

In the localization of Brazilian cities it is a legacy of the colonial experience that many are located on the coast or on navigable waterways. Of the nine largest cities, only São Paulo, Belo Horizonte, and Curitiba are not coastal. Of the 26 state and territorial capitals, only these three plus Teresina, Goiânia and Cuiabá are not located on the coast or navigable rivers. Only in the South-east are there substantial clusters of towns inland. Elsewhere the main concentrations of urban settlement are close to the coast – in the colonization zones of Rio Grande do Sul and Santa Catarina, and around Curitiba in the South, in the Bahian Recôncavo and the Zona da Mata of the North-east.

In terms of function Brazilian geographers have categorized towns into multi-functional national and regional metropolises; industrial towns; administrative and commercial centres of various scales; and a miscellaneous group. The administrative and commercial category includes both cities such as Teresina and Cuiabá, which are state capitals, and other places of merely local significance, with populations of less than 5000, which function as municipal seats and service centres for rural areas. The miscellaneous category includes towns with specialized functions, such as the spa towns and hill stations of southern Minas Gerais and the serras of São Paulo and Rio de Janeiro; centres of religious pilgrimage such as Aparecida and Bom Jesus da Lapa; seaside resorts such as Tôrres, Guarujá, Cabo Frio and Guarapari. Also identified are the *cidades mortes*; literally the 'dead cities'. Perhaps better described as decadent, these are towns left behind after the decline of economic cycles, where commodity booms sustained urban growth, but after the collapse of the boom, the towns have found little or no alternative *raison d'être*, and have stagnated. Because of this they have become 'museum pieces' of the urban landscapes fashionable during their particular period of prosperity and have recently begun to function as tourist centres. Examples include coffee ports such as Parati, mining towns such as Diamantina or Vila Bela da Santissima Trinidade de Mato Grosso and Oeiras, one of the earliest towns to secure city status, but superseded by Teresina as the capital of Piaui.

The nature of Brazilian towns and cities therefore varies profoundly. There are no 'typical' towns; each varies with its origins, history, function and so on. A majority of Brazilians now live in urban places. They have in common some experiences which, by definition, differentiate them from their fellow-nationals still living in the countryside. Yet the nature of that experience, and the urban landscapes within which they normally live will vary in response to many factors – the size of town; its location; their location within it and movement through it; its functions; their socio-economic status; its form and so on.

The sociologist Florestan Fernandes (1972) in his study of community and society in Brazil, identifies three broad urban forms, the *vila* (town), the traditional city and the modern city. Ideally these form a sequence, by which the primitive agglomeration acquires some limited urban functions and grows progressively in population, extent and diversity, to become a modern city. Brazil, in common with other countries, has urban places at various points along this continuum.

For Fernandes the *vila* is a semi-urban agglomeration set into an essentially agricultural context and, in form and function, is concerned with servicing that rural – agricultural environment. Many examples survive, impoverished and rustic in character, small in size, with limited functions and few of the trappings of urban life. Where such settlements, because of location, some economic, politico-administrative, or other impulse have grown, they have taken on a more recognizably urban character. Their population has increased and there has been an accretion of urban functions. They become the foci of administrative, political, commercial, educational and religious activities.

For much of Brazil's history the rural mode has been dominant, and the *vila* and traditional city have operated to service its interests. The modern city represents a shift in the balance of power, as urban-based activities have become dominant in their own right. This trend began to emerge in Brazil in the latter part of the nineteenth century, but has become characteristic in the twentieth. In form and function Brazilian cities have begun to resemble their counterparts elsewhere in western capitalist civilization. Urban-based functions of manufacturing and the tertiary sector have become significant; they have become the foci of political and administrative control; and a distinctive urban life-style has emerged.

It is impossible to provide a comprehensive portrait of the nuances of the varying urban landscapes of contemporary Brazil; there is much diversity in detail. Some broad themes, however, are identifiable and capable of exploration. These include the survival of traditional elements of the small towns, the emergence of modern, metropolitan forms, and the deliberate creation of urban features in new towns and townscapes.

Small townscapes

In the case of small town Brazil, some impression of the character of such towns is given in studies such as those of Wagley (1964) in Amazonia and Harris (1971) in the Bahian *sertão*. Wagley's Itá is a small river bank settlement. It consists of a few streets, with a grid-iron layout, and three public squares. The principal buildings are the church, town hall and school. Close to the waterfront there is a row of brightly painted houses, and the main shops. Further back not all the building plots are occupied, some of the houses are in poor condition, and are thatched huts, rather than the wood and tile houses of the waterfront. The streets are unpaved. Itá experienced some prosperity during the rubber boom, but then lapsed into a limited role as administrative and service centre for a large *municipio*. Its urban services are poor and transport links limited. Over the period 1948 to 1962 it acquired electricity, radios, more shops, a new soccer pitch and some road links. Its population increased and the town had added two more streets. But it remained in essence a small town with few facilities or opportunities.

Harris's Minas Velhas is an old mining town in upland central Bahia. Harris considered it a premature town, created by the mining boom, but once that had collapsed, the town was stranded, with a local population and agricultural potential incapable of sustaining it. In 1951 it had no cars, electricity, telephone, cinema, steel or concrete. Access was by dirt road, and the town was 80 km from the railway. The streets and squares were unpaved, the streets lined with mainly single storey limewashed houses. Most of the houses are sun-dried brick, painted white, pink, green or maroon, with the woodwork picked out in blue. Roofs are tiled. Only the church and courthouse are stone built. The best streets are the ones leading to the main square; housing quality declines with distance from the square, and the more distant streets are generally the poorest parts of the town. In the villages which are satellites of Minas Velhas, houses are simpler, mainly of wattle and daub, and thatched. These houses are generally detached, not in rows. There are few shops or public buildings, whereas Minas Velhas has shops, a weekly fair and craft industries.

Fig. 6.4 A small town in eastern Minas Gerais. Clustered around the church, the settlement acts as a service centre for the surrounding countryside.

In 1951 the town was technologically backward. There was no power-driven machinery; tools and techniques were simple; the hoe was the principal agricultural implement; the mule train the principal form of local transport. Its main function was as the service and bureaucratic centre for the surrounding municipio, together with some surviving metal and leather craft activities. Despite its simplicity, Harris regards Minas Velhas as urban, distinct in form and function from its satellite villages and the countryside.

Such portraits are perhaps limited and dated; Itá and Minas Velhas may have progressed over the past two or three decades but there are still in interior Brazil many such towns. In the São Paulo coffee lands, the advance of coffee and the railway created numerous small towns. Some have since grown and diversified; others have stagnated, with monotonous townscapes, little variation in their urban plan and diversity only in detail. Similar agglomerations are to be found in the backlands of the North-east, the rural interior of the South and South-east and, in more rudimentary form, in the pioneer fringes of the Centre-West and North. They are small in size, simple in layout and fabric and restricted in function. They form the base of the urban pyramid and the bridge between country and town. They provide the tertiary functions necessary for surrounding and extensive rural areas; they provide the focus for commerce, transport and social life, but their secondary activities are negligible and their provision of basic urban facilities of water and electricity supply, medical services and cultural activities is often restricted. Such small towns still form a distinctive element in the landscape. In 1970, 2845 of Brazil's *cidades* had under 5000 inhabitants; in addition there were 3791 *vilas* of similar limited size.

Big cityscapes

The nine metropolitan areas and other large cities are increasingly becoming the familiar landscape for a majority of Brazilians. In these cities, in the perceptive phrase of Beaujeu-Garnier and Chabot (1967), the dominating trends have been Americanization and Africanization. The former is represented by the growth upwards of skyscraper cores of office blocks and apartment houses; the latter by the sprawl on the periphery (and on inner city marginal land) of the simple shacks of the shanty town dweller. Both symbolize urbanizing aspirations, with the high-rise buildings symbolizing fulfilment of these aspirations and the shanties symbolic of frustrated anticipation.

In sheer scale the growth of these major cities has been enormous. Greater São Paulo has increased from 5.3 million inhabitants in 1950 to 12.7 million in 1980, Greater Rio de Janeiro from 3 million to 9.1 million, and the other seven metropolitan centres from 2.5 million to 13 millions. In consequence of this rapid increase in population these cities have expanded both vertically and horizontally, with the emergence of a high-rise central core and a rapidly advancing periphery.

The increase in population stems from both natural increase and in-migra-

Fig. 6.5 Growth upwards. The town of Ribeirão Preto, São Paulo, a product of the coffee boom, had few buildings above two storeys in 1944. Most of the high-rise buildings are apartment blocks.

tion. In the inter-censal period 1970–80 the national population increased by 2.48 per cent a year; in six of the metropolitan areas the rate of increase was in excess of 4 per cent. Such rates reflect the rejection of rural and small town life by Brazilians and the attractions of a more sophisticated urban scene. People are pushed out of the rural areas by lack of employment, by seasonal underemployment, by the limited opportunities to acquire land and by the lack of basic services for themselves and their families; they are seduced into the cities by the belief that there are greater job opportunities, that there is greater provision of health, education and urban services, and by the less precise 'bright lights' syndrome. Migrants to the north-eastern city of Fortaleza in the late 1960s cited the desire to improve their situation, to find a job, to educate their children, or to live in the city, where life was less difficult, as major reasons for their move. Some had also fled from drought, the natural

Fig. 6.6 The setting of Rio de Janeiro. The city grew over the limited flat lands available between the hills and mountains of its spectacular site. This view, from Sugar Loaf mountain towards Corcovado, shows the Botafogo district, which developed in the nineteenth century. Fig. 6.7 is a later photograph of the central area shown here, taken from Corcovado, and reveals considerable change in the urban landscape.

hazard of the *sertão* which periodically forces outmigration to the coastal cities of the North-east or to those of the South-east. Few of the migrants to Fortaleza wished to return to the interior – there everything is difficult, there are no jobs, it is unhealthy, it is remote! (Governo do Estado Ceará, 1967).

Brazil's two principal cities present profound contrasts. Evenson (1973) suggests Rio de Janeiro is a city which, more than any other, interweaves man and nature. It is, she suggests, one of the few cities in the world whose name conjures up an immediate visual image, even to strangers, with the most prominent landmarks natural rather than man-made. This juxtaposition of man and nature has been a persistent theme in the appraisal of the city and in its townscape since the colonial period. The setting is one of great beauty in which the sea and the mountains create, in the words of Roger Bastide, 'a luminous symphony' which no one can tire of admiring. The sea, the mountains and the forest provide a setting in which man has placed a city. According to Bastide, the statue of Christ on Corcovado stands above the confusion of rocks, vegetation and waves, pronouncing a blessing on this city of 'offices, ministries, import-export depots, banks and cabarets' (Bastide 1969: 142). If man has forced back the forest it remains ready, like a green monster, to reinvade the city.

If the beauty of Rio is that of nature, the beauty, such as it is, of São Paulo is artificial. São Paulo is a man-made city of concrete from which nature has been expelled. There are no mountains or waves to constrain it, so it has sprawled over the plateau, creating a continuously advancing tide of buildings, covering all the space available, and incorporating formerly independent settlements which stood in its path. The city's role in the principal economic focus in Brazil has been a crucial factor in its growth upwards, creating an enormous skyscraper central business district.

The beautiful site of Rio de Janeiro has had a profound effect on the form of the city. Small hills surrounded by marsh provided its early site. Expansion saw the infilling of the marshland and later growth has resulted in both removal of some of the hills and reclamation of the bay shore. At a larger scale the site is divided by a mountain range forming the west side of the narrow entrance to Guanabara Bay. The colonial city was between the eastern edge of the mountains and the bay, and this area still forms the downtown core of Rio de Janeiro, but the city has spread south and west along the narrow strips of land between the mountains and the Atlantic, and north along the large plains alongside the bay. The focusing of economic activity and traffic on the constrained downtown area has placed great pressure on limited land and prompted skyscraper construction, urban motorways and, most recently, an underground railway system. Despite the early occupance of the hilltops, relatively few have been built on, and those mainly close to downtown, in Santa Teresa, Glória and Catete. The lack of transport and other urban services and the risk of landslides has made them unattractive; left otherwise unoccupied they have been claimed by the shanty town dwellers. The more affluent have preferred to live on the restricted lowlands of the Zona Sul,

Fig. 6.7 Rio de Janeiro: the pressure on urban land. In the foreground growth upwards of apartment blocks in Botafogo, and in the background the very high densities of Copacabana. The small area of uniform housing on the hillslope in the centre is a BNH housing project on the site of a former favela.

with easier access to the beaches beloved of the Cariocas. Population increase and improving transport have pushed these residential suburbs outwards along the Atlantic shore, from Botafogo to Copacabana, Ipanema, Leblon and now into Barra da Tijuca, more than 20 km from downtown. Despite this horizontal growth, demand has also generated growth upwards in these fashionable residential areas, giving extremely high population densities, reaching over 30 000 per km^2 in Copacabana. Such areas represent an extreme form of urban living, of crowding, noise, bustle and excitement, from which the beach is the area of escape. Although late nineteenth and early twentieth century growth of the city was facilitated by the tram and the railway, more recent expansion based on the car and the bus, combined with sheer pressure of numbers, has necessitated major engineering works, building highways on land reclaimed from the sea or cut into the rock, tunnelling through the mountains, or in extreme cases building double-decker highways.

As national capital the Federal District formed the city-state of Rio de Janeiro. After the capital was transferred to Brasília, Rio became the city-state of Guanabara. More recently it has been absorbed into the much larger State of Rio de Janeiro. A number of contiguous settlements, mainly industrial and residential, had grown up to the north. These communities, such as Nova Iguaçu and Duque de Caxias, together with Niterói and São Gonçalo across the bay now form part of this major conurbation. Its unity has been improved by the bridging of Guanabara Bay. In 1980 the city of Rio de Janeiro had over 5 million inhabitants, Nova Iguaçu over 1 million and Duque de Caxias, Niterói, São Gonçalo and São João de Meriti all had over 400 000. Despite its enormous expansion the physical sub-division of its site has preserved some local characteristics, so that identifiable communities persist, with a sense of place and identity, and often some architectural distinctiveness deriving from the period during which the district developed.

Nonetheless the transfer of the national capital function from Rio de Janeiro was at least partially a reflection that the 'Marvellous City' was flawed – it was too big, too crowded, too noisy. Increasingly it was incapable of sustaining services to its bulging population. The city itself increasingly failed to match the beauty of its natural setting.

Its initial growth was uncontrolled. At the beginning of the twentieth century there was considerable reconstruction and reclamation in the downtown area. Subsequent attempts at planning have endeavoured to improve this area, creating new land, more open space and new buildings. In the inter-war period a major new multi-lane artery was driven out from the city centre towards the northern suburbs and factories – and the rest of Brazil. In the post-war period the continuing focus of commercial activity in the central area resulted in further improvements and a growing tendency to build upwards, but there was increasing congestion on the business district, roads, the port and industrial sites. Recent planning, at both city and national level, has sought to counter this congestion by development strategies for the whole metropolis, with various projects for the periphery of the city and beyond. These improvements notwithstanding the city remains under pressure. It has not coped with the increase in either its human or automobile population. The prolonged construction of an underground system to ease the journey to work has compounded the problems by its excavations and delays.

Despite its role as capital for two centuries Rio de Janeiro never acquired a core of distinguished public buildings or a symbolic focus. It also lacks the cultural trappings of a great city. Having lost its capital function its *raison d'être* has become essentially commercial. The downtown core is evolving as an office landscape of capitalism, with fashionable images of glass, metal and concrete, but still incorporates ill-maintained buildings and streets and inadequate services. Away from the core there are marked contrasts between the crowded but generally affluent residential areas of the south and the more diverse north zone. The latter is a haphazard mixture of docks, warehouses, factories, routeways, working class housing, slums and shanties, extending out to encompass the scarcely distinguishable settlements of Nova Iguaçu, Duque de Caxias and others. Substantial land reclamation in this area, incorporating bay islands, has provided sites for an impressive international airport and the federal university.

Rio is a far from perfect city, both for its inhabitants and in its urban form. It is a haphazard, piecemeal place, yet it is distinctively Brazilian. It has been replaced as capital by Brasília, a symbol of a different kind. Yet for many Brazilians and foreigners the city is symbolic of an enviable urban life-style. Norma Evenson claims that it is a Brazilian city not through the intent of its planners, but because its inhabitants made it so. It symbolizes the Brazilian way of living. Its urban form reflects both the past and the uneven progress of the present. Perhaps its greatest symbolism lies in its site, where this major conurbation is still dominated by its physical setting, which is a powerful reminder of the still unconquered interior.

If Rio de Janeiro is distinctively Brazilian, and retains powerful influences of the natural environment, São Paulo is the very antithesis. It is quintessentially a man-made urban environment; and it is a city firmly wedded to the ethos of aggressive and dynamic capitalism. From its roots in the coffee plantations it has boomed, expanded and diversified to become a world city in both function and form. In 1872 the municipio of São Paulo had a population of less than 32 000. In 1980 metropolitan São Paulo had 12 708 000 inhabitants.

Unlike Rio de Janeiro the site of São Paulo is unimpressive and plain. As it prospered the town grew easily and laterally across the plateau. Initially the affluent lived in substantial villas, later in garden-cities and elegant residential suburbs. The extraordinary economic growth and prosperity of the city, its massive population increase and urban sprawl, engendered an escalation in land prices, such that the expanding inner city began to grow upwards, providing not only industrial, commercial and professional office blocks, but also apartment blocks.

It is a disordered, higgledy-piggledy, dynamic city. It has become an ill-assorted agglomeration of offices, factories, dwellings, highways, destruction, construction, noise, pollution, progress and chaos. For over three centuries it was a modest little place. Unlike Rio de Janeiro, it had virtually no historical legacy worth preserving; nor did it have a physical setting to challenge. Nonetheless in the cause of progress it has destroyed even its recent past several times over, building new skyscrapers, urban motorways, factories and so on. There is no history, only novelty. Until very recently there has been no order and little planning. Here man has triumphed firmly over nature. Concrete has masked the land and eradicated the forest. Nature in Sáo Paulo is a vanquished enemy; skyscrapers, viaducts and motorways are the symbols of progress. It has become, both literally and metaphorically, an urban jungle.

If, for Brazilians, Rio de Janeiro is the city in which to enjoy life, São Paulo is the place to earn a living. It has become the dominant focus of Brazil, one of the principal cities of Latin America and one which, in form and function,

DISBRAU
DISBRAU
TAXI
HF 9269

is closely akin to the great capitalist cities of the 'Rich North'. It is a dynamic, booming city. Its core symbolizes its success. For those who have benefited from that success it offers affluence and the trappings of a great city. For others it has become the symbol of their aspirations. It has become a magnet for migratory Brazilians seeking new and better opportunities. Not all of these dreams have been realizable, for São Paulo's progress has been bought at a price. Its demographic growth has outstripped its ability to provide adequate services for all its inhabitants, while its economic growth has not been sufficient to provide jobs for all who have come in search of them.

Although its prosperity has enabled it to undertake major projects of urban improvement, creating open spaces, pedestrian streets and a metro system; urban renewal with new housing schemes; and conservation of some of its older structures (including, for examples, a viaduct dating from 1913 and a skyscraper of 1934), it has also experienced major urban problems. It represents not only the showpiece of Brazil's economic miracle but also what has been described as the 'perverse process of urbanization in an underdeveloped country' (Arns 1978: 11). Extreme contrasts have emerged between the townscapes of affluence and those of poverty, in which the working classes, the marginally employed and the unemployed lack access to proper housing, water, drains and transport.

Planned townscapes

The widely held view that towns in colonial Brazil were unplanned has recently been called into question (Delson 1979). It has been demonstrated that some settlements at least were subject to controls over their layout. However, although many colonial towns were deliberate foundations, their growth was uncontrolled and disordered. Others were spontaneous expansions from early nuclei of forts, missions, sugar mills and so on, acquiring urban function and form by the accretion of people and buildings. There was little planning of their layout, control over their buildings or provision of essential services, a pattern which continued in many cases in the period after independence.

However a number of towns have been deliberately created in the post-colonial period, and have been planned and developed as substantial entities. The most obvious examples are the state capital cities of Teresina (1851), Aracaju (1858), Belo Horizonte (1898) and Goiânia (1937), constructed to replace earlier capitals considered unsatisfactory for various reasons, and the federal capital of Brasília (1960), which replaced Rio de Janeiro.

Of these planned cities Teresina and Aracaju have simple grid-iron layouts, with few embellishments, and little evidence of any attempt to create a distinctive urban environment. Belo Horizonte was planned to replace the former capital and gold mining town Ouro Prêto, which was regarded as rather inaccessible and constrained in its mountain site. Its plan, by Aarão Reis, was

Fig. 6.8 and 6.9 The urban jungle of downtown São Paulo.

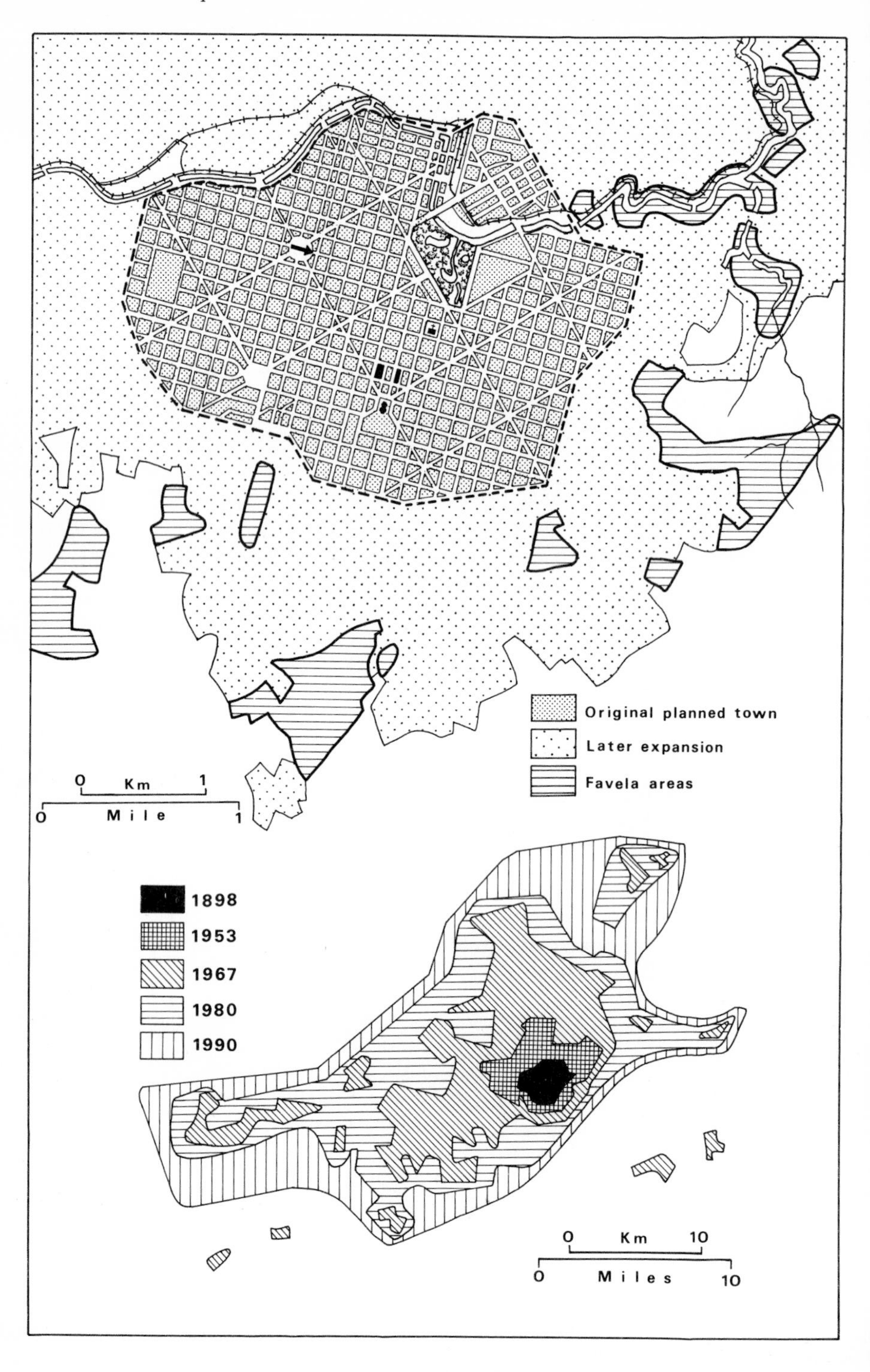
Original planned town
Later expansion
Favela areas
0 Km 1
0 Mile 1
1898
1953
1967
1980
1990
0 Km 10
0 Miles 10

inspired by that of La Plata in Argentina and by Washington DC. It consisted of a regular grid layout of roads, forming city blocks of 120 m × 120 m, cut by a large-scale grid of avenues running at 45° to this road system. The whole site was bounded by a 12 km peripheral treelined avenue. Width of roads and avenues was precisely defined, roads at 20 m, avenues at 35 m and the principal north-south avenue at 50 m. There was some intention of making it a 'garden city'. Street width was to be adequate not only for the movement of traffic, but for the planting of trees. Intersections were to be landscaped and there was to be a 100 000 ha municipal part adjacent to the main avenue. The governor's palace and state government agencies were ranged around a formal square at a high point on the site. The designed city was to accommodate 200 000 people. Its initial growth was relatively slow. In 1900 the population was 13 000, and it did not reach the target figure until 1940. In the early part of the century it was in essence a provincial capital, growing slowly and changing little. In 1945 it had few buildings above two storeys. In the past 40 years it has growth rapidly, as a major industrial amd commercial centre, and has shot upwards and sprawled outwards. By 1960 the population of the municipio was almost 700 000 and in 1980 1.8 million. By that date it had become a major conurbation, the third largest settlement in Brazil. A planned industrial district developed on its periphery had, by 1980, become an urban area with over 250 000 inhabitants and the total population of the metropolitan area was over 2.5 millions.

This explosive growth has clearly demonstrated the limitations of such formally planned layouts. The late nineteenth century plan made no provision for expansion beyond the target population, now exceeded tenfold. Expansion has been chaotic and uncontrolled, with extensive speculative building and the incorporation of previously separate settlements. The economic boom and pressure on downtown land has generated a substantial, and expanding, skyscraper core in the heart of the planned city, which is now surrounded by sprawling middle and working class suburbs, and with an emerging upper class district of apartment blocks and mansions on the slopes of the serra overlooking the city.

In addition to its failure to anticipate the expansion of the city, the original design did not, and indeed could not, anticipate the consequences of a revolution in transport. Its design was elegant and appropriate for the turn of the century; for the late twentieth century city of the automobile revolution it is a recipe for chaos, noise, congestion and pollution. The double grid layout creates a complexity of traffic intersections. At the principal intersections of the major grid no less than eight roads and avenues converge. It was claimed in the early 1970s that one of them received daily the equivalent of half of all the vehicles registered in the city.

Belo Horizonte provides an early example of a carefully planned town in

Map 11 Belo Horizonte: the original town plan and later expansion. The arrow on the upper map indicates the position from which illustration 6.10 was taken.

Fig. 6.10 An aerial view of Belo Horizonte, showing the original planned layout, the emerging skyscraper core and the later urban sprawl.

Brazil. Its precise and finite design was appropriate for the time in which it was designed; it has proved wholly inappropriate for the pressures and dynamism of the 1970s. It was designed as a 'City of Trees'; it has become the repository for a great range of urban problems. Even the beautiful horizons from which it took its name are disappearing in the cause of progress, as the rich iron ore they contain is removed!

The fourth, and most recent, planned state capital, Goiânia, has suffered less from the impact of recent pressures. Designed in the late 1930s by Attilia Corrêa Lima, it shows a somewhat more imaginative urban design than the other three planned state capitals. The formal curves which dominate its layout contrast strongly with the grid-iron or irregular designs of most Brazilian cities. As essentially the administrative and service centre of a primarily agricultural and pastoral state it has, until recently, grown less rapidly than Belo Horizonte. By the 1960s it had fewer than two dozen multi-storey buildings, and even adjacent to its formal core of state offices, land was primarily in single storey residences. The growth of Brasília and the focusing of federal highways on the south of Goiás state has stimulated its recent expansion. Its site, in 1933, had a population of 800, and it was planned to be a city housing 50 000 people by the 1980s; in 1980 it had 738 000 inhabitants.

Map 12 Goiânia: The planned core. In common with other such planned settlements, streets are mainly given numbers rather than names.

Brasília of course represents the acme of planned townscapes, not only in Brazil, but on the world scene also. It is a carefully circumscribed urban entity and at the same time a symbol of Brazil and of modern urban planning. The idea of a new national capital dates back to the eighteenth century and was written into successive constitutions from 1891. Surveys of potential sites were undertaken in 1947 and 1953, but it was not until 1956 that the project was finally implemented, as part of the spirit of dynamism and growth that characterized Brazil in the late 1950s.

The case for the move rested on several factors. A major one was the desire to counter the persisting dominance of the coast, and to occupy and possess the interior. As economic development at a truly national scale increased, it became necessary to integrate more fully the regional cores of the North-east, South-east and South, and to provide a jumping off point for penetration of the North and Centre-West. It was also felt that Rio de Janeiro was increasingly inappropriate as a capital city, both because it was divorced from the needs, aspirations and realities of the rest of the country, and because its constrained site was an obstacle to further growth.

What was needed therefore was a new capital city, which would symbolise national aspirations and achievements, integrate the nation and, at a different level, come to terms with the problems of late twentieth century urban life. What was required therefore was a monumental, modern, model city. Furthermore, despite the long gestation of the idea, the reality had to be created rapidly. The patron of the project was President Juscelino Kubitschek and it was vital that the city be inaugurated during his term of office, otherwise it was likely to lapse, given the reluctance of Brazilian politicians to continue projects begun by their predecessors.

The competition to decide the design of the city was announced in September 1956; the winning design was chosen in March 1957, and the city inaugurated in April 1960. It was an 'instant' city both in the speed of its development and in the formality of its design. The competition was won by the architect and urbanist Lúcio Costa, who saw the founding of a city in the wilderness as a deliberate act of conquest, a gesture in the tradition of the colonial pioneers. Costa therefore took the elementary gesture of one who takes possession of a place, the cross, as the fundamental element of his design. Brasília was to be not merely a place fulfilling the essential functions of any modern city, as an '*urbs*', but as possessing the inherent attributes of a capital city, as a '*civitas*'. The basic form of Costa's layout has been variously compared to a bird, bow and arrow or aeroplane. His own original sketches demonstrate the evolution of form from cross to aeroplane. The city, he suggested, should be appropriate for orderly and efficient work, but also vital and pleasing. It was also to be the cause of regional planning and development, not the consequence of it; development of the interior would follow the foundation of the city.

Brasília provided the first opportunity to apply contemporary ideas of design to a modern city. It provided a unique opportunity to apply such ideas *in toto*, rather than adding yet another dimension to the accreting form of the traditional Western city. It took account of current concepts of urban design that there should be spatial separation of function, that traffic and people should also be separated, and that there should be some unity of design. It was to be an urban utopia, combining the qualities of a technically advanced modern city with those of pleasing suburbia. As a complete and closed plan it would solve the conflicts and contradictions generated by the evolution of the traditional city.

Costa's design provided two axes, one essentially residential, and the other, transverse to it, containing the principal functional areas of the city. These functions were further separated along the axis including, from east to west, national government, church, culture and entertainment, shopping, commerce, hotels, media, sport, local government, military and light industry. There was much internal symbolism in the design. Its national and monumental functions are bought together in the Square of the Three Powers, where the three autonomous functions of government, legislature, executive and judiciary, are symbolized by the siting of the National Congress, Executive Palace and Supreme Court, at the three corners of an equilateral triangle. The government ministries are housed in uniform blocks on either side of the monumental mall; only the Ministries of Foreign Affairs and Justice have more

Fig. 6.11 The symbolic landscape of Brasília, with the National Congress building and the ministerial blocks behind.

individualistic buildings. Further along the mall the cathedral is symbolically separated from the activities of the State. In its overall layout there is spatial separation of symbolic and bureaucratic public building, commerce, recreation, housing – and traffic. For Costa it was to be a park and a city (Costa 1966: 16).

Costa provided a grand design, a monumental plan. Brasília has become a symbolic national capital and a deliberately created, new, full-scale, urban environment. Andre Malraux described it as the 'first capital of twentieth-century civilization' (Spade 1971: 17). It is the symbol of Brazil's need and desire to conquer its enormous territory, physically, economically and culturally. Its form was only possible in the creation of a new city at a virgin site. The contrast of function and form between the old capital of Rio de Janeiro and the new capital of Brasília is also profound. Rio was a traditional, evolving city, constrained and dominated by its magnificent physical setting. Brasília is essentially a man-made city, in which the simple empty space of its site is dominated by the creations of man.

If the impetus for its creation came from Juscelino Kubitschek and the inspiration of its design from Lúcio Costa, the striking visual features of its townscape are also derived from one individual, the architect Oscar Niemeyer. Brasília has been described as an architect's city, and Niemeyer, at the invitation of President Kubitschek, was the architect of many of the principal buildings, which have come to form part of the image of the city and of the country. In particular, his Congress building has become a widely known symbol. Niemeyer suggested that architectural work should be a challenge to the imagination, creating modern and beautiful forms that might astonish and which might create a mood of ecstasy, of dreams and of poetry (Niemeyer 1966: 21). The centrepiece of his work in Brasília is around the Praça dos Três Poderes, in which the three principal buildings around the praça, and the adjacent Ministries of Justice and Foreign Affairs are striking examples of his genius. Niemeyer has created new forms, startling in their originality and lightness 'airy, floating light and white in the endless night of the Brazilian highland' (ibid. 23).

In addition to the splendour of these five buildings, and others such as the cathedral and president's palace, Niemeyer was responsible for many other buildings in the city, and for defining the criteria for its development. Control over the size and height of buildings, extent of open spaces, and building materials used, imposed some coherence to the appearance of the city, inhibiting the disordered and confused growth characteristic of recent urban growth elsewhere in Brazil and abroad.

By no means all of the city matches up to the splendour of its set piece architecture. The original residential axis was designed on a neighbourhood basis with 'superblocks' of apartment buildings sustaining schools, shops and other local services. The six-storey apartment blocks, perhaps understandably, do not show the same originality or diversity as the showpiece public buildings, although in the more recently developed northern sector there is greater variety.

The city has not been without critics, of both its design and its architectural detail. The original notion of a classless city has been broken by the differential housing demands of different social classes, so that some of the original unity of Costa's design has been modified by the development of extensive areas of upper class single-unit dwellings, and the shores of the artificial lake, an integral part of the original design, have not been subject to carefully controlled developments. The great virtue of Costa's design, as a complete entity, has also become a vice in consequence of the growth of population. Conceived as a city of 500 000 inhabitants, by 1970 the planned city had 241 000 inhabitants, with a further 305 000 in other settlements within the Federal District. In 1980 the population of the Federal District was 1.2 million. This growth of population has substantially modified the original concept of the city. The rapid influx of population was such that satellite towns were developed away from the pilot plan area to house migrants and to rehouse inhabitants of *favelas* which developed within the city during the early phases of its construction. Such developments have contributed to social segregation within the Federal District, for they tend to house the low income population. There is less planned housing in the satellites. Instead of the uniform superblocks of the city core, there is a diversity of brick-built bungalows, wooden houses and shacks. Urban amenities of shops, educational and health services, planned open spaces, and paved roads, are also deficient.

There is then a less organized and less spectacular side to the growth of Brasília. Nonetheless it must be seen as a success in becoming the functioning national capital, the seventh largest conurbation in Brazil, and a national and international symbol. The core at least of the Costa – Niemeyer city is a very distinct urban landscape, which has been created rather than evolving. It is in

Fig. 6.12 Instant townscape. Palm trees being planted in front of Oscar Niemeyer's Itamarati Palace, the Brazilian Ministry of Foreign Affairs, Brasília, 1968.

essence a man-made landscape where, in contrast to its predecessor as national capital, the contribution of the physical setting is negligible. It is a particular vision of a late twentieth century urban life-style. It has also come to represent the country's collective Ego, burgeoning in the thickness of the green wilderness of the interior (Tuan 1974: 171).

All of these planned cities represent attempts to provide settlements appropriate to their function as capitals. Their layouts represent changing fashions in urban design over more than a century. In their own terms they might be regarded as successful, in providing some form of public symbol of their age. They all demonstrate however the limitations of planning for a finite city, since all have been overtaken by the unanticipated growth of population, changes in urban life-style and technology. The planned areas now form the cores of much larger settlements; they provide examples of changing approaches to the deliberate creation of urban landscapes, but they have been encompassed by more spontaneous and disordered expansion horizontally and, with the exception of Brasília, been disrupted internally by vertical growth.

Company towns

Less spectacular in scale but more numerous than the planned capital cities are settlements established to house workers engaged in particular economic activities. Such settlements, defined by J. B. Allen (1966) as communities owned and operated by a particular company, are usually single enterprise communities. Such a description could include the nucleations associated with sugar or coffee plantations, but these are generally small and essentially rural. Company towns have emerged in Brazil in the process of economic diversification, particularly in the development of mining and manufacturing. In the former case minerals occur at specific sites which may have little or no previous associated settlement. A company wishing to exploit such a resource has, therefore, to provide not only the infrastructure to extract the mineral, but to attract and retain population, by providing housing and essential services. In the case of manufacturing much industry has accreted on to existing towns, but in some cases pioneer sites or small settlements have provided attractions, such as power sources or raw materials, for factories, so that housing is necessary. It is also the case that substantial company-owned estates have been grafted on to the existing towns.

J. D. Porteous (1970) has suggested that control of an area of land by a single entrepreneur will have distinctive modifying effects on the local landscape. Company towns are dominated by the parent firm, both physically by the mine or factory, and in the creation, ownership and organization of the community. The company provides the public facilities of schools, stores and other buildings for community use, and housing for its employees. This latter is characterized by uniformity of architectural style and building age. In resource-exploiting communities such housing may be simple but elsewhere more substantial dwellings may be constructed. Town layout follows some form of predetermined plan, and there may be internal segregation in house type and social provision for different grades of employee.

In Brazil the relatively recent development of large-scale mining and of factory-based industry has been an important factor in the creation of these single enterprise dominated settlements. They have been responsible for the introduction into the tropical landscape of the artifacts of industrialization – pits and spoil heaps, factory chimneys, freight routes and vehicles, noise and pollution.

One of the most striking company towns is that of Volta Redonda, the location of the Companhia Siderúrgica Nacional steelworks, in the Paraíba valley. When the plant was developed, on the site of an old *fazenda*, the population of the district was 3000; by 1980 it was almost 200 000. In addition to creating an integrated steelworks with a capacity of 250 000 ingot tons of steel (substantially increased subsequently), the company has established a large town, providing housing, medical facilities, schools, stores, canteens and sports facilities. The steelworks dominates the town. These symbiotic elements of town and factory are separated by the railway, and extend parallel to one another along the valley. The town core and most of the workers houses are located on the valley floor, with better class housing up on the

Fig. 6.13 The company town of Volta Redonda in the Paraíba valley, showing the steelworks and workers' housing.

valley side. In addition to Volta Redonda, the company also provides communities for its coal miners in Santa Catarina and iron miners in Minas Gerais.

The state of Minas Gerais has numerous examples of company towns linked to recent economic developments, in mining, textiles and metallurgical industries, either as entirely new settlements or else as substantial company estates grafted on to older small towns. The colonial gold mining towns were spontaneous and haphazard, but the later deep mining of gold by a foreign company did result in the creation of a prime example of a community whose structure and form was shaped by the mining company. Nova Lima became dependent on the Morro Velho mine of the St John d'El Rei Mining Company. The pit headworks and ancillary plant formed the core of the town, surrounded by uniform workers' dwellings. Even more crucially, during the period of British control of the company, the significance of the mine was so great that it was impossible to comprehend the life of the community without reference to the company, which monopolized the economy and all the social, cultural and political activities of the population. The company was the principal employer, principal rural and urban proprietor and principal purchaser of all commerce (Instituto Brasileiro de Geografia e Estatística 1959: 195).

Elsewhere in the state the development of the cotton industry prompted other nucleations. Cotton mills were established at water power sites, at Caetenópolis and São Vicente for example, and around the mill clustered a small settlement of uniform, company built and owned houses. Some of these settlements have expanded into more diverse towns, but others persist as small towns of 1500–3000 inhabitants, still dependent on the cotton mill. (Dickenson 1970: 379–414).

The exploitation of the local iron ore prompted not only mining towns, at Casa da Pedra and Itabira, but also settlements associated with iron and steel working. Some were grafted on to existing settlements, such as Sabará, where the standardized housing estate of the Belgo-Mineira steelworks contrasts with the disordered colonial baroque settlement. Elsewhere the development of virgin sites has given rise to independent and uniform company towns. In the Rio Doce valley the Belgo-Mineira steelworks at Monlevade, Acesita at Timotéo and Usiminas at Ipatinga provide examples of such creations. In all three cases the companies concerned had to develop not only steelworks but accommodation and urban services. Such settlements are similar in character, providing dwellings for families and for single men, hospitals, sports facilities, stores, cinemas, canteens, schools and technical colleges to train workers. The companies also provide electricity, water and drainage services. Timotéo, developed from 1944, has a commercial core adjacent to the steelworks, with employees, living in six residential districts (*vilas*), with some differentiation between grades of employees. In the case of Ipatinga, the jointly owned Japanese/Brazilian steelworks was developed in 1958. At that time the area had 60 houses and 300 inhabitants. Usiminas constructed an architect-designed town with, in its first phase, 3700 dwellings plus accommodation for 2500 single men. The initial planned site was for a community of 90 000 people,

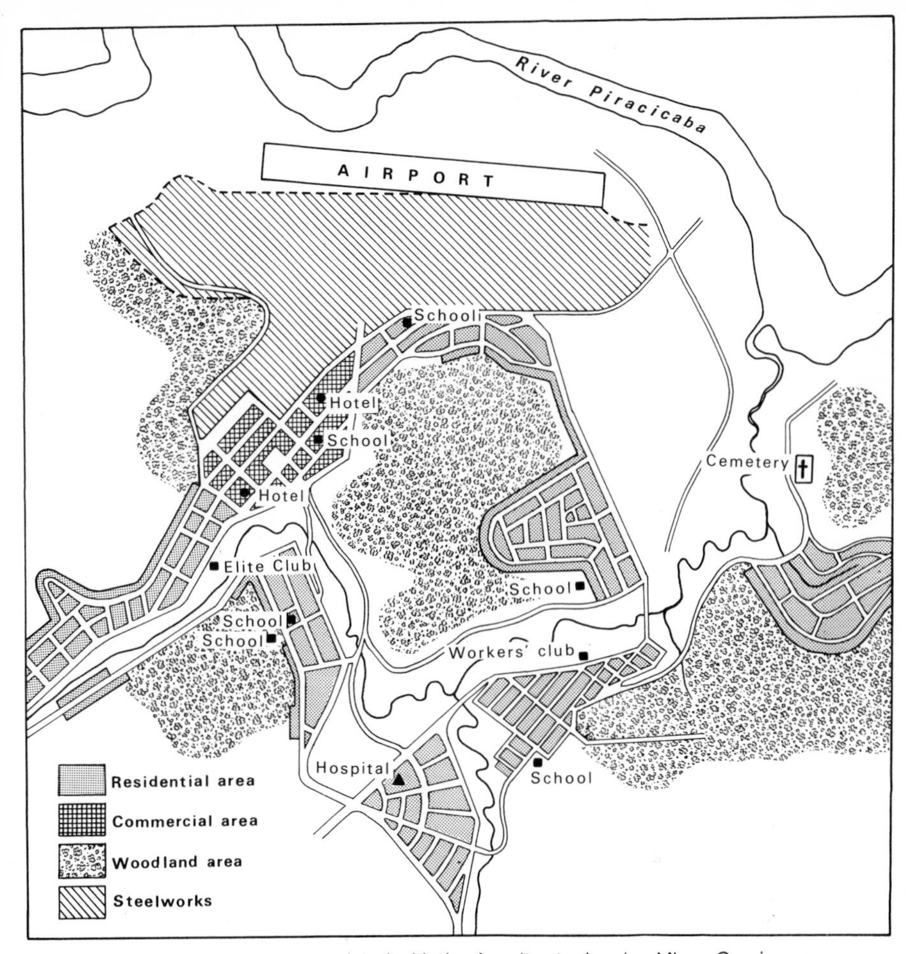

Map 13 The company town associated with the Acesita steelworks, Minas Gerais.

to take account of envisaged expansions of the steelworks. By 1970 Ipatinga had a population of 48 000; by 1980, 153 000. The residential area is segregated from the works by a green belt, and is subdivided into neighbourhood units which each provide schools, shops and health and sports facilities. Properties vary in quality and area with family size and job status. Dwellings in the original town ranged from 40 m^2 to 250 m^2, and house plots from 240 to 1300 m^2.

Such communities provide an integral part of the urban landscape of modernizing Brazil. The term 'company town' often carries derogatory implications and these towns are characterized by regimentation, standardization and uniformity. They do, however, provide housing of a basically sound standard, and give access to the amenities of water and electricity and to urban functions. They have been an essential component in the development process, and have given rise to distinctive urban forms. In some cases, once the settlements have become established, companies have sold off the dwellings, or have permitted private, speculative, building. Where the growth of the town has made it less acutely dependent on the parent company, spontaneous development has attracted yet more people, so that the ex-company towns become mixtures of planned estates, private housing and shanty towns. The two company towns of Ipatinga and Timotéo are located 10 km apart. Between them is the older settlement of Coronel Fabriciano. As a consequence of the expansion of the steelworks and the stimulus to other activities all three settlements have expanded, and there has also been the growth of spontaneous and shanty settlements. In 1950 the then *municipio* of Coronel Fabriciano had a population of 22 000; by 1980, when it had been divided into the *municipios* of Coronel Fabriciano, Timotéo and Ipatinga, the population had risen to 282 000.

Company dominated towns similar to those of Minas Gerais exist elsewhere in Brazil. There are, for example, a number of small mining towns in the coalfields of Santa Catarina, and Monte Alegre is a company town developed by the Klabim paper mill in the Paraná pine forest. Resource development in the interior is likely to generate new company towns. Exploitation of the Carajás iron ore deposits in Pará requires the creation of a town of 6000 inhabitants at the mine and two small settlements on the 970 km railway linking it to the coast.

Urban embellishments

In addition to the broad trend whereby the familiar landscape for most Brazilians is an urban one, the country has begun to evolve distinctive features within its urban landscapes, derived primarily from the talents of a group of modern Brazilian artists.

During the colonial period and in the nineteenth century the arts in Brazil were heavily derivative, based on Portuguese and other European models. The inspiration for change was again external, derived from Modernist trends in Europe, but in this case the consequence was the creation of original and new art forms, with unique and distinctively Brazilian characteristics. The two principal catalysts to this change were the Week of Modern Art in São Paulo in 1922 and the political revolution of 1930. The former introduced new ideas in literature, music, painting, sculpture and architecture, and sought to break from inherited European traditions and create more indigenous and nationalistic art forms; revolution induced profound change in the social, economic and administrative life of the country, and facilitated the introduction of these new artistic concepts.

These advances began to find expression in the built environment and thus came to form part of the landscape. A number of buildings incorporating new ideas were constructed in the early 1930s but the real starting point for the new Brazilian architecture was the Ministry of Education and Health in Rio de Janeiro. The Swiss architect Le Corbusier was consultant to a group of Brazilian architects which included Lúcio Costa, Oscar Niemeyer, Affonso

Reidy and others. The building made use of several of Le Corbusier's ideas. It was raised above ground level on free standing columns (*pilotis*), giving space underneath; it was divorced from the street line and incorporated sunbreakers (*brise soleil*) against the tropical light. It also utilized Brazilian elements. Extensive use was made of the decorative tiles (*azulejos*) inherited from colonial Portugal, but in this case designed by the Brazilian artist Candido Portinari, and its surrounding garden was designed by Roberto Burle Marx.

From the group of architects and artists involved on this project and the techniques used, have evolved many of the distinguishing features of modern Brazilian architecture and urban design. Two major factors have been the considerations given to the tropical climate, and the building materials used. Concern with countering the effect of heat and sun glare has encouraged use of the *brise soleil*, which also functions as a mobile feature in architectural design. The distinction between indoor and outdoor living has been made less rigid by the use of metal and concrete grillwork to enclose spaces, the use of open plan layouts and of thin partition walls. The use of reinforced concrete as a building material has been an important factor in the development of the characteristic free flowing, plastic and exuberant forms of modern Brazilian buildings, permitting a fluidity in design and not possible in buildings using structural steel. Early examples of this new Brazilian architecture are the Santos Dumont airport, Brazilian Press Association building (both by the Roberto brothers) and a day nursery by Niemeyer, all in Rio de Janeiro.

In addition to architectural advances, Brazilian modernism began to evolve an integrated form of urban design, incorporating the sculptural and spatial of architecture and the visual arts of murals, decorated *azulejos*, sculpture and landscape gardening. Oscar Niemeyer has been a leading figure in the creation of distinctive architectural forms, and has argued that architecture is a work of art (Niemeyer 1963: 68); certainly some of his major works, such as those at Pampulha and Brasília, must be seen in this light. Pampulha is an important milestone in the evolution of the modern Brazilian urban landscape. It is an upper class residential district sponsored by the then mayor of Belo Horizonte, Juscelino Kubitschek, and several of its major projects brought together the talents of Niemeyer, Portinari and Burle Marx.

Marx has also been a major figure in the evolution of Brazil's distinctive urbanscapes. His landscape gardens have been described as providing the natural habitat for Brazilian buildings, and Brazil's greatest contribution to the contemporary visual environment (Bullrich 1969: 26). They are designed expressly to complement buildings, and derive inspiration from the luxuriance of the tropical landscape. Marx incorporates natural features, varying levels, still and running water, and the texture, shape, colour and volume of plants to create abstract designs. Much of his work is in private gardens but in addition to gardens for the Ministry of Education, Pampulha and Santos Dumont airport, a major public work is the landscaping of the bayside reclamation in the Glória-Flamengo district of Rio de Janeiro. Using rocks, peb-

Fig. 6.14 Urban design in Rio de Janeiro: the Glória-Flamengo park designed by Roberto Burle Marx. The wavy pattern in the foreground using different grasses echoes street paving designs in Rio de Janeiro and Lisbon. In the background the Glória church is a hill-top remnant of colonial Rio.

bles, sculptured stones, grasses, palm trees and a variety of native and foreign flora he has created a remarkable setting for the Museum of Modern Art, War Memorial, the baroque Glória church and the urban motorway linking downtown Rio to Copacabana.

These developments in Brazilian architecture and design attracted domestic and international acclaim. Within Brazil these styles were rapidly accepted and both the State and private enterprise have been important sponsors of major projects. Government officials during the Vargas regimes and President Kubitschek were influential patrons of the new architecture. The development process has generated a need for a diversity of public buildings, such as government offices, hospitals and universities. Many of these have been built with some concern for architectural quality and not mere function. Private companies have similarly sponsored prestigious and distinctive office buildings.

At a lesser scale private housing for affluent society is frequently architect designed. Upper class districts in major Brazilian cities contain luxurious and beautiful houses, which are individualistic in design, modern in style and well adapted to the tropical climate. Like the larger public buildings, they take account not only of architectural fashion but incorporate art, murals, *azulejos* and tropical landscaped gardens. Pressure on land in fashionable areas of the major cities has also prompted the construction of apartment houses of similar quality and originality, incorporating balconies, roof gardens, tiled façades and *brise soleil*.

Such developments of striking buildings and the synthesis of architecture, art, sculpture, landscape gardening and urban planning are the products of a few individual talents and the result of patronage by the State, business and the rich. It represents in effect official and public landscape taste. It is in essence the preferred landscape of mid and late twentieth century Brazil.

Yet these landscapes are essentially symbolic. They constitute only a small part of the urban scene and only a minority of the urban population have direct experience of them. Much of the literature on landscapes is concerned with landscapes that are aesthetically pleasing, that is with landscapes which represent and are shaped by landscape tastes (Lowenthal and Prince 1965). Usually such landscapes are desired by, created for, and described by, an élite. Aesthetically pleasing landscapes are usually those of an affluent élite and judged by their standards, while essentially economic landscapes, which may well be aesthetically unpleasing, are also created primarily in the interests of the élite group of government and affluent society. But in a developing country like Brazil, many people are excluded, by lack of wealth and education, from these aesthetic judgements. They do not shape fashionable landscape tastes; they may not necessarily even participate in the economic landscape.

Landscapes of poverty

In Brazil, as in other developing countries, there are substantial variations in levels of well-being. There are contrasts, as measured by shares of income distribution, between regions, between urban and rural areas, and within society. In 1970 average income in Rio de Janeiro and São Paulo was above the national average; in all other areas it was below that figure. Income levels in Rio de Janeiro were more than twice those of Minas Gerais and the North-east. At a national scale income levels in the rural areas were only about one-third of those of the urban areas. Within the rural and urban areas there were also pronounced inequalities. In both areas 70 per cent of the population had incomes below the respective rural and urban averages. In the countryside the poorest 10 per cent of the population shares 2 per cent of the total rural income; the richest 10 per cent shares 36 per cent. In the towns the equivalent figures were less than one per cent and 44 per cent respectively. (Langoni 1973: 36–39). More recent work (Bacha and Balthazar 1980) has suggested that about two-fifths of Brazilian families did not earn sufficient income to meet their basic human needs of food and other essentials.

Not only is there relative poverty, but also absolute poverty. In Brazil *per*

capita gross domestic product in 1978 was US$1500 and, as indicated above, the distribution of income is markedly skewed in favour of a rich minority and against a poor majority. In such circumstances living standards for many people are inevitably low. What people can afford in the way of food, clothing and shelter is minimal. Although poverty is probably more acute in the countryside, concentrations of the impoverished within cities create more obvious landscapes of poverty. Such concentrations of poverty and their associated landscapes derive from the rapid growth of the cities in response to natural increase and in-migration, the failure of the urban economy to generate a commensurate number of jobs to absorb this increase and the failure of urban authorities to make adequate provision of transport, drainage, water and electricity supply, and other basic services. The degree of urbanization and particularly the concentration of population in large cities has increased markedly in recent decades but the capital-intensive nature of the industrialization process has not been sufficiently labour absorptive. Even in São Paulo, the core of Brazil's recent economic advance, open unemployment has been calculated at between 6 and 9 per cent of the labour force, and a further 34 per cent underemployed – that is, it is engaged in relatively unproductive work which yields an income inadequate to sustain a minimum living standard. An index of the inadequacy of urban service provision is indicated by the fact that in 1970 70 per cent of Brazil's urban private houses lacked mains drainage and 45 per cent lacked piped water supply.

Substantial areas of the cities are thus occupied by people with low incomes, deficient urban services, and employed at best in low-paid, marginal or irregular jobs. The most striking expressions of this poverty are the shanty towns or *favelas*, which have become familiar features of the big city scene in Brazil, and which frequently occupy land which is in some way marginal. They consist of clusters of simple dwellings, improvised from a variety of materials, without urban zoning or provision of services, and occupy land illegally. They locate on a variety of sites, usually unattractive to conventional housing, such as hillsides, ravines, swamps and tidal flats.

The emergence of the shanty towns appears to be largely a phenomena of the present century. In the nineteenth century the urban poor occupied overcrowded tenements and court dwellings (*cortiço* and *cabeça de porco*). The earliest *favelas* in Rio de Janeiro date from the last decade of last century, but grew rapidly from the 1930s, when the push of falling agricultural prices combined with the pull of industrial development. In Fortaleza in the North-east, the earliest *favelas* date from the 1930s. Both Belo Horizonte and Brasília acquired shanty towns soon after their construction began. In the big cities shanties have come to house a significant proportion of their population. The proportion of *favelados* in the population of Rio de Janeiro rose from about 8 per cent in 1950 to almost one-third in 1970 (Perlman 1976: 14); they con-

Fig. 6.15 A *favela* in north Rio de Janeiro.

stituted about one-fifth of the population of Fortaleza and one-third of that of Belo Horizonte.

The shanty towns form substantial communities, ranging from a few hundred people to several thousand. The *favela* of Jacarezinho in Rio had an estimated population of almost 30 000 and that of Marmiteiros in Belo Horizonte had 32 000, part of an estimated total of 100 000 *favelados* who live on the banks of the River Arrudas flowing through the city.

The shanty towns of Brazil and elsewhere provide a familiar image of Third World poverty – small, crowded, crude shacks of wood, tin, cardboard, rags or wattle and daub, and acutely deficient in basic services. The shacks frequently have only a single dirt-floored room, no facilities for hygienic food preparation and lack piped water or drains. For many observers they have been seen as foci of abject poverty, crime and political unrest. A fairly typical description sees the Brazilian *favela* as a grouping of impoverished people, avoiding the control of local authorities, and living in deplorable promiscuity in poor, unhygienic cabins which are potential sources of disease and perversion, and inimical to normal family life (Teulieres 1957). Negative stereotypes such as this are primarily derived from national and foreign élite observers, horrified and scandalized by these spectres of poverty, and the contrasts they make with the striking modernity of the office core or the tourist strip, and the criteria of 'normal' standards of living!

Recent work has suggested that shanty towns are far from homogeneous. Population densities vary, some have a degree of ordered layout, communal piped water may be available, there may be illicit provision of electricity. The simple houses may be reasonable adjustments to climate and available building materials, and well maintained by their inhabitants. Over time they may be improved, using more permanent building materials. The communities sustain shops and may try to provide schools, churches and other community buildings. Traditionally *favelados* have been seen as migrants from the rural areas,and as temporary residents in the shanties. Recent evidence suggests that the pattern is more complex, with migrants from a diversity of sources, including those with prior urban experience, and with people moving into the shanties from other parts of the city. Many become long-term residents of the *favela*. While particular *favelas* may be notorious as centres of crime and vice, others provide the only homes available to those employed in the lowest sectors of the formal economy, engaged in quasi-legal activities, or seeking employment. Shanty town dwellers contribute to the unskilled labour force, in the construction industry and in low-paid urban service jobs – road-sweepers, bus conductors, caretakers, dustmen, porters and similar jobs. Many of the females work as domestic servants. Less secure income may be derived from odd jobs such as street vending, car washing, shoe-shining, or *in extremis* by scavenging street refuse and garbage dumps.

A corollary of this type of employment and the low level of income is a need to be close to the place of work. Many *favelas* are thus to be found in close proximity to the inner city or to affluent neighbourhoods. The location

Fig. 6.16 Landscapes of wealth and poverty: the juxtaposition of shanties and middle class housing, Rio de Janeiro.

of some of Rio's shanties on spectacular sites on the hillsides adjacent to the city's tourist and better class residential areas gave them high visibility. Attempts to eradicate these 'eyesores' by destroying them and decanting the population to simple housing estates on the city periphery undermined the shanty dwellers' economy, involving them in increased expenditure on rent and transport. Eradication of *favelas* has tended to be the dominant official strategy towards them, but there have also been some efforts at encouraging their self-improvement.

As long as the cities remain incapable of providing sufficient jobs and urban services, landscapes of urban poverty are likely to persist, for even life in a shanty may be more attractive than the poverty of the countryside. For the rural poor the city offers greater opportunity, real or imagined. In the case of Fortaleza, for example, where occasional drought is an additional push factor, migrants to the city were motivated by the desire for a job, a house or simply to improve their lot (Governo do Ceará 1967: 107).

Such motivations clearly shape the urban perceptions of migrants to the city and the shanty – it is a better place than the place of current residence. Peter Lloyd (1979) has recently queried the notion that the shanty dwellers are merely passive victims of circumstance. He argues that the decision to migrate, to participate in a land invasion and to improve their shanty dwelling indicates much more positive attitudes. Lloyd suggests (ibid. 69) that the shanty town poor are creating an environment of their own, within the constraints of the wider society. The motivations of house, job, better education and health are similar to those of that wider society. The level at which these aspirations are fulfilled in the shanty are, to external observers, at best low. Yet we know little of the *favelados'* own perception of his environment. Presumably settlement in the city is a fundamental goal of the *favelado*, but how does he or she perceive the 'poverty and squalor' which so disturbs middle class bureaucrats, academics and tourists? Sources of such information are inevitably few; *favelado's* have minimal access to the conventional media, and high levels of illiteracy are a common feature of shanty populations. Some slight insight into such perceptions may be derived from the diary of Carolina Maria de Jesus, a record of life in a São Paulo shanty in the 1950s (de Jesus 1962). It may be untypical both because of the author's literacy, and because she subsequently moved out of the shanty. It portrays a life-style of hardship and poverty, of hunger, and the need to scavenge for food and for refuse to sell to buy food, clothes and other essentials. Her views of the poverty, noise, smell and life-style of the shanty are essentially negative. She suggests her need to create an atmosphere of fantasy in order to forget that she is living in a *favela*. There are frequent contrasts between the 'city' (the ideal of the *favelado*?) and the actuality of the *favela*. The city is seen as a world of luxury; the *favela* as a garbage dump; it is the city's backyard, where the garbage is thrown. The city of São Paulo is a paradise, but is scarred by the ulcers of the shanty towns.

The *favelas* have become, and remain, a substantial and striking feature of the Brazilian urban landscape. For many city dwellers they provide the day-to-day landscape. If they lack the bright lights to which their residents aspire, they at least give access to them.

Although the shanty towns provide the most obvious landscapes of urban poverty, there are also substantial areas of the principal cities inhabited by people of low income, and where urban services are deficient. In the city of São Paulo in the early 1970s about one-tenth of the population lived in slum properties and about one-third in poor housing on the periphery. In some of parts of city over half the housing lacked access to water, drainage, paved roads or refuse collection. Dwellings are overcrowded and the provision of public open space is limited.

The contrasts between wealth and poverty are perhaps most acute in the cities of São Paulo and Rio de Janeiro, though most of the large cities have their *favelas, malocas* and *mocambos* as their shanties are variously called. The contrasted townscapes, of wealth and poverty, are both products of Brazil's recent economic progress, which has generated and sustained spectacular city centre growth of skyscraper office blocks, apartment houses and department stores, and which has also prompted and sustained large areas of crude shacks and slums.

Housing provision in Brazil has largely been in private hands, whether of

Fig. 6.17 The regularity of BNH-financed, low-cost housing, near Angra dos Reis, Rio de Janeiro.

architect-designed mansions and apartment blocks for the well-to-do, speculative development for other segments of society or self-help by the *favelados*. Between 1938 and 1963 the public sector had provided less than 150 000 housing units (Banco Nacional de Habitação 1970), and there was an estimated housing deficit of 7 million units. In 1964 the government created a housing bank, the Banco Nacional de Habitação, to tackle this housing problem. Its tasks were to build housing projects into which shanty town dwellers could be moved, and support State, municipal and co-operative projects which would increase the housing stock. Subsequently its role was widened to include the provision of urban services such as water supply and drainage. By the mid 1970s it had been involved in the construction of over 1 million housing units, mainly concentrated in the larger cities. The bank's strategy has been criticized as tending to favour the provision of housing for middle rather than low income groups. The simplicity of the housing styles used and the regularity of the layout of housing estates and apartment block complexes have also received criticism. Heterogeneity and individuality have been traditional features of Brazilian urban housing, at all levels from wealthy suburbs to shanty towns, so that the uniformity and monotony of public housing estates introduces an unfamiliar element to the urban scene.

The frontier

It can be argued that most of the present-day cultural landscape of Brazil is essentially the product of the advance of the frontier. From 1500 the settlement and development of the country has been associated with penetration towards the interior from the coast, with the progress of the cutting edge of the frontier to exploit a particular commodity such as sugar, gold, coffee or the product of one of the lesser economic cycles. In contrast to the Turnerian frontier in North America, the Brazilian frontier has not been a continuous, advancing sweep but instead piecemeal and hesitant, and it is still active. Map 14 indicates that a substantial part of the country has a population density of less than one person per square kilometre. Densities in excess of 5 per km^2 are mostly within 500 km of the coast, so that large areas remain to be significantly and substantially settled. Advance of the frontier has been sustained by the mys-

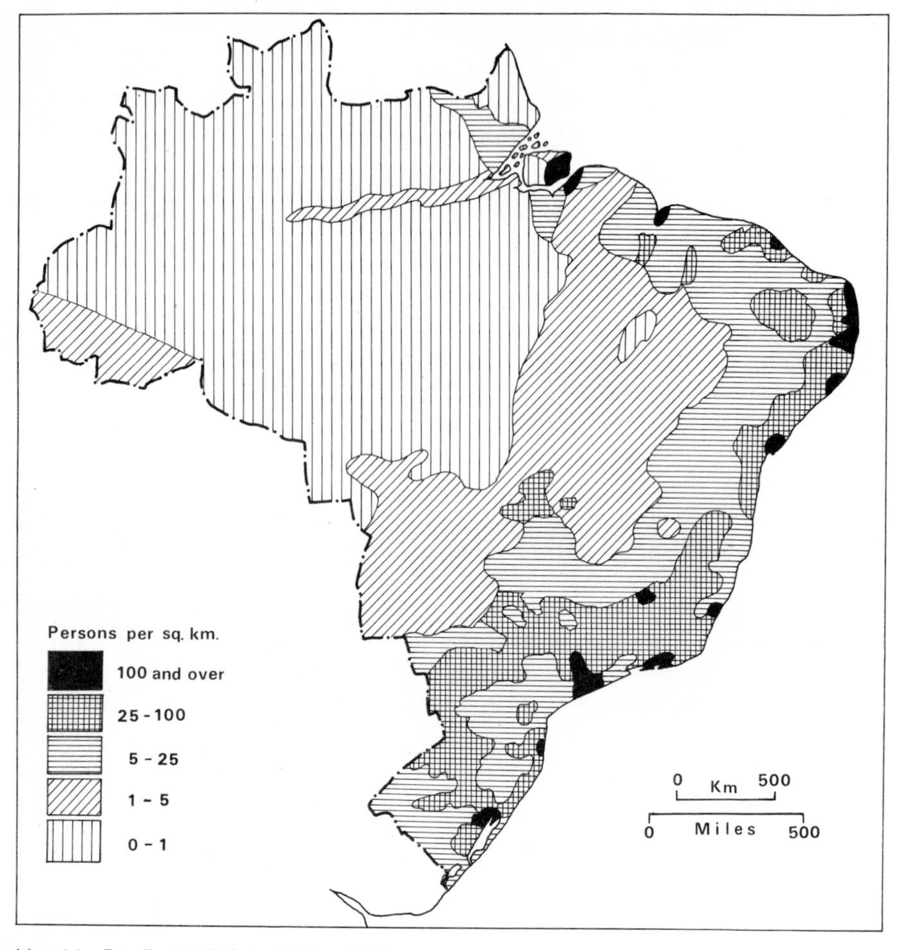

Map 14 Brazil: population density, 1970.

tique of the interior and the persisting myths of undiscovered riches, obsessions articulated as the '*Marcha para Oeste*' – the 'march to the West'. This phrase however conveys an image of coherence and uniformity to the advance of the frontier, when in fact the process has not been a single experience but a series of sequential and spatially separated advances. Most of these have been in response to external demands, provoking advance to exploit particular areas and resources to provide commodities for overseas markets. Richard Morse (1965) has noted that the Brazilian frontier was not a clear line but consisted of a number of multiple, complex and imprecisely demarcated frontiers, which generated not a continuous zone of settlement but a pattern of settlement archipelagos. This process and pattern characterizes both past and current frontiers. The process has been one of interpenetration rather than precise advance, and an intermittent quest rather than a systematic programme. Its consequences have been the creation of a discontinuous and imprecise frontier zone.

Much of the frontier advance in the twentieth century has been a continuation of trends established previously. The most important and dynamic area of advance has been effectively the continuing pulse of the coffee frontier, pushing into western São Paulo and then beyond, into lands marginal for coffee in northern Paraná and more recently beyond the political frontier of Brazil into Paraguay. A distinguishing feature of this advance, compared to its early progress through São Paulo, is that the role of coffee has been less exclusive.

Fig. 6.18 The advance of the coffee frontier resulted in the replacement of the diverse natural vegetation cover of large areas of southeast Brazil by the uniform dark green ranks of the coffee bushes.

The advance of the coffee frontier into western São Paulo and Paraná was sustained by continuing world demand, the support given to coffee cultivation by the national government, and was facilitated by the continuing existence of vacant land, mobile labour and the advance of railways and roads. The prolonged availability of virgin land has been a crucial element in the continuing dynamics of the frontier. So long as such land was available there was little incentive to improve the usage of existing farmed land. To the present time there has always been empty land to take, so that the agricultural frontier has been able to move on as yields have begun to decline, rather than intensify production methods.

The coffee frontier had spread across São Paulo, following the interfluves and the railways to the far west by the 1930s. Subsequently the frontier of cultivation spread out of São Paulo, north-westwards into Mato Grosso, Goiás and the Triângulo Mineiro, and south into Paraná. Advance into these two areas provided very different patterns of development and landscape change however, with one showing traditional features of unordered development on large land holdings and the other a closely regulated pattern dominated by small farms.

The colonization process in north Paraná has been characterized as one of the most dynamic in Latin America and as an outstanding example of planned development in the tropics. This pattern derives primarily from the activities of a single company, originally British, which in 1925 bought 12 600 km^2 of land, about one-twentieth of the total area of Paraná. The coffee frontier had already advanced into north-east Paraná in the early 1930s. The founders of the company recognized the potential of the lands in the north, with extensive areas of *terra roxa* soils and reliable rainfall, for its further advance, but in contrast to the process in São Paulo, this was carefully controlled by the company. Occupation of the territory was progressive, with one area being settled before another was opened up. The extension westwards of the São Paulo – Paraná Railway was an essential part of the colonization process, for the railway provided the spine of penetration into the territory. The railway and the principal road run along the interfluve between the Tibagi and Ivai rivers, and from these transport lines a series of feeder roads have been built. Layout of the project was carefully designed, with land lots running from the hillcrest roads to the valley bottoms, giving each lot access to transport and water and a diversity of terrain. It was recognized that because of frost risk the area was marginal for coffee cultivation, so that coffee was planted on the crests and upper slopes, and the valley bottoms were given over to other crops and pasture. The size of lots varied. The most common were '*sitios*', of about 40 ha, but there were smaller holdings, '*chacaras*', of about 12.5 ha around the town, and some larger *fazendas* were permitted in more distant areas. The foundation of towns was an integral part of the development programme, with the regional centre, Londrina, on the eastern edge of the property, and major settlements along the line of rail at intervals of about 100 km. Smaller service centres were planned and laid out at intervals of about

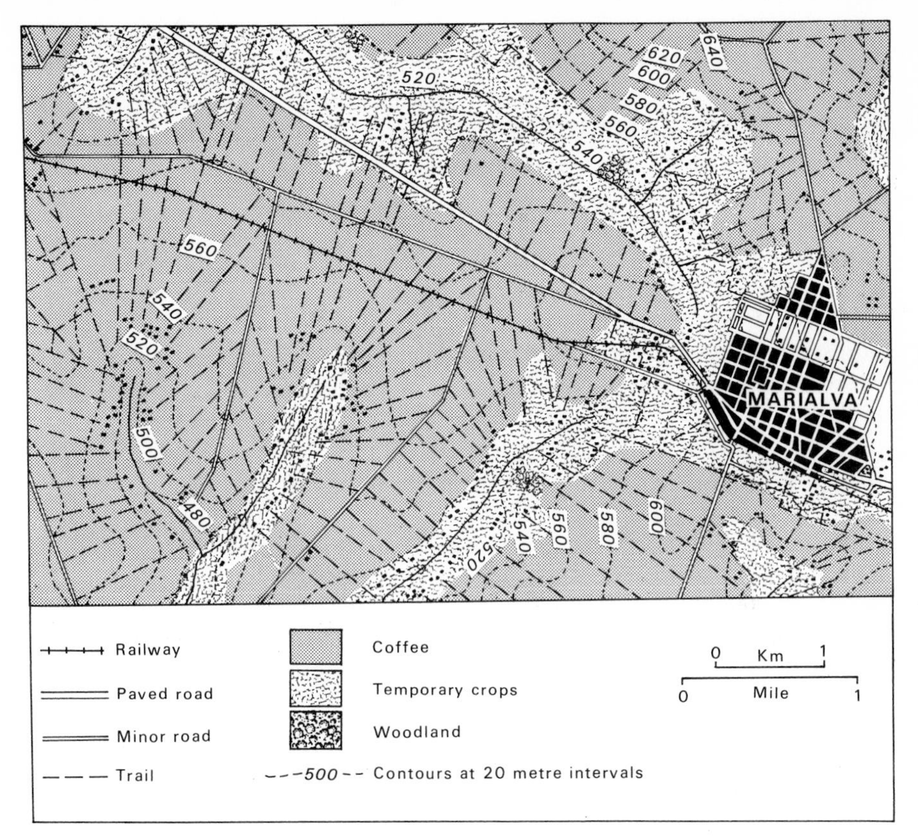

Map 15 North Paraná: the patterns created by organized colonization, with the small service town of Marialva, transport routes along the hill crests and farm lots running downslope. Coffee covers the hill crests and slopes and other, more frost-resistant, crops the valley bottoms.

15 km along the feeder roads. This provision of towns and their very rapid growth have been one of the distinguishing features of the north Paraná scheme. Creation of such a dense urban network is uncharacteristic of most Brazilian development. It reflects the careful planning and success of the project and the close inter-action between the rural and urban sector, for the predominance of small farmers called for greater provision of commercial and other services than is generally required by the large-landowner dominated pattern of other areas.

The rate of growth of the project was phenomenal. Because of the depressed economy of the 1930s initial progress was slow, but by 1944 over one-third of the concession was taken up, the railway had advanced 40 km from Londrina and over 900 km of road had been built. By 1950, 75 per cent of the land had been sold and the length of railway and road had been doubled, and by the early 1970s occupation of the territory was virtually complete. It had created a distinct rural landscape of small mixed farms worked by family labour. The distribution of land provided a regularity of farm layout and a rural settlement pattern of fairly evenly distributed dispersed farmsteads, and regularly spaced, planned towns.

The visual pattern of the farmed landscape initially bore some resemblance to that described in older coffee areas, of a 'green wave', generated here by the practice of cultivating coffee on the plateau tops, with other crops hidden in the valleys. This development made Paraná Brazil's principal source of coffee. In 1939 the state produced about 500 000 sacks of coffee, about 2 per cent of national output. By 1960 it had overtaken São Paulo and by 1963 was producing almost two-thirds of national production, from a 'forest' of almost 1300 million coffee trees. However, the marginality of the area for coffee was exposed by frosts in 1964, 1966 and 1975, which has resulted in a retreat of the coffee frontier, and the conversion of much of its fertile soil to other crops and pasture.

A measure of the dynamism generated by this scheme is reflected in the growth in population of the region, increasing from just below 500 000 in 1950 to almost 1.5 million in 1970. Two-thirds of the 1970 population were migrants. The growth of the towns is particularly spectacular. The two major settlements, Londrina and Maringá, founded in 1929 and 1946, had populations of 228 000 and 121 000 respectively in 1970; in 1980 the figures were 309 000 and 172 000.

If expansion of the frontier into Paraná saw the advance of a traditional crop, coffee, in the framework of a new and carefully planned agrarian structure, the advance northwards from São Paulo into the Centre-West region of Mato Grosso and Goiás was characterized by the persistence of traditional structure but very different crop patterns. This frontier has been identified as distinctive in being the first not to be associated with responses to external demand, but with the supply of internal needs.

Part of the area had been penetrated during the colonial gold rush, and there had developed extensive pastoralism and collecting activities of prospecting and rubber tapping. The significant advance of the frontier has come, however, with penetration into the area of improved transport links, the railway in the 1930s and federal highways in the 1950s. The advance of the frontier from São Paulo did not bring with it coffee, but rather the production of food and raw materials for the urban markets of São Paulo. In addition, the foundation of a new state capital, Goiânia, in 1937, and of Brasília, has created important local markets. In consequence the southern part of the Centre-West has become an important producer of rice, maize and cotton. This has been associated with the movement of small-scale farmers to the frontier, using traditional methods of land rotation, but there has also been some organized colonization, and some development, of larger, more advanced holdings producing wheat and soya beans. Greater access to market has also led to change in the pastoral economy, with improvement of pasture, and the development of cattle raising and local fattening, replacing the earlier pattern of very extensive raising of cattle which were then moved nearer the urban markets for fattening. The overall impact of these developments has been to extend the agricultural landscape of the South-east, and to integrate the area into the core region of Brazil.

The advance of the twentieth century frontier has been closely linked to the construction of transport lines, whether the railways into western São Paulo and Paraná in the inter-war period, or the highways into the Centre-West and Amazonia since 1950. Such lines have been crucial for the opening up of new territories and in providing access between new sources of forest and agricultural products and established markets. Seen in a positive light these route-ways are axes of modernization, advancing into a virgin land. The Brazilian Ministry of Transport (1970) saw the Belém – Brasília highway, built in the 1950s, as having such a role, a decisive factor in the occupation of the hinterland,transforming virgin regions. Between 1960 and 1970 almost 2 million people settled in the area opened up by the highway, over 100 settlements were established, a substantial pastoral economy developed, as well as extractive industries exploiting lumber and other forest products. The highway provided the spine for the construction of over 2000 km of feeder roads.

A more negative view would see much of that 'progress' as destructive, as squatters without title to land or large landholders move in along the route, clearing the forest to plant a few crops or to establish extensive grazing lands.

Fig. 6.19 The impact of spontaneous colonization near the São Paulo–Paraná border. An untidy landscape of cropping, simple dwellings, cultivation of the hill slope and clearance of the forest.

In both cases the pattern of clearance is to fell the forest and burn it off, replacing the forest landscape with one of burnt tree stumps, poor grass, and large herds of cattle (Smith 1971: 215 –72).

The last frontier?

Highway construction has been an integral part of the advance of Brazil's latest, and perhaps last, frontier, that into Amazonia. This has been intimately associated with the construction of the Transamazônica an other highways pushed into the region since 1970.

After the collapse of the rubber boom Amazonia lapsed into stagnation, except for abortive attempts to establish rubber plantations by the Ford Motor Company and a brief flurry of renewed production of natural rubber during the Second World War. The awakening of interest in regional development programmes in Brazil after 1945 saw some attempts to improve infrastructural provision for the existing population. This interest intensified during the 1960s with the creation of a regional development agency, the Superintendência do Desenvolvimento da Amazônia (SUDAM), to encourage the settlement and increase the productive utilization of the region. The area defined as classic Amazonia occupied 40 per cent of the land area of Brazil, but contained about 4 per cent of the national population, at a density of about one person per square kilometre. It was essentially a deserted forest. Such economic activity as existed was limited and mainly small scale, and knowledge of the region's resources and potential was scanty. Yet for Brazilians, and others, it was a fabulous and challenging storehouse of unrealized wealth. SUDAM'S early work focused on improving the infrastructure and encouraging development in industry and agriculture. Such developments tended to focus on the pre-existing areas of settlement, along the river line and particularly in the principal towns of Belém and Manaus. The latter was particularly stimulated and began a new phase as a 'boom' town by becoming a free port, which generated much commercial activity and some industrialization. There were however few spin-offs from this into the rest of the region.

The simple explanation of the proposal to build a 1200 km highway across Amazonia can be seen as a response to the impact of yet another drought on the impoverished North-east region of Brazil. Amazonia was an empty but seemingly fertile land; the North-eastern *sertão* was a harsh, marginal environment with a population in excess of its apparent capacity to sustain them. What could be simpler than to use Nordestinos to build a road into Amazonia and then encourage them to settle along it as small farmers? Broader considerations can be seen in a much more explicit concern to explore the region's resources, particularly in areas remote from the existing lines of penetration along the rivers. In addition much of this land had been theoretically Spanish during the colonial period but had become Brazilian by right of possession. Growing interest by other Latin American countries in their Amazonian lands, the building of highways, and the discovery of petroleum prompted geo-political concern by Brazil to reaffirm possession of what might prove to be the unmasking of a late twentieth century El Dorado.

The Transamazônica highway between Estreito and Humaitá was completed by 1975. In 1973 another highway north of the Amazon, the Perimetral Norte, was announced, and other linking highways were developed or proposed. These were to provide lines of settlement. Organized colonization schemes along the Transamazônica were to provide 100 000 families with landholdings within five years. A network of planned settlements – designated *agrovilas*, *agrópoles* and *rurópoles* in ascending order of their planned population and range of service provision – were to be located at set intervals along the highway. These communities were to provide basic services of electricity, water, education and health facilities. The organizing agency, Instituto Nacional de Colonização e Reforma Agrária (INCRA), was to transport selected colonists from their source area, settle them on plots of 100 ha, provide them with subsistence for 6 months, and with credit for the purchase of the plot, farm implements, and to construct a house.

In theory this was a well-organized settlement scheme, but its implementation did not match its objectives. By 1974 only 6000 families were settled along the highway, less than 10 per cent of the predicted target, and less than 2 per cent of the 'excess' population claimed to exist in the North-east.

The reasons for the limited success of the scheme are manifold. The original scheme was a spectacular and grandiose government showpiece – it would be an 'opening of frontiers which would change the face of Brazil' (Delfim Netto 1971: 136). However, because it was to be an instant solution to a problem it was hastily and rigidly planned, with limited knowledge of the environment into which it was to be set, and limited appraisal of its consequences. Although the road was speedily constructed, the resources necessary to co-ordinate and implement the colonization process were inadequate. There were insufficient technicians to plan and execute the settlement process. Layout of holdings was initially planned with great rigidity, with no concessions to variations in terrain or soil quality. Some plots were thus incapable of sustaining cultivation, and were abandoned after partial clearance. Later plots on such lands were increased in size to provide pastoral holdings, or the lands were left untouched. In some attempt at conservation 50 per cent of plot area was to be left in forest; initially INCRA tried to insist that this reserve should be a continuous stand of forest across each block of plots, but this was later modified to leave the reserves in those areas unsuitable for clearance. The settlement of most colonists in the *agrovilas* meant they were remote from their plots, and in addition plots on the poorly maintained side roads were sometimes seasonally inaccessible to the colonists, agronomists and health visitors. Some colonists chose to build simple dwellings on their plots which gave direct access to their land, but isolated them from planned support services, and made the *agrovilas* less viable. In fact provision of *agrovilas* was not at an adequate rate, and many of the proposed services were delayed or absent.

In addition to the limitations of the planning *per se* of colonization, there were broader inhibitions to its success. The Amazon environment was poorly known and, coupled with a basic deficiency of technicians, advice on how best to utilize it was largely unavailable. A fundamental flaw may well have been this difficult and unknown environment was an unsuitable combination with the refugees from the North-east. Many colonists were ex-farm labourers, used to working for a *fazendeiro* and not to independent farm management; they were poorly educated, and certainly ill-equipped to cope with the utilization of a rain forest environment totally alien to the semi-arid experience with which they were familiar. The methods they used to clear their land were traditional and slow, using slash and burn techniques and family labour, with few tools, fertilizers or other inputs. In addition to a lack of agricultural advice, colonists lacked other supportive elements. Many chose to grow cash crops of rice, manioc, maize and beans, which meant dependence on a seasonal harvest, and thus periods in which both subsistence and income was deficient. Longer term crops required time to reach maturity, but credit was not always easily available. Concentration on a few cash crops when markets were limited and storage inadequate tended to force down prices.

In consequence of such checks, by the mid 1970s, the advance of the frontier in this particular form was beginning to stagnate. Progress was much slower

Fig. 6.20 Agricultural colonization in Amazonia. A simple dwelling provided in a clearing along the Manaus–Pôrto Velho highway. The land has been cleared by slash and burn techniques, leaving major trees and fallen trunks amongst which crops are planted.

than had been envisaged and the emergent pattern of colonization bore limited resemblance to the regular plots and neat little towns demarcated on the planners' drawing boards. In addition the neat symbiosis between the over-populated North-east and empty Amazonia had broken down. Increasingly colonists from other regions were settled, partly in the hope that more able farmers from the South-east and South would provide a 'demonstration effect' for North-easterners, and partly under the sheer weight of numbers of aspirant colonists from these areas.

In response to this limited success other 'frontier' strategies have been applied to Amazonia. Even before 1970 SUDAM had been fostering larger scale, pastoral farm enterprises. Funds were available for investment in a range of development fields, including industry, tourism and agriculture, and a majority of the projects approved were for developments in pastoralism. Between 1966 and 1976 over 300 such projects were approved, relating to 7.8 million ha, an average size of over 20 000 ha. Most of these projects were located in southern Amazonia, in the northern parts of Mato Grosso and Goiás, and south Pará, as highways from South-east Brazil penetrated northwards. Such schemes provide a secure investment in land, will generate substantial meat output for the national and world market; they provide few jobs and result in extensive clearance of the vegetation, as once again fire clearance is used to improve grassland and clear forests.

After 1973 this process was further stimulated by INCRA's granting of holdings of up to 3000 ha along the Transamazônica, again attractive to pastoral farmers. Clearance of holdings of this scale, even if the rule about preserving 50 per cent of the forest cover is observed, profoundly transforms the landscape, from one of dense tropical forest or the more open *cerrado*, into extensive, low-quality grassland. Figures relating to the scale of the impact of this clearance vary considerably. One estimate (Mahar 1979: 128) suggests that by 1978, 30 000 km^2 had been cleared. This can be variously perceived as deforesting less than 1 per cent of the area of Amazonia; or of a piece of territory as large as Belgium!

In 1975 federal planning introduced a new element into the development of the Amazon frontier. Instead of being seen as an area for the advance of a substantial frontier of settlement, it was identified as a resource frontier, within which certain specific resources – minerals, forest products, pasture, for example – might be exploited to generate export earnings or substitute imports. To foster this development 15 growth poles were identified, some related to specific resource locations, such as mineral deposits and others to more extensive areas based on lumbering, rubber extraction or pastoralism. In consequence the frontier of development will be nuclear rather than linear, with the hope that growth will diffuse outwards from these poles.

In addition to the planned advance of the frontier of Amazonia, along the Transamazônica, on large ranches or from growth poles, there has also been a more spontaneous and traditional frontier development in the far west. The territory of Rondônia was made accessible from the South-east with the completion of the Cuiabá – Pôrto Velho highway and has been subject to substantial immigration, of both small farmers and pastoralists. In consequence there has been much uncontrolled settling and destruction of the forest cover, to plant cash crops and raise cattle. Lack of control has meant dispute over land ownership and environmental destruction, generating a pattern of landscape and living reminiscent of the 'Wild West'. A few agricultural colonization schemes have been organized. However, Rondônia, along with other parts of Amazonia opened up by highway schemes, has been flooded with immigrants in search of land. Such spontaneous movement and settlement is based on squatting, slash and burn clearance of land and planting of a few hectares of subsistence and cash crops. This process is less spectacular or notorious than the large-scale pastoral schemes of south-eastern and multinational corporations, but it is more insidious, less easily controlled and probably at least as destructive of the natural resources and landscape of Amazonia. The dynamism of change and the absence of close control over this spontaneous development makes precise assessment of its scale extremely difficult. However, the 1975 Agricultural Census recorded an increase in the area in farms in Rondônia from 1.6 million ha in 1970 to 3 million in 1975, and in Pará the farm area increased from 10.7 million to 16 million ha!

Some measure of the scale of dynamism of the Amazon frontier is given in the preliminary report of the 1980 census (IBGE 1980), which shows that the regional population grew from 3.6 million in 1970 to 6 million in 1980, an annual rate of increase twice the national average. Rondônia experienced a rate of 15.8 per cent a year. All but one of the territory's seven *municipios* at least doubled its population, and the population of Cacaol *municipio* increased from just over 1000 to 68 000 during the decade. High rates of increase were also experienced in Pará, particularly along the line of the Transamazônica; Altamira, the focus of much of the organized colonization, increased its population from 15 000 to almost 50 000.

Rates of growth of this magnitude are indices of the rapidity of change in Amazonia, transforming it by ordered colonies, planned towns, mining and lumbering camps, the slashing scars of highways, vast extensions of pasture, and the disordered chaos of spontaneous small clearings and frontier towns.

All of these developments represent the advance of man-made landscapes and the retreat of the primeval forest. The presumed wealth of the forest has motivated its penetration since the early colonial period, but until recently the impact of man has been negligible against the greatness of the forest. The potential scale of the impact of development, both planned and unplanned, in the region since 1970 has, however, prompted a fierce debate about the propriety of opening up this last frontier. For the Brazilian government development of Amazonia presents the logical continuation of the long standing obsession with the area, it provides land for the settlement of population, a possible resource base for the process of national development and confirmation of the possession of territory against the perceived threats of peripheral states. Development of the region is thus seen as a symbol of progress, and the new landscapes those of progress.

For the conservationist lobby, within and outside Brazil, such development and its associated landscapes is essentially destructive. At best development is seen as premature, for the potential use of forest resources is unknown, and may be lost for ever by wanton clearance; while limited knowledge of the area means that the likely consequence for the natural environment of deforestation and agricultural use are uncertain. What is increasingly clear is that the lush, diverse and dense forest cover does not indicate rich soils awaiting cultivation. Instead it has become apparent that this is a fragile ecosystem, and that once the nutrient cycle has been disrupted by extensive deforestation, soil fertility and crop yields decline rapidly. While virgin forest remains new land can be taken into cultivation but there is an obvious limit to this process. Amazonia presents the last area where Brazilians can follow a mobile frontier, but in this case it is finite. Moreover in this area such a frontier does appear, under present practice, to leave behind it land with little alternative use.

Increasing knowledge of the area has begun to reveal its internal diversity. Furley (1980) has indicated that the region's landscapes are not homogeneous and should not be subject to a single pattern of utilization. There are some areas of higher potential, along the seasonally flooded *várzeas* and in limited areas of better soil. Elsewhere small-scale slash and burn shifting cultivation may be the best available method of utilization, doing least permanent damage to the environment; the problem with such an approach is that it is primarily concerned with subsistence and is perceived as 'backward', rather than contributing spectacularly to national economic growth. Even this strategy would require some degree of control, since excessive population using such techniques would be as effective at deforesting large tracts as a large corporation.

To some extent the limited success of organized development on the Amazon frontier and doubts about the environmental impact of such development have slowed down the official onslaught on the forest, so that the natural landscape might survive a little longer than the more pessimistic environmentalists have predicted. It is possible that less destructive policies towards this frontier may emerge, or even that alternative areas, such as the *cerrado*, may form the focus of late twentieth century frontier expansion. Such a strategy would also require greater control over the impact of spontaneous, unplanned clearance by migrants, whose individual impact may be tiny, but whose cumulative consequences may be substantial.

In addition to recent concern about the destructive impact of the Amazon frontier on the natural landscape, this area also provides the last refuge of the primitive landscapes of the surviving Amerindians. In the face of the advance of highways, squatter clearings and company lands the simple Indian landscapes have been reduced by genocide, absorption of Indians into Brazilian society or further retreat of the tribal Indians. These groups are particularly at risk because the prime motivator in the advance of the Brazilian frontier is land, which is also used by the Indians. As over the previous four centuries it is the Indians who have lost ground, both literally and metaphorically. In recent years concern for their rights and claims has tended to be neglected. The establishment of Indian reserves has created what are in effect artificial Indian lands and landscapes. Furthermore, even these reserves have not been inviolable against alternative developments in the cause of 'progress'.

Throughout the past 480 years Brazil has had a frontier, or frontiers. Its advance has given the country its shape and contributed substantially to the present form of much of its cultural landscape. The continuing availability of virgin land has both drawn on the frontier and diminished the need to be careful with land behind the frontier. The fragility of the Amazon environment and the fact that it represents the last, even if substantial, frontier makes it increasingly likely that future developments in agriculture will be derived from increases in the intensity of use of existing farmlands rather than the opening up of new ones.

Behind the frontier

The frontier has been a major theme in the history and geography of Brazil, shaping both the land and the landscape. It remains an active and important theme up to the present. But the advance of the frontier has left behind it an area of occupation and settlement. If the frontier is a zone of dynamic change the lands behind are subject to more stable and ordered development. If a majority of Brazilians are now urban dwellers, there are still large numbers of people, in absolute terms, who live in rural areas and find employment in agriculture, creating and maintaining farming landscapes. The 1975 agricultural census of Brazil recorded 3.2 million km^2 of land in farms, employing 21 million people. The country is a major agricultural producer in world terms, ranking among the top five producers of coffee, cocoa, maize and soya beans, and with the fourth largest cattle herd.

Yet in spite of its importance, Brazilian agriculture rarely creates a neat ordered farming landscape. Few areas are characterized by regular bounded fields, extensive continuous tracts of crops and grassland, or trim, picturesque villages, for even behind the frontier use of land is incomplete. Substantial areas of territory are not in agricultural use. In 1975 just over one-third of the national territory was actually in farms. If the Centre-West and North regions are excluded as containing most of the active frontier, the proportion of land in farms in the more settled areas is about two-thirds of the total. In addition to the incomplete incorporation of land into farms, utilization of land within farms is often incomplete, with substantial areas remaining in forest, in secondary growth recovering from shifting cultivation or in poor, extensive natural pasture. In 1975 only 2.5 per cent of total farmland was under permanent crops and 9.4 per cent under temporary crops. In total less than 5 per cent of Brazilian territory is actually under crops. Relatively little of the substantial area used for pasture is improved grassland, so that the non-cropped areas include substantial tracts of natural vegetation – natural grassland, scrub, cleared woodland or native forest. In consequence much of the farming landscape of Brazil is not a neat patchwork of fields under a variety of crops and pasture, but an irregular pattern of cropland inter-mixed with extensive pasture and unused land.

At a macro-scale the pattern of Brazilian agriculture has remained relatively static over a long period, with the principal areas of cultivation close to the coast and the interior farmlands under pasture. In the North-east the *zona da mata* retains much of the legacy, in land use and land ownership, of the sugar economy, and the interior that of very extensive pastoralism. Both areas also have some element of subsistence cultivation, and between the two areas has emerged, since the colonial period, a transitional area, the *agreste*, of better pastoralism and small-scale cultivation. The South-east still bears some of the marks of the sugar and coffee economy, but has made most progress in diversification, in some break up of large holdings, the cultivation of a wider range of crops and the development of improved pastoralism for meat and dairy produce for the urban markets. The South, too, part of which includes the recent frontier of Paraná, includes some element of modernization in its small-scale cultivation and improved pastoralism. The long-established pastoral zone of the south of Rio Grande do Sul has also been associated with improvements in grassland and stock.

It is also the case that Brazilian agriculture has remained largely traditional in its landholding practices and techniques of land use. The granting of large holdings was an integral part of the colonial process, and these persist, either as a historical legacy or as an element in modern commercial farming. In some areas, such as the colonization zones of the South, smallholdings were granted. Elsewhere the process of squatting or the break up of old estates after the decline of a boom crop have generated some smaller farm units. There is a basic contrast between a relatively small number of large holdings, and many small ones. In 1975, 52 per cent of farm holdings were below 10 ha; they controlled about 3 per cent of the farmed land. Holdings over 1000 ha made up less than 1 per cent of the total; they controlled 43 per cent of farmland. In fact 14 per cent of Brazil's farm area was held by 1824 farms of over 10 000 ha each. In general the larger units are farmed less intensively. Much of Brazilian agriculture remains traditional. Land is cleared by slash and burn techniques. Rotation of crops is limited; instead, as yields decline, plots are abandoned and new ones opened up. Where new land is not available former plots may be used, in a system of land rotation. Modern inputs of improved seed, better stock, fertilizers and so on are limited. Manual labour, or at best animal traction, are still widely used; the mechanization of agriculture is still limited, and the hoe and the axe are important farm implements. In 1950 the country had less than 10 000 tractors. The development of a domestic tractor industry has improved this, but the level of mechanization remains low. In 1970 there was only one tractor per 218 ha of arable land, as opposed to 1 : 27 in the USA.

A further index of the stagnation of Brazilian agriculture and the persistence of traditional patterns and practices is evidenced by the limited improvement

in productivity. Over the past two decades Brazilian agriculture has shown high rates of growth in output. However, this has been largely derived from the added production of new land, and not from increased productivity from established farmed areas. Total production in many crops has increased substantially, as in the case of maize, rice and sugar; but so too did the cultivated area under these crops. In numerous cases – cotton, rice, beans for example – average yields per hectare have tended to fall, not increase. Such patterns are not uniform across the established farm area, there are regions where there is greater innovation, particularly in the South-east and South, where there is greater input of more modern methods. There is more use of machinery and fertilizer, and of improved seeds and stock, and of more intensive land use to meet the demands of the growing urban markets. The introduction or substantial expansion of certain crops has also brought change, particularly the cultivation of soya beans and wheat. Elsewhere traditional methods and low yields persist, with substantial under utilization of land on the *latifundios*.

In general then the pattern of the rural landscape behind the frontier is relatively long established and little changing. The oldest and most static are those of the North-east. The colonial contrast between the sugar zone of the coastlands and the extensive pastoralism of the interior persists. These landscapes have changed little in more than three centuries. In the humid *zona da mata* sugar remains dominant over large areas, providing an unbroken monocultural sea of green cane, the principal change being the factory scale processing of the *usina*. Although the factory chimneys and buildings of the *usina* are a new element in the landscape, their need for larger cane inputs has served to strengthen the dominance of the canelands. In the semi-arid interior the poor scrub of the *caatinga* still sustains extensive pastoralism. The dreary greyness of the *sertão* extends over very large areas, changing into a brief lush greenness with the rains. Some modification has been introduced into this region by the cultivation of tree cotton in the nineteenth century, and more recently by the introduction of drought-resistant cash and fodder crops. The uplands and other areas of more reliable water supply form small oases of cultivation, and the river lines strands of subsistence crops. Although storage dams have been constructed as part of an anti-drought strategy in the *sertão* for over a century, they have done little to alter the basic nature of the pastoral landscape. Only in the last decade have large-scale irrigation schemes introduced new elements into the *sertão*, with dams, lakes, irrigation channels and new croplands.

A somewhat similar dichotomy may be noted in the South, between the grazing landscapes of the Campanha Gaúcha, and the agricultural landscapes of the serras. The region has experienced a greater degree of modernization than the North-east. The pastoral economy established in the colonial period has seen some change, with the improvement of stock and grazing. The Cam-

Fig. 6.21 Agricultural landscape in Rio Grande do Sul. Land is being prepared using an ox-plough, and there is some regularity in field layout and the use of field boundaries.

panha landscape has also been diversified by the development of large-scale, mechanized cultivation of wheat, rice and soya beans. On the serras the distinctive patterns created by the foreign colonists persist, with small farms, polyculture and specialty activities of maize/pig production, viticulture and tobacco growing.

The South-east has the greatest internal diversity in its rural landscapes and also has experienced the greatest degree of change. The area has made most progress in agricultural modernization, not only in new crops, stock and machinery, but in inputs of credit, improved transport, rural electrification and the development of co-operatives. All of these trends give a more 'commercial' dimension to the farming landscapes of the region, with the development of modern cash crop farms for domestic and foreign markets, intensification of land use, particularly in the development of horticulture and in improved pastoralism using more productive stock.

There are, then, broad regional contrasts in the established rural landscapes of Brazil and there are significant internal contrasts in the farming pattern within these macro-regions. Given the persistence in Brazil of agricultural specialization, it is also possible to identify distinctive landscapes associated with particular products. These are expressed not only in near monocultural land use but in characteristic settlement patterns and the accoutrements of agricultural processing. Such specialized landscapes would include the sugar lands of the North-east, the cocoa district of Bahia, the coffee lands of Paraná and specialized areas of viticulture, tobacco growing and rice cultivation in Rio Grande do Sul.

One other element of significance in the rural landscape is the form and pattern of settlement. While the recent trend has been towards urbanization and the consequent significance of urban landscapes, a large number of Brazilians still live in small towns, villages, hamlets and dispersed houses, with their life-style still closely linked to rural activities. There were, in 1970, 42 million Brazilians living in settlements with less than 200 inhabitants or in isolated farmsteads.

The small towns and villages have acquired some minimal service functions as well as housing rural labourers, small landholders and providing town houses for *fazendeiros*. Other nucleations have developed as part of the farm economy, on cane and coffee plantations and linked to other cash crops. For many rural Brazilians, though, the pattern of settlement is a dispersed one.

Within the rural landscapes, house types are an important element, reflecting the relations between man and environment. Their character is influenced by the nature of the local agricultural economy, the type of building material available and the social status of the inhabitants. Within Brazil there is considerable diversity in the pattern of agriculture, while the limited level of

Fig. 6.22 Rural landscape in the interior North-east. Although it is in the heart of the *sertão*, the Cariri region of Ceará is a prosperous agricultural area because of the availability of reliable spring-line water. The houses in the foreground are of wattle and daub, with tiled or thatched roofs.

economic development means that there is still a substantial dependence on local building materials, rather than on industrially produced construction materials. The most commonly used are thatch, wood, wattle and daub, and crude bricks. The use of stone is uncommon. Certain types of farm activity generate ancillary buildings for processing and storage, but in many cases the farm consists only of the dwellinghouse. In this climate, too, there is little need of stabling for stock.

The Brazilian social historian Gilberto Freyre distinguished between the *casa grande* (the mansion) and the *senzala* (the slave quarter). Though the *senzala* has disappeared, this classification points to the distinction between landowner and labourer, and one can identify in the rural landscape the substantial residence of the large landowner, and the simpler dwelling of the rural labourer or small farmer.

The *casa grande* is particularly characteristic of the plantation lands of cane and coffee and, on a rather more modest scale, on the cattle estates of the *sertão* and the *campanha*. The archetypal *casa grande* is that of the North-eastern sugar zone, where it formed the hub of the cluster of dwellings and processing plant of the *engenho*. The *casa grande* itself was a substantial single-storey building in colonial style, often with an adjacent chapel. The *casa grande* also formed the nucleus of the cluster of dwellings and processing plant on the nineteenth century coffee plantation. This had a timber frame built on a stone foundation, with walls of wattle and daub and roofed with tiles made on the *fazenda*. They were usually of one storey, but sometimes of two, or with storerooms below the living quarters. Walls were limewashed, usually in white, with the woodwork picked out in another colour. In addition to the processing plant the slave quarters were usually adjacent. In the late nineteenth century these were replaced by simple houses for the immigrant *colonos*.

In the pastoral areas the *fazendas* tend to be less substantial than those of the plantation lands and less associated with ancillary buildings. Limewashed wattle and daub or plastered brick are the most common building materials, with roofs made of interlocking curved tiles. A veranda is a common feature on the *fazendas* of the *sertão*. They are less common on the cattle *fazendas* of the Planalto Central, a response to the milder climatic conditions, though projecting eaves may provide shelter against sun and rain. On the Campanha Gaúcha, the *estancia* may be protected from wind and sun by a wind break of trees. The main building is relatively simple, a whitewashed brick and tile dwelling.

On all of these estates, whether plantation or pastoral, there is a marked contrast between the substantial dwelling of the landowner and the house of the rural labourer. These are small, simple buildings, of brick or more commonly wattle and daub, which is whitewashed, with a ridge roof of thatch or tile. They may be single dwellings or, on the sugar and coffee plantations, in rows. They consist at most of two or three rooms, with few furnishings, contrasting with the multi-room, richly furnished *casa grande*. On the plantations these dwellings may have been constructed by the landowners and have some degree of uniformity.

Elsewhere the dispersed housing of the rural poor, whether smallholder, rural labourer, squatter or cowboy, are simple and crude. They reflect the limited resources of their inhabitants. There is little if any use of commercially produced building materials and there are in consequence regional variations in these dwellings, reflecting local building materials and environmental conditions. The basic house plan is a simple rectangle, of one or two rooms, of simple materials and with few, and frequently unglazed, windows. Walls are made of wattle and daub, or clay. Roofs are rarely tiled; instead, local vegetation of palm or grasses is used for thatching, forming a ridge roof.

In Amazonia dwellings are usually raised above the ground to avoid flooding and humidity, and even in areas above the flood level some form of foundation is common. Along the rivers houses are sometimes built on rafts, to counter seasonal fluctuations in river level. Building materials are vertical boards of locally abundant palms or cedar wood, and thatch. Simpler dwellings, of squatters or forest-gatherers, may consist only of a timber frame and thatched roof–walls of palm leaves.

In contrast, in the backlands of the North-east the absence of substantial timber makes wattle and daub a much more common building material. Bamboo canes or the branches of contorted *caatinga* bushes are interwoven, lashed together with lianas and covered with local clay. This is rarely smoothed or whitewashed. Grass, straw or palm leaves are used for the ridge roof. The house is built without foundations and has an earth floor. This house form is common in the open lands of the *caatingas* and *cerrados*.

In the South-east the survival of some of the forest cover permits greater use of construction timber, giving more substantial houses, though using wattle and daub or brick as their principal building materials. Tiled roofs are more common. In the more accidented topography of Minas Gerais, dwellings may be built against the hillside, and partially supported on pillars. If this latter space is enclosed it may be used for stock and storage.

In the far South different building materials and non-Luso-Brazilian traditions provide profound contrasts to the house types of the rest of the country. Much greater use is made of wood. Sawn planks of *Araucaria* pine, placed vertically, are most commonly used. The ridged roof, also frequently of wood, is steeply pitched to facilitate run-off of the higher rainfall of the South. The use of details of carved wood betrays areas of Germanic settlement. Some areas of German settlement, particularly the Itajaí valley, are also distinguished by the existence of half timbered houses, in which a dark wood frame is filled with dark red bricks, the mortar often being painted white. Flat tiles or wooden tiles are used for roofing. Such German dwellings are also associated with a cluster of outbuildings, usually of wood, providing stables, hen coops, maize stores and pigsties. Elsewhere the two-storeyed dwellings of Italian colonists provide a feature unusual in other parts of Brazil. In the viticultural

Fig. 6.23 Half-timbered farmhouse of a German colonist in the Itajaí valley, Santa Catarina. The cluster of house and barns is a characteristic feature of this area.

areas of Rio Grande do Sul the stone-built lower storey provides the wine cellar, and the upper storey of wood the living quarters.

In a small area on the coast of Santa Catarina are survivals of early colonist settlement, constructed by the Acorians. These are quite similar to traditional Luso-Brazilian houses, simple, one-storey dwellings of whitewashed brick or clay, with a tiled roof. Also increasingly uncommon are the sod houses of the Campanha Gaúcha, the rudimentary dwellings of rural labourers, constructed of earth and grass blocks, with a thatched roof.

In Amazonia Japanese colonists near Belém and Manaus have also constructed some distinctive house forms, the more prosperous of them being plank dwellings of two storeys. Simpler, single-storey dwellings are also wood-built, with horizontal planking, a distinction from those of Brazilian settlers. In the last decade a new house form has been introduced into Amazonia by the provision of housing for colonists along the highways, though neither the number of colonists nor the provision of housing has been on the scale originally projected. Located in the centre of the lots along the highways, the houses are neat and uniform, of regular planks which are painted. The houses are raised on piles, and frequently with a front porch and veranda. Roofing material is often manufactured, such as asbestos sheeting.

Given the poverty of much of the rural population of Brazil, the rural house types are a reflection of local geographical conditions, of the nature of the agricultural economy and the local availability of raw materials. Though there is still a dynamic frontier area, with characteristic rudimentary or uniformly planned dwellings, elsewhere traditional rural house types may be declining in response to the drift to the towns. In addition, particularly in more modern agricultural areas, there is an increasing tendency to employ temporary, casual labour (the so-called *boias-frias*), breaking traditional patriarchal patterns whereby rural workers might receive a small plot and house in return for necessary labour. A consequence has been for these casual labourers to live in shanties in the small towns, from where they are transported when needed, and for the dwellings in the countryside to fall into decay.

Landscape destruction and conservation

Critics of the development process in Brazil, both in the past and currently, argue that the country's resource use has been essentially destructive and to the general detriment of the natural environment. Brazilian development has been associated with the rape of the soil and the devastation of the forest. Yet the clearance of the forest and the use of the soil was as inevitably a part of the process of settlement in this new land as it was in Europe in the Middle Ages or in the colonial United States. Profligate resource use in Brazil has perhaps been a response to the seeming superabundance of land, forest, minerals and other resources. With such seeming wealth there was no need to be conservative.

As settlement has advanced the natural landscapes of the tropics have been replaced by those of agriculture. The forest has retreated before the monocultural landscapes of cane, coffee and extensive pastoralism, and the depredations of small farmers and squatters. Much of the land has been cleared by traditional methods of slash and burn, felling the vegetation cover, burning it off and cultivating the land. As a system used on a small scale by the Amerindian its impact was limited, but used more extensively, as a system of land rotation, its impact has been more severe, especially when coupled with overcropping, overgrazing and the cultivation of unsuitable terrain, resulting in a decline in soil fertility and the erosion of soil.

Although such practices represented a careless, exploitative and ephemeral use of land, considerable areas so worked in the early frontier areas remain in use. Developments on the current frontiers of Amazonia and the Centre-West are spectacular, and have contributed to the increase in Brazilian food output, but the older areas remain as significant agricultural producers. Some land usage has been destructive and has left behind devastated landscapes, but Brazil has considerable potential for agricultural expansion and improvement. Much of the national territory remains outside farms, so that there is virgin land beyond the frontier; even within the farmed area land use is incomplete and often extensive. Such land could be brought into use. The possibility also exists of more intensive use of land through mechanization and the application of chemical inputs, though both carry risks of destruction and pollution of the environment.

It seems likely that in the immediate future continued replacement of the natural landscape by an agricultural one along the frontier will be a major dimension in increases in agricultural output. Reserves of virgin land tend to be those less accessible to use because of distance, topography or climate, but current highway programmes are likely to bring lines of penetration of farm landscapes into these areas. At the same time there is growing evidence of more careful, intensive and conservative use of land in older areas in the North-east and South-east.

Advance of agricultural landscapes at the expense of natural ones has not only been to expose land for farming, but to exploit forest reserves *per se*, for fuel, construction and industrial use. From the earliest colonial exploitation of *pau brasil* the forest has been an important resource, the exploitation of which has tended to be destructive. São Paulo is reckoned to be the most deforested state in Brazil. In its primitive condition forest covered almost 82 per cent of its area of 248 000 km^2; in 1854 almost 80 per cent was still in forest, but as a result of the sweep of the coffee frontier and other economic advance, by 1973 less than 8 per cent remained under natural forest (Bicudo and Santiago 1977: 294–5).

Throughout settled Brazil the forest has been exploited for construction timber, and for fuel for industrial and domestic use. The 'zone of the woods' of the North-east lost its tree cover to provide land for cane plantations and wood for the sugar mills. In a land deficient in coal, wood and charcoal have been important fuel sources for locomotives, lime making and iron smelting. It was estimated that in the early 1960s the charcoal-based iron industry of Minas Gerais required 27 000 ha of forest a year to meet its needs (Dickenson 1967: 418). The exploitation of timber for construction and for paper production has also had a profound effect. In Paraná staté the Paraná pine *Araucaria angustifolia* provides one of Brazil's few areas of uniform forest cover. Before settlement this forest is thought to have covered 180 000 km^2; by 1930, 40 000 km^2 had been cleared for settlement and timber; in the next two decades a further 50 000 km^2 disappeared (Sternberg 1968: 423).

In addition to this large-scale use, the forest has been eroded by individuals for building material and fuel for cooking. As recently as 1941 an estimated 53 per cent of Brazil's energy use was derived from wood. This proportion has fallen with the development of electric power and oil and the use of bottled gas for cooking, but in small towns and rural areas charcoal is still used for the latter. It is also the case that large areas of forest have been lost by accident. In 1963 fires set for land clearance in Paraná got out of control and destroyed 2 million ha of forest and other vegetation (Sternberg op.cit. 419).

Against this destruction of the forest landscape, Brazil has begun programmes of reafforestation. Initially the consequence of private initiatives by railway, metallurgical and paper companies, the federal government has begun

Fig. 6.24 Re-afforestation in Minas Gerais. Land being planted to trees to supply charcoal for the local iron and steel industry.

to foster reafforestation through the Instituto Brasileiro de Desenvolvimento Florestal (IBDF). In the inter-war period railway companies in São Paulo began to plant eucalypts to replenish their sources of locomotive fuel. More recently, major charcoal-based steelworks in Minas Gerais such as Acesita and Belgo-Mineira have undertaken substantial programmes of planting to provide reliable, uniform and more substantial fuel supplies. Between 1953 and 1974 Acesita, for example, planted 53 500 ha to forest, and has subsequently embarked on an even larger programme, to meet its needs of 3 million cubic metres of charcoal a year (Florestal Acesita n.d.). Such programmes replace some of the destroyed forest cover, though generally substituting a fast-growing uniform forest of eucalypts and pines for the diversity of the original forest. Financial support to reafforestation by IBDF has given rise to the re-creation of woodland cover. Between 1969 and 1974 reafforestation projects affecting 1.1 million ha were approved by IBDF, over 80 per cent of the area being in São Paulo, Paraná, Minas Gerais and Santa Catarina.

The recent perceived threat to the Amazon rain forest as a consequence of proposed highway schemes has generated much debate. To many Brazilians this advance is merely a continuation of the process of the movement of the frontier, which has been a continuing fact of the country's history since 1500, and a logical step in the 'March to the West'. To the government it represents the securing of territory, a possible solution to the population problems of the North-east and a likely revelation of new resources. To critics it represents the loss of the 'last great forest', the destruction of as yet unknown forest resources, the creation of a 'red desert', and, to some, a threat to the world's oxygen supplies. (For varying viewpoints on this debate see Goodland and Irwin 1975; Davis 1977; Mahar 1979; Barbira-Scazzochio 1980). The scale of deforestation in Amazonia is imprecise and interpretation of its consequences varies with the viewpoint of the observer. Barbira-Scazzochio quotes a loss of 100 000 ha per year. Such a rate would not support critics who suggest that the forest will be gone by AD 2005. In the development programme for the region IBDF tried to ensure that half the forest cover would remain, but this policy was not consistently applied and easily circumvented. However, slow-down in the programmes of highway construction and colonization, and reappraisal of its regional strategy by the government, have checked the development process recently, such that exploitation may be delayed, be more conservationist or may be diverted elsewhere, to less vulnerable ecosystems. One positive by-product of the Amazon development programme has been the activities of RADAM, an air-photographic survey of the region, now being extended to other parts of the country. This has provided the first reasonably detailed survey and mapping of the geology, landforms, soils and vegetation of the interior, and has provided some assessment of potential land-use, such that future exploitation of the natural environment will have a more rational base.

The exploitation of minerals must inevitably be a destructive use of resources. Minerals have been important in the Brazilian economy, whether precious metals and gemstones in the colonial material or more mundane metals such as iron and manganese in the present. The country is well endowed with a diversity of mineral resources, but the impact of their exploitation on the landscape has generally been limited. There are some spectacular mining sites such as the iron mines of Casa de Pedra and Itabira in Minas Gerais, but their landscape impact is very localized. There are no extensive mining landscapes such as characterize some areas of the developed world. In the principal coalfield of Santa Catarina, workings are small scale and there is little dereliction due to colliery waste, and little coal-based industrialization. In Rio de Janeiro and the North-east the salt pans add an almost picturesque element to the coastal scenery.

Since destruction and pollution of the environment is a consequence of human action, it is likely that the concentration of man in limited areas will have adverse environmental consequences. The rapidity of Brazilian urbanization, with its consequences in urban sprawl and the growth of landscapes of deprivation in the shanty towns, has been noted above. The inability of urban authorities to cope with city growth has resulted in increasing pollution of rivers and coasts due to the inadequacy of water supply and drainage. The absence or weakness of planning control has fostered severe problems of

Fig. 6.25 Mining landscape. The Casa de Pedra iron ore mine, Congonhas, Minas Gerais.

industrial pollution which, with the automobile boom, has contributed to serious problems of air pollution in the major cities. It is also claimed (Costa n.d.: 17) that Rio de Janeiro and São Paulo rank first and second as the world's noisiest cities.

Increasing awareness of the problems of the urban environment has prompted federal concern within the framework of national planning. Since 1975 there have been efforts to counter the 'premature metropolitanization' focused on São Paulo and Rio de Janeiro and to a lesser extent the other big cities, by controlling their growth, encouraging the expansion of other towns, especially those with populations of 50 000 and more and providing counter-magnets to would-be migrants. Action has begun against the 'pollution of development' caused by industry and automobiles and the 'pollution of poverty' due to inadequate water, drainage and medical provision.

Areas with particular pollution problems have been identified. They include the metropolitan areas of São Paulo, Rio de Janeiro, Belo Horizonte, Recife, Salvador and Pôrto Alegre; the industrial districts of Cubatão and Volta Redonda; and the river basins of the Tietê, Paraíba do Sul, Jacuí, and Pernambuco. Measures include greater planning control and land zonation, the establishment of pollution standards and the relocation of major polluters.

On balance it is probably the case that much of the exploitation of the Brazilian environment has been destructive. Given the seeming luxury of the natural endowment there was little apparent need to carefully husband resources. In consequence the landscape bears many scars of careless usage and of rapid, uncontrolled development.

In recent years growing global concern about the destruction and pollution of the environment have found an echo in Brazil. However, commitment to conservation policies is qualified, on the ground that the problems are less acute in Brazil because there are still extensive areas of the country which are undamaged; that a balance must be drawn between the needs of rapid development and those of minimizing damage to the environment; and at a larger scale that Brazil's industrialization process should not be inhibited by other counter-concerns about pollution.

The need to defend natural resources of soil, air, water, flora and fauna has been recognized, with greater concern for accurate survey of their potential, rational exploitation of those which are of value and defence of those which are vulnerable. This concern includes not only resources *per se* but also areas of merit. These include areas of attractive coastline, of natural beauty and of historic interest.

To date concern to establish landscapes of conservation is an objective rather than an achievement. Available evidence relating to earlier efforts in this field suggest they may be vulnerable to other pressures. The limited success of the IBDF in preserving 50 per cent of the forest cover on Amazonian colonization schemes has been mentioned above. Changes in the status of reserves for the Amerindians also suggest inconsistencies in conservation policy. Though their prime role is to provide homelands for the surviving tribal Indians, the exclusion of European developments from them should also make them areas of conservation of the natural environment, which would be little affected by the limited scale of Indian activities. However, the government has not always succeeded in protecting these lands, or the Indians, from the depredations of white squatters and developers, and has itself modified the reserves in the interests of highway construction and resource development (Brooks 1973).

Brazil has attempted to establish a series of National Parks, to preserve areas of outstanding natural attributes, protecting their physical features, flora and fauna. Of 17 Parques Nacionais proposed by 1972, with a total area of over 3 million ha, less than 10 per cent of this area had been formalized by 1977. Much of the land remains in private hands, and had been modified by fire, deforestation and erosion. Some proposed sites such as those adjacent to the spectacular waterfalls of Paulo Afonso, Sete Quedas and Iguaçu had been modified in the interests of national priorities for hydroelectric power (Strang 1977).

One other sphere in which there has been some government attempt to conserve landscapes has been in the preservation of cultural features of historic or architectural interest. In 1937 the Instituto do Patrimonio Historico e Artistico Nacional was established to oversee the protection of the country's historical and artistic inheritance. This includes material of archaeological, ethnological, historical and artistic interest as well as natural features, sites and landscapes. Designated sites could not be destroyed, demolished or modified without the permission of the Institute. By 1974 almost 200 sites had been designated. These included buildings of architectural merit or associated with famous Brazilians, old *fazendas* and *engenhos*, and physical features such as Corcovado and Pão de Açucar in Rio. Also included were all or part of over a dozen settlements which constituted major and coherent urban landscapes. Included were parts of Pôrto Seguro, the first landfall of the Portuguese, much of colonial Salvador, baroque mining towns such as Mariana, Diamantina and Tiradentes, and towns associated with the early phase of the coffee boom such as Parati and Vassouras (IPHAN 1973). Such preservation implies some concern for landscape conservation, and does leave within the present-day scene specific features or substantial areas which provide impressions at least of past landscapes.

If Brazil's record of environmental and landscape conservation in the past was weak, there are increasing signs of greater awareness of the threats to the natural and cultural landscapes, and of greater recognition of the desirability of trying to reconcile development and conservation.

7

Media landscapes

Previous chapters have dealt with the Brazilian landscape in relatively conventional terms, seeking to indicate the factors which have shaped its evolution, and to describe past and present landscapes. Some parts of the country have virtually pristine natural landscapes; in others, cultural landscapes have been shaped in response to the social organization, economic needs and aesthetic preferences of Amerindians, Portuguese, Africans, Brazilians, South and Central Europeans and Japanese. Such groups have modified their physical milieu in response to their needs, wishes and skills. The degree of modification has varied; in some areas it has been limited and ephemeral, in other profound and permanent. These influences have created the present-day landscape which we can identify and describe; that is, the world about us.

But there is, as Goodey (1971: 1) reminds us, the world outside and the images inside our heads, of environments we perceive. In an early paper on environmental perception David Lowenthal (1967) suggested that there were three realms of geographical study: the nature of the environment; what we think and feel about that environment; and how we behave in, and alter, that environment. He suggested that geographers had largely confined themselves to the exploration of the first of these, that is, what they considered to be the 'real world'. However, in daily life people subordinate reality to the world they perceive and experience. Behaviour in the environment and visions of it are influenced by the perceptions of the individual, by groups and cultures. Lowenthal argued that 'what we see, what we study, and the way we shape and build in the landscape is selected and structured for each of us by custom, culture, desire and faith' (ibid.1). Such influences affect the way we see, act in, and shape our environment and landscape.

In a later paper with Hugh Prince, Lowenthal suggested that 'Landscapes are formed by landscape tastes. People in any country see their terrain through preferred and accustomed spectacles, and they tend to make it over as they see it' (Lowenthal and Prince 1965: 186). The arbiters of landscape taste are often a minority, who influence and shape the landscape of the majority.

The Brazilian landscape of the present has been shaped by the needs and tastes of individuals, groups and cultures before and since Cabral. In the late twentieth century the landscape and tastes in landscape are subject to the influence of at least three potent and growing forces. The landscapes which are evolving may not be 'desirable' in any aesthetic sense, but they are the direct and indirect consequences of the wishes and actions of individuals and groups. The three influences are the growing involvements of the State in Brazilian society and economy, the intertwined impact of multi-national corporations, advertising and the mass media, and the growth of the 'fourth wave' of leisure and tourism. These agencies are involved in both changing the landscape and in the moulding of landscape tastes.

Official landscapes

The State is an increasingly powerful agent in the shaping of landscape. As previously indicated (Chap. 6) in the process of fostering economic development, government has had an important role in changing the Brazilian landscape. But in addition to this direct role the State has an indirect role in influencing the landscapes which we perceive. As Goodey (1971) has indicated, decision-makers operating in an environment base decisions on the environment as they see it, not as it is. The State makes decisions in accordance with its perceptions and objectives, it influences the perceptions and actions of its citizens and can provide an image for outsiders. Lowenthal (1961) suggested that each society and culture organizes its world in accordance with its structure and requirements. National landscapes reflect the attitudes and ideas of inhabitants and government, so that patriotism and national aspirations are powerful forces in shaping attitudes to environment and environmental change. The State is an increasingly powerful agent in shaping such attitudes, through education, influence in the media and publicity and propaganda. Such influences can create a powerful image of a country, as it is, or as it should be. It can create an ideal landscape to be aspired to; to create a notion of a landscape not as it is, but as it is going to be. In addition, State-fostered images may serve to convey a particular image abroad, simply as part of the national image, or to attract investors or migrants.

Such images are usually positive. The State wishes to create an attractive image of itself, its achievements and aspirations. Such images are inevitably selective and partial. They reflect the imposition of a particular value system, with specific images of the environment as it is and might be. Ideological attitudes distort reality to serve some particular interest. In a developing country the landscape change due to a development project is in the 'national' or 'public' interest, though that interest may in fact be the narrow interest of a particular political, social or economic group, rather than the interests of the whole population or territory. The State can therefore create particular landscapes; because as central authority it can influence the entire national territory, it can foster a cultural uniformity, through the standardization of State-funded facilities or the fiat of national legislation. It can also create powerful internal and external images of past, present and future landscapes.

Shortly after the Brazilian revolution of 1964, official posters appeared repeating the old adage that 'Brazil is the country of the future' but adding that, in 1964, 'the future had arrived'! Examination of literature produced by government agencies over the past two decades reveals an overriding concern for the future and for change, and to portray Brazil as a dynamic country. The preamble to the IInd National Development Plan 1975–79 indicated the crossing of the boundary between underdevelopment and development as a major objective. The whole tenor is for change, innovation and dynamism. Over the period 1965–75 Brazil had carried out 'a highly dynamic experiment in development, associating the public will, through national mobilization, to the capacity to accomplish through action in the public sector, and private and community initiative' (Federative Republic of Brazil 1974: 23). The dominant traits which are stressed are dynamism and modernity – of agricultural change, rapid industrialization, social advance and urban growth, transport innovation and participation in scientific advances in telecommunications and nuclear energy.

Important elements in Brazil's external image which emerge from official literature are those of sheer scale, of space available for development, of a rich and diverse resource endowment, of economic progress and of multi-racial harmony. There is an emphasis on impressive facts and figures – the fifth largest country, the seventh most populous; rapid rates of demographic, urban and economic growth; the world's largest river basin; Latin America's largest industrial complex, and so on. Such figures provide statements of fact, expressions of aspirations, and convey an image. Illustrative material associated with such literature supports this image, with some concessions to spectacular natural landscapes, historical legacies and cultural influences. The principal stress though again is on modernity – steelworks, car factories, iron mines, new roads, schools and housing, people on the move, sporting prowess, modernity in arts and architecture.

Some idea of Brazil's self-image can be gleaned from the following quotations:-

> 'An up-to-date picture of modern Brazil : her expanding economy surging forward from a striking post-war boom; the cumulative impact of the application of new technologies; the consistent drive to effectively develop an enormous territory and the determination to spread education to all levels of a dynamic society' (Brazilian Embassy 1972: 3);
>
> 'A young and cosmopolitan country ... the world's most advanced tropical civilization.' 'With her cultural vitality, her economic potential, her national stability Brazil is dedicated to far more than merely solving her problems. She is a modern nation' (Federative Republic of Brazil 1976: 14–15);
>
> 'Brazil is remarkable for what it is and for what it is likely to become ... whatever Brazil's present attractions, its resources are so great and its progress now so rapid that in the near future it is bound ... to become a much more prosperous land' (Brazilian Government Trade Bureau 1961: 1).

Such imagery conveys the sense and notion of change. As a developing country which has experienced rapid economic growth in recent years, considerable modification of the landscape is essential and inevitable; the State has contributed directly to such change; it has sought to foster desire for progress amongst Brazilians; and it has tried to create a portrait of a dynamic country to external observers.

Landscapes of mass media and mass consumption

The State is a potent influence in creating particular landscapes and landscape images, introducing familiar and standard elements such as highways, factories and dams and creating more universal landscapes of modernization. Another significant influence on landscape and landscape taste is the penetration of foreign and multi-national capital and its associated advertising.

Brazil has been firmly committed to a programme of economic development, closely affiliated to the pattern of Western capitalism. The State has had a significant role in this, in shaping the broad strategy, and in direct participation in certain sectors of the economy. Elsewhere there has been a large role for private domestic and foreign capital. The development process in general and the commitment to a capitalist economy have had three substantial impacts – the introduction of the technology of development, increasing demand for its products and the intrusion of agents to prompt such demand, through mass advertising.

The landscapes of modernization have been largely discussed above (Ch. 6), with the construction of factories, dams, schools, highways and so on. These provide new and distinct intrusions into natural and traditional landscapes, but at the same time they are common elements of the development process, irrespective of location. Steelworks, car factories, oil refineries or office blocks have a technical uniformity such that they provide a globally similar contribution to landscape, rather than a peculiarly national or local one. They contribute to the evolution of a more standardized international landscape of economic development, rather than a peculiarly Brazilian one. This pattern is compounded by the role in the Brazilian development process of multinational corporations, with their own standardizations of plant and product. This process, sometimes identified as Coca-Colonization, is neatly satirized by Paulo Martins (1961) in his study of a day in the life of an average Brazilian, *Brasilino*, dependent on foreign corporations for his food, transport, public utilities and entertainment, because Gillette, Palmolive, Johnson and Johnson, British American Tobacco Co, General Motors, General Electric, Armour, Coca-Cola are as much part of the Brazilian life-style as they are in other capitalist countries. Their plants, products and symbols are an ever increasing part of the Brazilian scene. It is also the case that certain public utilities make a significant impact on the landscape. The federal petroleum monopoly, Petrobrás, is Brazil's largest company, and the role of road transport is such that 'Petrobrás' is a widely diffused element in the roadside and urban scene.

In addition to this direct impact of the trappings of capitalist development on the landscape, commitment to such a model has a less tangible impact on changing the landscape. Brazil and Brazilians have become desirous of change. The country has become, at least in aspiration, a 'consumer society' and its inhabitants have succumbed to the 'revolution of rising expectations'. These trends mean that the life-styles of the high mass consumption of developed capitalism are envied and sought after and to be achieved by the migrant to the city, the urban worker and the aspiring middle class. Such a pattern again fosters a trend to greater uniformity – to live in town, dress fashionably, own a car, TV, fridge, etc, such that the trappings of North Atlantic technology and the culture of consumption become the normal experience of the affluent and the objective of the rural and urban poor. Because many of the sought-after accoutrements are the products of multi-national corporations, they further compound the move towards reducing dissimilarities in cultural landscape within Brazil, and between Brazil and countries of the First World.

In the evolution of landscapes of capitalist development and of the aspired-to landscapes of conspicuous consumption, the media have a particular role, fuelling demand for particular commodities and life-styles and thus having potential impact on the landscape. In Brazil government education programmes have substantially reduced illiteracy, the percentage of literate adults rising from 60 per cent in 1960 to 76 per cent in 1976. Education, access to books, magazines and newspapers, and the spread of transistors and television have made more Brazilians aware of alternative life-styles. McLuhan's notions that 'the medium is the message' and of the emergence of the 'global village' are at least indicative of the potential impact of greater access to the media. Such media – printed, spoken or photographic – have given Brazilians greater awareness of distant places, their life-styles and landscapes.

This awareness has been compounded by the deliberate influence of commercial advertising. Advertising is an integral part of the capitalist economy, seeking to promote mass-consumption of non-essential goods such as household gadgets, non-staple food and drink, vehicles, entertainment and travel. It seeks to sell products and to foster the impulse to buy. Advertising serves to generate a way of life for all to aspire to. It tries to make its audience dissatisfied with its present way of life, and offers a better alternative, already followed by those who have succumbed to its attractions. It teaches the receiver what to want, offering the possibility of escape to a beautiful, rich, easier, better, problem-free, good life. If we buy what is offered, we, our life-style, and possibly our environment, will be transformed.

The increasing skill of the practitioners of advertising is such that advertisements can manipulate cultural viewpoints; they influence opinions and attitudes and promote a desirable way of life. Advertisements have become one of the most significant cultural factors of the present, in reflecting and shaping our lives. They are, according to Berger (1972: 139), an essential element in the culture of the consumer society. They are ubiquitous, an unavoidable part of capitalist society and landscape, whether in neon lights on

Fig. 7.1 Multi-national billboard, Recife. Swedish winner of an English tennis tournament advertises a Brazilian-made whisky produced by a Canadian owned company!

Sugar Loaf or painted on a rock in the barren *sertão*. In Brazil the importance of the multinational corporation means that the images propagated form part of a process of cultural imperialism fostering the substitution of traditional values, beliefs and scenes by a process of Americanization. In the late 1960s multinationals were the principal advertisers in Brazil (Serra 1972: 62), leading firms being Willys Overland, Sydney Ross, Volkswagen, Gessy Lever, Gillette, Nestlé, Ford and Rhodia.

Advertising has been identified as a major factor in the socio-economic life of Brazil (Camargo and Noya Pinto 1975: 49) and, with the mass media in general, is seen to affect behavioural patterns, develop motivations, create expectations and modify ways of life. Advertising takes up over 15 per cent of radio and television time (ibid. 71–73). Mass-circulation magazines such as *Manchete, Fatos e Fotos* and *Veja* are also influential both in their contents and in their advertising material, fostering the homogenization of culture, fashion, life-style and so on. Bardi (1970: 124) argues that advertising, when it arrived in Brazil, was welcomed, absorbed and soon became a normal feature of the nation's life. The style of publicity which has evolved is essentially North American, with some Brazilian elements.

It has been suggested (Brookfield 1969: 65) that in addition to fulfilling its prime aim of selling a commodity, advertising widens and distorts the perceived environment. Advertising and the mass media in general generate mass fashions and tastes. The evolution of such mass values create uniform products and places. Common and standardized tastes and fashions reduce the diversity of place and foster increased uniformity of landscape (Relph 1976: 92). They promote a banalization of landscape.

To date the impact of these trends in Brazil has been uneven. They have had most impact on those areas where the population is best able to acquire the goods and services purveyed, that is in the cities, particularly those of the more prosperous South-east. In these areas more people have the purchasing power to obtain the trappings of the 'good life' and are most exposed to its siren calls. Elsewhere the consequences are less substantial; the media create the aspirations; new lives and new landscapes are for tomorrow, or in the city.

One other contribution of mass advertising to landscape change is in its direct intrusion into the landscape, as billboard, poster, neon sign, slogan and so on. Such elements have become an integral part of the cityscape and of the roadside. Great hoardings and neon signs have become as much of the urban environment of Rio de Janeiro or São Paulo as they are of other capitalist cities. They promote new images within the environment, and a ubiquitous feature

Fig. 7.2 The contradiction of advertising. Billboards advertising nutritious yoghurt, 'the coffee of good taste', and Hollywood cigarettes, 'the secret of success', mask a *favela*, Belo Horizonte.

of the urban scene. For some they are a lively, dynamic and artistic addition to that scene; for others they are a further element in the disorder and visual blight of the city. Such features have become an integral part of the landscape of both the towns and countryside of Brazil. They provide images of a different world, and sometimes stand in pronounced contrast to the realities of the world about them.

Landscapes of tourism

Tourist landscapes take three forms: the landscapes which exist to attract tourists; the landscapes which are constructed to provide for tourists; and the landscapes, real or imagined, which are created by the media to generate tourism.

Tourism is a phenomenon of growing economic and social significance, increasing in response to greater affluence and leisure time, and easier and more rapid travel. It has been transformed from an élite privilege to a mass pastime, with increasingly profound consequences on the landscape. The development of tourism in Brazil is a relatively recent phenomenon, for both domestic and foreign tourists. The poverty of many Brazilians inhibits domestic tourism, but for the affluent middle and upper classes domestic and foreign tourism is of increasing significance. International tourism to Brazil has been inhibited by its relative remoteness from the main tourist-generating areas of Europe and North America, deficiencies in basic infrastructural facilities of all-weather roads and reliable water and electricity supplies, and more specific deficiencies in hotel provision. In recent years the economic potential of tourism has been recognized, and government encouragement has been given to the industry. The country continues to have a deficit on its foreign tourist account, with greater expenditure by Brazilians abroad than by foreigners in Brazil, but the number of foreign tourists is rising. Between 1967 and 1977 the number of foreign tourists entering the country rose from 158 000 to 635 000.

Sun, sea and sand are major stimuli to a good deal of domestic and foreign tourism in Brazil, but in these the country is competing with other similarly endowed countries. More distinctive attractions occur in the areas of culture, tradition, scenery and entertainment . There are few pre-Colombian legacies to compete with those of Peru or Mexico, but there is a wealth of colonial sites, in the coastal towns of the North-east, and the mining towns of Minas Gerais and the Centre-West. The country has neither the traditions nor the resources to sustain concentrations of museums and art galleries comparable with the great European centres, but São Paulo has developed an impressive diversity of traditional, domestic, fine and modern art galleries, and other cities have capitalized on local traditional and religious art to provide worthwhile tourist attractions.

Traditional elements which provide actual or potential attractions stem largely from Amerindian or African origins. The former are limited, simple and relatively remote from the main centres of population. Former slave areas preserve elements of African traditions but these tend to be part of the general scene rather than explicit tourist attractions, though religious and musical legacies of candomblé, macumba, capoeira and samba form part of the tourist circuit and the national image. In the South cultural traditions and festivals preserved by immigrants from nineteenth century Europe provide current and potential attractions.

Natural landscapes provide attractions for tourists, but the remoteness and dispersion of the most striking inhibits their exploitation. Such features include the Amazon jungle, the scenery of Rio and the Serra do Mar, the falls of Iguaçu, the limestone caves of Minas Gerais and the wind-eroded rocks of Vila Velha. The beaches attract both Brazilian and foreigners, while a series of mountain resorts, primarily hill station retreats from lowland high temperatures, were among the earliest domestic resorts. These include Teresópolis, Petrópolis and Campos do Jordão. Also in the mountains of the South-east spas and health resorts such as Caxambu, Araxá, Poços de Caldas and Águas de Lindóia are domestic tourist centres.

The best known tourist attraction of Brazil is probably the Rio Carnival, which brings a seasonal influx of domestic and foreign tourists. The samba school processions and spectacular fancy dress balls contribute a particular image of Brazil. Other entertainments, in the form of cinema, theatre and other cultural activities, are limited to the main metropolitan centres, which also have the most extensive night life. International tourism tends to generate 'international' cuisine, but in addition to basic dietary elements of rice, black beans, manioc and tropical fruit, there are regional specialities of spicey African-influenced food in the Northeast, churrasco (grilled meat) in the South, and Indian dishes in Amazonia.

To capitalize on these resources the government created EMBRATUR, the Empresa Brasileiro de Turismo, in 1966, to stimulate the industry by providing funds for hotel construction, labour training and publicity. The development of tourism has come to form part of national planning strategy, while general infrastructural improvement has also facilitated tourism. Specific support for tourism by EMBRATUR has resulted in a substantial increase in hotel space, though two-thirds of new accommodation is located in Rio de Janeiro, São Paulo and the three southern states.

It is in the 'seaside' resorts of Rio de Janeiro, Guarujá, Tôrres, Guarapari and Camboriú that the most 'traditional' tourist landscapes of sea, beach, hotel, restaurants, bars and so on have emerged. The peculiar importance of the culture of the beach in the life-style of affluent Brazilians makes a pilgrimage to the seashore an integral part of the weekly ritual of residents of coastal cities. For those who do not live on the coast, cottage second homes, apartments

Fig. 7.3 Tourist landscape and the cult of the beach: Copacabana, Rio de Janeiro.

and condominiums in resorts such as São Vincente, Parati and Cabo Frio provide for weekend escape to the seashore, and create distinctive landscapes. The spas and hill stations also form particular resort townscapes.

Perhaps the most interesting role of tourism is in its creation of images of place. People travel to seek changes of environment, to explore new and different places, and to undergo new experiences. They move for relaxation, escape, for educational and cultural experiences, for health, sport, a change of climate, or to conform. To capitalise on these aspirations in the competitive world of tourism various agencies – government departments, travel agents, airlines, guidebooks – purvey attractive images. The media of films, books, brochures and maps provide information which reflects the wants or perceived wants of the tourist. The tourist arrives expecting to have these images realized; the reality he sees is selective; he sees what he expects to see. As Tuan has noted (1974: 63–64) the visitors' view of the environment is generally fleeting, simple and aesthetic, and it may be highly coloured by his expectations, for much travel literature tells you what you are supposed to see. Indeed, in the era of package tours, what the tourist 'must' see is carefully selected. Moreover, for those who cannot afford the luxury of travel, travel literature provides powerful images of far places. Brian Goodey (1971) has noted that we have images in our heads of far places, which are unvisited by us, but which have been displayed to us by the media. These geographically distant physical and human environments are made familiar by film, television, books, magazines and pamphlets, but they manipulate and influence our images of places. The skills of the advertiser create a consciousness of place for both tourist and armchair traveller.

An examination of tourist literature produced by EMBRATUR, by VARIG, Brazil's principal airline, and by travel agencies, suggests that major elements in the tourist landscape of Brazil are beaches, sun, scenery, forest, Indians, baroque and immigrants, carnival and soccer, girls and gemstones. The country offers 'the admirable combination of splendid beaches, forests, mountains and flatlands with which Nature has blessed this tropical land', 'the carefree, restless spirit of its people', 'the unique spectacle of frantic fans in Maracana stadium and the contagious enthusiasm of carnival, coupled with rich folklore, tranquil interior towns', and 'the fascinating scenario of baroque cities, permanent witnesses to its colonial past, its history and its culture'. The lure of the tropics is carefully cultivated. Brazil is described as a 'paradise of enchantment and magic, an unsurpassable tropical spectacle of lush forests, bleached-white beaches fringed by coconut palms, an ever present sun, magnificent waterfalls and golden fields'. It is a 'wonderland of splendor and exoticism', of 'breathtaking variety, of forest and grassland teeming with wildlife, of lofty mountains and mighty rivers; a land rich in popular traditions, rites and dances and songs'. It is a land of contrasts. There are of course 'many other lands throughout the world that offer contrasting colours. What makes Brazil different, as a country of striking unlikeness, is the subtle blending of its peculiarities'! At the broadest scale, then, the image conveyed is of tropical exoticism, but there are also internal contrasts which are exploited to create other images for tourists.

In the restless search for 'new' tourist experiences Amazonia is projected as likely to become Brazil's second most popular tourist destination. Here the landscapes which are exploited are those which have fascinated the white man since the sixteenth century – the jungle and the Indian. The dense and luxuriant jungle offers tourists the vision of 'an almost unrealistic world within which everything is immense. It is a veritable paradise of verdure, water and sun. It is one of the last land frontiers to be civilized, an unexplored and primitive landscape, where the limits between reality and imagination, legend and mystery, are far from precise'! Nonetheless Belém and Manaus are 'significant examples of cities in which man has managed to implant all the comforts of civilization in the heart of the jungle'!

In the North-east 'the sound of drums is pure Africa, but the architecture of the huge mansions is old European baroque. Tall coconut palms among the white, unspoilt beaches bend in the breeze like those of the South Seas'. It is portrayed as a mysterious and poetic region, whose attractions are its beaches, its early colonial legacy and its African traditions in music and cuisine.

The South-east is a microcosm for, 'if you're on a tourist trip to Brazil, you'll find the image you already have of the country confirmed by the states which form the South-east region – here in this most developed part of Brazil you will see the whole range of scenery, settings and human types to be found in the rest of the country', – beaches, mountains, spas, historical towns, great cities. It offers beaches of all kinds on the Gold Coast and the Green Coast, pure mountain air and waters, the Gold and Diamond Trail leading to the Baroque, and the special attractions of Rio de Janeiro and São Paulo. The literature on these two cities presents differing and interesting emphases. The 'marvellous city' is a place of pleasure – sea, sun, sand, scenery, soccer, samba, beaches and bikinis. Its landscape of rare beauty enables the tourist to enjoy all that is best in nature. The happy, carefree welcoming Cariocas seem able to combine business and the pleasures generously provided by Nature. Their 'demi-paradise offers the most breathless, awe-inspiring urban scenery the world has ever known, as well as sophisticated urban fun'! 'Rio is the compulsory stop-over for any tourist who wants to say he has been to Brazil'.

Tourism is not confined to holiday makers alone; business visitors contribute to the influx of foreigners. For them São Paulo, as the economic focus of the country, is the main centre of attraction and tourist literature is geared partly to their requirements. If Rio is the 'marvellous city', São Paulo is the 'incredible city', dynamic, lively, competitive. 'Despite all its activity, the city has a conspicuous charm, being clean and pleasant looking'! 'Here one doesn't care much about tradition, at least in the material sense'. Instead the attractions include the ABC industrial towns, multi-lane highways and the port of Santos. Few centres, other than aggressive São Paulo, would wish themselves advertised in a tourist brochure as 'a tangled urban conglomerate'. The work

Map 16 Brazil: tourist images. Alan Hodgkiss (1981: 15) has noted the persuasive role maps may exercise in promoting tourism. This map has been specially drawn by him using Brazilian tourist maps, brochures and guide books in an attempt to convey the principal tourist 'markers' of Brazil. Inset: proposed national and state parks.

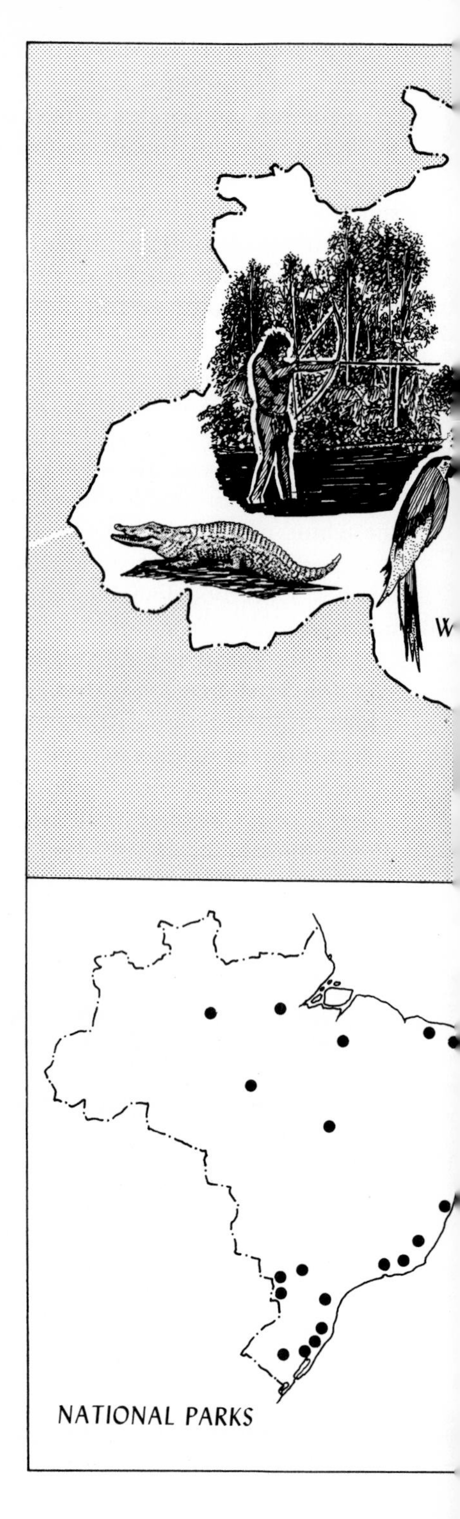

0 Km 500
0 Miles 500
Teatro Amazonas
Manaus
Ver-o-Peso Market, Belem
Jangada
zonas
Araguaia River
National Congress, Brasília
Ouro Prêto
Spas
Carnival
ATLANTIC
OCEAN
Iguaçu Falls
Vila Velha
Gaucho
German style
building
São Miguel of the Missions
Sugar Loaf from Corcovado
Rio de Janeiro

ethic dominates – the skyscraper boom encompasses offices and banks, the city is Brazil's main industrial centre, there are industrial fairs and excellent hotels. But Paulistas and businessmen do 'not live by work alone'. There are beaches and golf courses 'nearby', horse racing 'at the weekends', the 'gaiety of lively nights'!

In the interior South-east the legacy of the gold mining boom is a potent and increasingly exploited attraction of rich splendour 'as if time has stopped at the end of the eighteenth century in order to preserve this fabulous tale for the twentieth century tourist'. The mining towns provide unforgettable and romantic places, including Ouro Prêto, 'considered the most homogeneous artistic and architectonic complex in the western world', and Congonhas, 'one of the richest complexes of colonial art in the Americas', Minas Gerais offers 'the best climate, the richest land of the country and the most beautiful views. There are also artistic and historical treasures beyond measure', in all an impressive ensemble of steep crooked streets, splendid old houses and magnificent churches.

The South has two principal elements – some spectacular physical features and the distinctive landscapes of European immigrants. This legacy also makes the South distinct from tropical Brazil. The natural attractions are the eroded sandstone towers of Vila Velha, an 'eerie stone city' of strange shapes, and the massive cascades of the 80 m high Iguaçu falls, 'the most fabulous sight in the whole of the American continent'. In the cultural landscape the colonies are 'replicas of the small backland towns of Europe'. It also offers beaches, mountains, vineyards and colonial mission churches.

Nature and man are also the attractions of the Centre West. In the savannahs 'a magnificent explosion of wildlife has resisted the advances of civilization'. There are 'beautiful and fish filled rivers', and 'immense forest reserves which are still the natural habitat of indigenous Indian tribes'. These elements contrast with the world's 'most daring capital' and 'most modern city', the futuristic Brasília. The federal capital provides a stunning architectural wonder that rivals the most exuberant natural phenomena.

The setting for these specific attractions is essentially tropical with sun all the year round – 'it is always summer here'; 'translucid waters and clean sand, with none of the pollution which has invaded the sea resorts of other tourism centres'; 'the wild peace of deserted beaches, dark green forests and palm trees'; exotic tropical fruit – in all 'a unique show, where Nature and Man meet each other in a perfect harmony of colours and shapes'! Brazil is, according to a series of VARIG advertisements, the place of 'your wildest dreams'. 'Brazil is string bikinis, white sands, and nights that disappear in a samba. It's jewels. And carnival. It's Rio. Bahia. Brasília. It's Sugar Loaf Mountain. Iguaçu Falls. The Amazon Jungle', 'pristine beaches, mysterious jungles'. 'Exotic, erotic Brazil'. It also offers 'the romance of Paris, the adventure of Africa, the warmth of Spain and the quiet of a Jamaican afternoon'!

Such prose, of course, flatters to deceive. It tries to paint an attractive and distinctive portrait to draw in tourists, and to stress Brazil's attractions against those of other countries. But the power of publicity not only attracts tourists but is a powerful force in creating a distinct image to foreigners of the 'far place' of Brazil; this imagery becomes the perceived reality. It provides a powerful but partial portrait of the place. This partiality is compounded because particular elements become the foci of package tours. It is possible to 'do'. Brazil in a couple of weeks, such that 'Ouro Prêto/Congonhas can be seen in a day, all of Salvador in two days, Brasília merits a full day and overnight, and Natal is a pleasant overnight stop'. Places therefore become part of the schedule and the ritual, as do sights – Corcovado, Tijuca forest, Copacabana, Ipanema and a samba school encapsulate Rio.

The consequence is that tourist advertising and tourist experience generate a warped representation of reality, providing a particular vision of people and place. Both travel literature and travel experience can be agents for change in the landscape, improving and sanitizing areas so that they accord with tourist expectations and values. Tourist resorts and areas begin to shape their own images in advance of the arrival of the tourist. There is both confirmation of stereotypes and provision of essentials expected by the tourist, such that package landscapes evolve which incorporate the essential ingredients of a place or country, and at the same time the tourist is cocooned by his necessary home comforts. For example, the Sheraton hotel group, which includes the Rio-Sheraton, offers havens where the tourist can forget he is abroad, with no problems of language, currency, transport or shopping provision. 'Sheraton provides its own version of geography, safe, clean and comfortable' (Sampson 1974: 89).

Tourism also introduces 'foreign' elements and values into the landscape. Modern tourism is linked to mass movement, mass advertising and multinational provision of travel and accommodation facilities. There is an impact of external culture on the domestic, generating homogenized landscapes, replacing, in Relph's view, place by placelessness (Relph 1976).Distinctive local landscapes are modified by those of conventional tourist architecture and services, by synthetic landscapes and pseudo-places. Though 'flying down to Rio' is a well established jet set activity, Brazil is a relative newcomer to the age of mass tourism. The development of 'placeless' tourist landscapes is still limited, but the packaging of the country's tourist attractions creates increasingly pervasive images and, if successful, must prompt significant landscape change in popular areas.

Landscapes of literature

If tourist brochures, propaganda posters and billboard advertisements contribute to the landscape we see and desire, another medium which records landscape perception and shapes landscape taste is that of literature. The landscapes of literature have been a concern for both geographers and writers. Several geographers have suggested that geography has much to learn from good literature. E. W. Gilbert (1972) noted the way in which novelists have illuminated the landscape, providing realistic and detailed portrayals of the real earth. Tuan (1978) suggests that literature is a source material for geographers and provides a perspective on how people experience their world. Pocock (1978) points to writers skills in the perceptive recording of the distinctive qualities of place, not only by felicitous literal description in prose and poetry, but also in terms of emotion and symbol. Interests in this field have prompted studies such as those of Pocock (1981) and the careful weaving of literary quotations into geographical prose by Watson (1979). Writers themselves have pursued similar concerns. Margaret Drabble's concern with the British landscape in literature (1979) notes that writers record both themselves and the age in which they live, and the places they describe. They provide their own perceptions of landscape, portraying a vanished past and the present that remains. Margaret Attwood's exploration of Canadian literature (1972) moves even closer to recent concern by geographers with literature as source, in her interest in place not simply as a space inhabited with the body but with the head. 'Literature', she argues 'is not only a mirror; it is also a map, a geography of the mind' (ibid. 18–19).

Literature then offers us a potential source of material on landscapes, as it has been perceived by a group skilled and practised in the effective use of language, conveying their impressions and visions of the land, and influencing ours.

Putnam (1948) argues that 'literature in Brazil began with landscape', in the prose descriptions of the early discoverers and explorers. He suggests that landscape and the economic motive are two major themes in Brazilian literature, describing the lush tropical environment and its potential for sustaining human well being, dependent on the will and ability to exploit the abundant resources. In the broader context of this book one might argue that these are two crucial themes in the shaping of the Brazilian landscape – the opulent beauty of the natural environment and the aggressive attempts to exploit it. Putnam suggests that the exuberance and grandeur of the natural environment have prompted a certain lushness in the style of Brazilian literature.

Other observers note the internal variations in the nature of Brazilian regional literature, concerned with portraying different and differing parts of the country. Verissimo (1945) suggests that Brazilian writers are concerned with various limited fields – a city, state or region, and only together do they provide a portrayal of the vast panorama of the national landscape. Vianna Moog argues that 'despite our territorial continuity, Brazil does not form a continent; we are a cultural archipelago. And this archipelago is made up of many cultural islands, all more or less autonomous and distinct' (Moog 1951: 17). He identifies seven nuclei or cultural islands – Amazonia, the North-east, Bahia, Minas Gerais, São Paulo, Rio Grande do Sul and metropolitan Rio de Janeiro.

The literature generated by these nuclei, especially that which gives us literary perceptions of landscape, is by no means even. The literature available provides some portrait of past and present landscape and of life-styles, such that we have descriptions of natural landscapes, the countryside, townscapes and economic activities. It should be noted that most of this work is the product of an urban literati, writing about a country in which much land remains unsettled, where until recently rural life dominated society and economy, and where a majority were illiterate. In addition, Brazilian letters have been markedly culturally dependent, deriving their models from Portuguese and later European current fashions.

Of the regional literature which provides potential source material, that relating to the North-east is perhaps the most clearly defined, particularly the work of authors such as da Cunha, Ramos and Queiroz, concerned with portraying the drought-ridden *sertão*. The writings of Jorge Amado are a major source of insight on Salvador, the cocoa coast of Bahia and the African inheritance of the North-east. There is also material on the sugar lands of the coast. Literature on Amazonia is limited, and tends to perpetuate the fascination and awe shown by Europeans to the water and forest wonderland of the river. From the South-east there is material on Minas Gerais, on the coffee lands of the region, and also on the townscapes of Rio de Janeiro and São Paulo. Materials on the South are much less abundant, as are those on the Centre-West. There are few portrayals of the frontier in these areas, nor, in the case of the south, of imigrant landscapes.

A major and inevitable theme in Brazilian writing relates to the lavish richness of this tropical world, particularly the abundance and exuberance of its forest cover – to be awed by, and later axed. Jorge Amado's *Terras do sem fim* (1942) captures the powerful influence exercised by the forest on the Portuguese and the Brazilians, a daunting jungle of tangled vegetation, creeping lianas, fierce jaguars, venomous snakes and fantastic beasts: 'The forest! It is not a mystery, it is not a danger, a menace. It is a god! . . . . The giant wood is the world's past, the beginning of the world'(Amado 1948: 29). Ribeiro provides a less hostile portrayal of the lavishness of this forest, 'with a thousand lianas, a thousand creepers, a thousand diverse orchids, with red, yellow, blue, scarlet, white flowers – all creating a multi-coloured mass, in an orgy of green, an excess of colours which overwhelms and tires the imagination' (Ribeiro n.d.: 37). José de Alencar, a master of the description of the natural landscape of Brazil, paints a more restrained picture of mountain, stream and forest in the Serra dos Órgãos, in the preamble to his *O Guarani* (1857). The Paquequer, a wild mountain stream, loses it savage beauty and becomes calm and serene like a lake when it joins the majestic Paraíba (de Alencar n.d.: 25).

Water and the forest are dominant elements in the limited literature generated by Amazonia (Preto-Rodas 1974). Among authors describing the Amazon scene are Verissimo, Inglês de Sousa, Cruls and Rangel. The latter captures the pessimistic view of the constraints of the hostile environment of climate, forest, flood, insect and disease on man in his *Inferno Verde* (*Green Hell*, 1927) where 'the banana grove crushed the hut, the forest suffocated the banana grove, and in turn, the very sky weighed down heavily on the forest' (Rangel 1974: 187). Peregrino Jnr's *Mata submersa* (*Submerged Forest*) and other stories describe the landscapes and human activities of the region, and 'the changing and inconstant image of the river' (Peregrino Jnr n.d.: 313).

The most substantial collection of regional writing is that relating to the North-east, particularly the *sertão* and the drought. José de Alencar was an early contributor to this literature. For me, the opening phrase of his '*Iracema*' will always evoke the Cearense shoreline, although 'wild green seas' is an inadequate translation of '*verdes mares bravios*', and points to one limitation of using literature as a source, particularly foreign literature. Is there a loss of sense, if not of strict meaning, in translation? Does direct experience of the scene described colour the impression conveyed by language? Alencar's work included Indianist novels such as *Iracema* (1865) and *Ubirajara* (1874), and portrayal of the colonial *sertão* in *O Sertanejo* (1876). The latter conveys the image of this region in drought, looking like the burning land of the prophet, through which fire had passed, consuming all the greenery, leaving the vast charnel house of the old forest.

A major contribution to the portrayal of the *sertão* is Euclides da Cunha's *Os sertões*, a documentary portrayal of the late nineteenth century rebellion at Canudos in Bahia. His study contains a wealth of precise and accurate geographical descriptions of the region and its environment. His portrayal of the onset of drought (da Cunha 1944: 104–10) or of the scorching midday heat of the region (ibid.: 182) are classic, if unfashionable, pieces of geographical writing. He also evokes some of the *sertão's* features with a phrase – 'the uniform and unvaryingly melancholy appearance' of the *caatinga* (ibid.: 183),'a shapeless mass of vegetation, the life drained from it, writhing in a painful spasm' (ibid. 35).

A regionalist conference organized in Recife in 1926 by Gilberto Freyre was an important stimulus to regional writing on the North-east, including Américo de Almeida's *A Bagaceira* (*Cane Trash* – 1928), Raquel de Queiróz' *O Quinze* (*The Year'15* – 1930), and Graciliano Ramos' *Vidas Secas* (*Barren Lives* – 1938). All three evoke the dry landscape of the *sertão*, the drought, and its victims, the *flagelados*. 'The brushland stretched in every direction, its vaguely reddish hue broken only by white heaps of dry bones' (Ramos 1965: 4).The *flagelados* are seen by Américo de Almeida as being 'driven by swords of fire out of their paradise'. 'They fled the sun and the sun led them in their forced nomadism' (Américo de Almeida 1978: 5). They move to work fronts, to the moister lands of the coast or to the cities. The refugees of *Vidas Secas* 'were on their way to an unknown land, a land of city ways. They would become its prisoners. And to the city from the backland would come even more of its sons' (Ramos 1965: 131). Although the *sertão* provides the major source of regional writing on the North-east, there are portrayals of other landscapes within the region. Jorge Amado has produced an extensive literature on the cocoa coast of southern Bahia, in novels such as *O pais do carnaval* (1932), *Cacaú* (1933), *Terras do Sem Fim* (1942), and *Gabriela, cravo e canela* (1958). The latter neatly contrasts the *sertão* with the coast. 'As the migrants moved southward, the landscape changed. The inhospitable dry scrubland gave way to fertile valleys, green meadows, dense woods, brooks and rivers' (Amado 1963: 89). Other work by Amado portrays life in Salvador – *Suor* (1934) and *Jubiabá* (1935).

The more fertile areas of the Northeast are also described by Ramos' *São Bernardo* (1975), which portrays life on an Alagoan fazenda, and Azevedo's *O mulato* (1881), which is set in Maranhão. Jose Lins do Rego's 'cane cycle' provides a detailed insight into sugar plantation economy and society in Paraíba, and other aspects of the North-eastern scene. The cycle consists of five novels: *Menino do engenho* (1932), *Doidinho* (1933), *Bangüê* (1934), *O moleque Ricardo* (1934) and *Usina* (1936).

Concern with economic activities is also a major theme in the literature of the South-east. Bernardo Guimarães *O Garimpeiro* (1872) describes the prospecting for mineral wealth in Minas Gerais, amid 'the most pleasant and enchanting landscapes it is possible to imagine', where each crest gives a new perspective and panorama of rounded hills separated by crystal streams (Guimarães, n.d.a,: 19). The landscapes of Minas Gerais are also described in his *O seminarista* (1872), in Palmerio's *Chapadão do Bugre* (1971) and in the writings of Guimarães Rosa – *Sagarana* (1946) and *Grande Sertão*' (1956).

Coffee has been a major source of regional writing, with a number of authors setting their stories in the coffee lands. The impact of the coffee frontiers on the land is a recurring theme, as is the dynamism of its advance. A rather striking element is the awareness of its instability and destructive impact. Bernardo Guimarães' *A escrava Isaura* (1875) portrays the contrast between the forest and farm during the early phase of the Rio coffee boom: 'In the distance nature displays itself still in all its primitive and savage wildness, but closer, around the delightful dwelling, the hand of man had converted the wild jungle into gardens and orchards, grassland and fat pasture, shaded here and there by giant figs, perobas, cedars and copaíba trees, reminders of the vigour of the ancient forest' (Guimarães n.d.b.: 19). Monteiro Lobato's *Cidades Mortas* (1919) describes the later decline and stagnation of the early coffee lands. His work also captures the nature of coffee's advance into western São Paulo, where the *fazendeiro's* 'fierce ambition prefers the regimented beauty of the tree which yields gold to the beauty of disordered nature' (Lobato 1977: 35). He saw the advance of coffee as a new and genuinely local phenomenon in which the natural forest cover was felled, cleared and burned, 'destroying in decades the works which nature had been composing since the beginning of time' (ibid: 36), with the 'tree of gold' producing only at the cost of the lifeblood of the earth. His *Negrinha* encapsulates the rapid and aggressive advance of the coffee frontier, 'clearing, felling, burning, open routes, cutting ditches, fixing wire, building bridges, erecting houses, clearing pastures, planting coffee' (ibid: 77). Rubens do Amaral captures the stimulus given to urban growth by coffee –'there were cities created in ten years, where formerly there was only virgin forest'; cities with electricity, polite society, prosperous agriculture and commerce (do Amaral 1977: 46). It was Lobato (1977: 60) who noted however 'the tremendous desert which Atilla Café created', for 'they destroyed, but did not know how to build' (ibid. 37).

The South-east also provides the setting for Graça Aranha's *Canaã* (1902), a study of the reaction of German immigrants to Espiríto Santo. He conveys idyllic images of a land blessed by nature, of sunshine, gentle breezes, perfumed flowers, incalculable treasure, abundant flocks and fruits and fertile soil. In this land of Canaan the immigrants saw the colonists' houses 'nestled in the green and peaceful abundance of the countryside. The little houses were strung all along the valleys, some sheltered by the hills, others perched on the slopes but all gracefully arranged' (Graça Aranha n.d.: 63).

Literature on the South is less abundant, though the *gaucho* landscape is forcefully described in Alcides Maya's *Ruínas Vivas* (1910), *Alma bárbara (1922)*. Augusto Meyer's *Coracão verde* (1926) and Verissimo's *O tempo e o vento* (1949: 62). The Centre-West also lacks literary description, though de Taunay's *Inocência* (1872) provides some of the earliest accurate descriptions of Mato Grosso with, for example, detailed observations on the *cerrado* and *campos* vegetation.

One other major theme in the landscapes of literature is that of the towns. In addition to Amado's portrayals of Salvador and Ilheus, Montello's *Os degraus do paraiso* (1976) explores São Luis do Maranhão in the early twentieth century, de Alcântara Machado's *Novelas paulistanas* (1961) the life-style of Italian immigrants in São Paulo, and Barreto's *Recordacões do escrivão Isaías Caminha* (1909) and other novels capture the bustle of Rio de Janeiro. Two novels by Azevedo contribute visions of the city. A would-be migrant from Maranhão seeks 'a great city, old, full of dark streets, full of mysteries, of hotels, sporting houses, of suspect places and fickle women' (Azevedo n.d.: 22). His *O Cortiço* (1890) is a realistic portrait of urban slum life in nineteenth century Rio.

Space does not permit a full exploration of the theme of landscape and literature, and quotations from literary sources have to be brief. Nonetheless such works of fiction are of significance for they describe landscape and provide a sense of place. Tuan (1961) has reminded us of the virtues of consulting such works of fiction are of significance, for they describe landscape and proways of looking at landscape and demonstrating skills in describing it.

8

Conclusion — retrospect and prospect

The present-day landscapes of Brazil are the product of the interplay between nature and man. In some areas almost pristine natural landscapes persist, little tampered with by man. Elsewhere the natural landscape has been substantially modified, creating distinctive cultural landscapes, whilst in some areas the landscapes which exist are largely man-made.

Two decades ago Pierre Gourou could indicate that almost two-thirds of Brazilian territory was unmodified by man, or consisted of predominantly natural landscapes with only a few small areas of human settlement (Gourou 1961: 3). Much of this area remains scarcely explored on the ground, even if our knowledge of it has been greatly increased by survey from the air. It is, however, in retreat before the line of the frontier advancing from the east and south, and along the penetration lines provided by new highways.

Elsewhere the lands of Brazil have been perceived, used and transformed by men in accordance with their needs and tastes. Lewis suggests that the human landscape is an unwitting autobiography of man's tastes, values, aspirations and fears (Lewis 1979: 12). Lowenthal and Prince, in their analyses of the English landscape (1964, 1965), identify preferences for the rural scene on the part of the English, in which the picturesque, the tidy, the bucolic and the past are important; nostalgia is a potent force in the perception and preservation of the English landscape. Judgement of such landscapes is primarily aesthetic, in which landscapes deliberately designed to please or accidentally made pleasant in the course of performing some economic function are deemed attractive and desirable. In the United States, though the dominant traits may be wilderness, formlessness, disorder and blight (Lowenthal 1968) there is nonetheless some notion of an idealized past and a preferred future.

In the Brazilian case concern for the past, and order, neatness and conservation are less influential forces in the landscape; concern for profit, progress and the future have greater impact. There is no overall uniformity to the Brazilian landscape, for in addition to the basic dichotomy between natural and man-modified landscapes, there are many variations, between regions, locales, and between country and town. The cultural landscapes which have evolved have been shaped by groups and by individuals, mainly over the past half-millenium. The impact of some groups has been short term and small scale; of others it has been extensive and substantial. In some cases countless nameless individuals have been the agents of change, elsewhere specific individuals have left major legacies.

In both the past and present landscapes of Brazil predominant themes have been disorder, progress and change. From the early colonial period there has been an ambivalence towards nature, and a fundamental contradiction in the approach to the land, initially perceived as both paradise and wilderness. The seeming super-abundance of the resources of this tropical paradise has prompted exploitation, with little or no care for the consequences; at the same time the sinister wilderness has been there to attack and drive back. If the early colonists saw Brazil as a paradise, at the hands of their heirs, part of that paradise might be seen as being lost, as soil, plants, wildlife and minerals have been exploited to meet the needs and desires of colonial Portugal, industrializing Europe, the booming heartland of the South-east and the aspiring affluent segment of Brazilian society.

Some critics would see the use of the lands of Brazil as entirely destructive; certainly some symbols of this destruction have passed firmly into the folklore of non-Brazilians – the Manaus opera house as totem of the rapacious and sybaritic rubber boom, the burning of coffee beans, and more recently the despoliation of Amazonia and the attack on a significant part of the global oxygen supply! While it cannot be denied that care has not been a strong element in Brazilian land use, the present pattern of the landscape does not sustain this external vision of wholesale destruction. The transformation of the natural landscape into a cultural one is an inherent part of the Brazilian development process, as were earlier transformations in Europe and North America. It is the case though that this process in Brazil has sometimes been careless and destructive, and has not produced the picturesque landscapes lovingly evolved by generations of European peasants, or neatly ordered by Parliamentary enclosure or Congressional townships.

The sheer scale of Brazil's territory and its apparent wealth encouraged profligacy in its use (in 1980 population density was still below 15 persons per square kilometre). The ratio of land to man encouraged extensive rather than intensive use, and the mobility of men and their farmed land. The desire to 'get rich' had also been a strong motivation for the individual and the nation. In the colonial period the demands of the crown and in the nineteenth century the desire for profits by landowners and shareholders influenced the style of development and its visible expression in the landscape. In the twentieth century, whatever the fashionable terminology applied to economically poorer nations, Brazil has been a 'developing' country. Critics might ask 'development for whom?' but there has been, since the 1930s, a strong commitment to economic advance. The prime concern has been to improve the economic position of the country; the consequence has been that 'progress' has been the principal priority, at the expense of other considerations, including conservation of the environment.

In such a situation it is inevitable that the natural landscape will be changed rapidly and dramatically. At the frontier between the natural and the cultural landscape that transformation will be profound. In 1975 Brazil had some 320 million hectares of land in farms, an area which has almost doubled since 1920, and increased by almost one-third since 1960. There are then landscapes of rapid and recent change at the frontier. But, the myth of the hollow frontier notwithstanding, there is a substantial area of consolidated and in some areas long established rural landscapes in the zones of earlier settlement. Even here though the landscape is not one of neat, ordered and continuous farmland. Abundance of land and large scale of holding means that not all of farm territory is in crops or pasture; they are inter-mixed with forest, secondary scrub and wasteland. Some farmed areas are dominated by extensive monoculture, with the green monotony of the canelands or the rigid regularity of coffee bushes. Field boundaries marked by trim hedges, stone walls or even barbed wire are uncommon, as are neat uniform villages. Much of the rural landscapes is irregular and untidy. Possibly because of the inherent mobility of Brazilian agriculture there has been less incentive to establish boundaries and permanent markers.

Such rural landscapes may not accord with Euro-American preferences and practices, but they are distinctively and essentially Brazilian. The lands of cane, coffee and colonization, for example, provide landscapes with some internal coherence and uniformity. Such landscapes have emerged spontaneously as a by-product of the development process, motivated by a desire for economic return, rather than having been consciously designed for aesthetic pleasure.

Some memorable landscapes in Brazil derive from purely natural features – the breathtaking splendour of Guanabara Bay and its encircling serras, the grandeur of the Iguaçu or Paulo Afonso falls, the spectacular coastal scarp, or the enormity of the Amazon. The sheer fact of scale is an essential element in some of these natural landscapes. The Amazon forest may be a never-ending monotonous green hell, or a complex and diverse wonderland; the *sertão* in the dry season may be a dull grey plain or, at twilight, a palette of pastel shades; the open plateau of the Centre-West may be an unending, scruffy scrubland, or a mysterious, empty and brooding place. The uniformity of these extensive natural features is an important ingredient in the landscape.

In total contrast, in the man-made landscape of the town and cities, unity derives from a lack of order. The charm of the hilltop towns of colonial Brazil, such as Olinda or Ouro Prêto, stems from the picturesque confusion of topography, vegetation, churches, public buildings and houses. The urban scene has increasingly become the norm for most Brazilians. The city is both the common experience and the aspiration of the majority. It is the place of opportunity and progress. In parallel with the basic thrust of Brazil's recent development, the pattern in the city has been dynamism and change. Cities have boomed and blossomed, spreading upwards and outwards. Both of these

Fig. 8.1 Elements in the urban future, Rio de Janeiro. From left to right – apartment block; the headquarters of Petrobrás, the federal petroleum monopoly; the new cathedral; the retreating remnant of the Morro do Santo Antonio, one of the hill top foci of colonial Rio; new office building.

trends have been largely uncontrolled, giving rise to spectacular skyscraper cores, even in medium-sized towns, and a surrounding sprawl of urban lots and shanties. Again the principal characteristic has been diversity, in the housing styles of the affluent, the working class and the *favelados*. Except for the BNH estates and the company towns, there are few areas of uniform standardized housing.

It is in the cities though where landscape taste in Brazil is perhaps most clearly expressed. The concern of Brazil and Brazilians is for the future, not the past. That future in terms of growth and opportunity, appears to lie in the city, generating a preference for the city and its landscapes. Rapid urban growth has also prompted change in the city, as attempts are made to provide essential urban services for the swelling population, and as the urban past is cleared to make way for the present and the future in the form of office blocks, urban motorways, hyper-markets, metro systems and factories. It is also in

Fig. 8.2 Elements in the Brazilian scene. A 'Bahiana' in 'traditional African' dress selling 'typical' foods; Coca-Colonization; hand mill for crushing sugar cane to produce syrup; religious pictures. In the background Volkswagens and the office core of Brasília.

Beba
Coca-Cola
Nº2

the cities that there has been some deliberate creation of aesthetic landscapes, whether in the comprehensive form of the Costa-Neimeyer Brasília, or in the detail of the distinctive work of Brazilian architects, artists and landscape gardeners.

The persistent concern for wealth and the more recent planning of paths to economic advance have been the prevailing forces in shaping the Brazilian landscape. In Brazil landscape 'taste' has been and is at best a minority concern. The evolution of pleasing landscapes has been accidental rather than deliberate. Though there has recently been greater awareness of problems of resource destruction, environmental pollution and uncontrolled urbanization, there is still some reluctance to give too great weight to conservation and preservation, whether of land, forest, Indian or historical inheritance, if they stand in the way of what is perceived as progress.

It seems likely that in the immediate future the priorities of progress and change will prevail. Over the past quarter century, successive Brazilian governments have been firmly committed to the economic development of the country. The intention is to transform Brazil into a developed country with a modern, competitive and dynamic economy. This implies a continuation of recent trends in which infrastructural provision, urbanization, industrialization, agricultural modernization and the further advance of the frontier are the dominant traits. The cultural landscapes characteristic of this process are likely to continue their advance against the surviving natural landscapes of the interior. Within the established and settled areas the commitment to development, the dependence on borrowed technology, the action of the State and the penetration of multi-national capital are likely to exert powerful influences on the evolution of the landscape. The 'Brazilian-ness' of present landscapes, themselves shaped by a variety of forces from abroad, is likely to be overlain by the pattern of the developed capitalism of the USA, Europe and Japan, a process compounded by the demonstration effect of the transistor, TV movie, advertisement and tourist. Such influences may generate an increasing homogenization of landscape, in which the uniqueness of evolved Brazilian landscape is masked or modified by the impact of modern technology and the influence of mass media.

Bibliography

The material included in the bibliography incorporates references cited in the text, other sources which have been utilized, and suggestions for further reading.

Introduction

Appleton, J. (1975) *The Experience of Landscape*, Wiley, New York and London

Brookfield, H. C. (1969) 'On the environment as perceived' in C. Board *et al.* (eds), *Progress in Geography*, vol. 1, Arnold, pp. 51–80

Burns, E. B. (1980) *The Poverty of Progress*, California Univ. Press, Berkeley and London

Hadfield, W. (1854) *Brazil, the River Plate and the Falklands*, Longman, London

Houston J. M. (1970) 'Editor's Preface' in Tuan, Y. E., *China*, Longman, London, pp. v–vi

Lowenthal, D. (1961) 'Geography, experience and imagination: towards a geographical epistemology', *Annals Association American Geographers* **51**, 241–60

Lowenthal, D. (ed.) (1967) 'Environmental perception and behaviour', *Department of Geography, University of Chicago, Research paper*, No. 109, Chicago

Lowenthal, D. (1968), 'The American scene', *Geographical Review* **58**, 61–88

Lowenthal, D. and Prince, H. (1964) 'The English landscape', *Geographical Review* **54,** 309–46

Lowenthal, D. and Prince, H. (1965) 'English landscape tastes', *Geographical Review* **55** , 186–222

Meinig, D. (ed.) (1979) *The Interpretation of Ordinary Landscapes*, Oxford Univ. Press, New York and London

Prince, H. (1971) 'Real, imagined and abstract worlds of the past' in C. Board *et al.* (eds) *Progress in Geography*, vol. 3, Arnold, pp. 1–86

Saarinen, T. F. (1976) *Environmental Planning: Perception and Behaviour*, Houghton Mifflin, Boston

Tuan, Y. F. (1974) *Topophilia*, Prentice Hall, Englewood Cliffs

The natural landscape

Azevedo, A. de (ed.) (1968) *Brasil: a terra e o homen*, Vol 1-*As bases físicas*, Cia. Editora Nacional, São Paulo (2nd edn)

Fittkau, E. J., Illies, J., Klinge, H., Schwabe, G. H. and Sioli, H. (eds)(1968) *Biogeography and Ecology in South America*, Junk, The Hague
Fundação IBGE (1968) *Novo paisagens do Brasil*, IBGE, Rio de Janeiro
Fundação IBGE (1968) *Subsidios a regionalização*, IBGE, Rio de Janeiro
James, P. E. (1969) *Latin America*, Odyssey, New York (4th edn)
King, L. C. (1956) 'A geomorfologia do Brasil oriental' *Revista Brasileira de Geografia*, Ano XVIII, pp. 147–265

The Amerindian landscape

Fittkau, E. J., *et al.*, op. cit.
Gross, D. R. (ed.) (1973) *Peoples and Cultures of Native South America*, Doubleday, New York
Heath, E. G. and Chiara, V. (1977) *Brazilian Indian Archery*, Simon Foundation, Manchester
Hemming, J. (1978) *Red Gold*, Macmillan, London
Hopper, J. (1967) *Indians of Brazil in the Twentieth Century*, Institute for Cross-Cultural Research, London
Meggers, B. J. (1971) *Amazonia: Man and Culture in a Counterfeit Paradise*, Aldine, Chicago.
Melatti, J. C. (1970) *Índios do Brasil*, Editora de Brasília, Brasília
Ribeiro, D. (1970) *Os indios e a civilização*, Civilização Brasileira, Rio de Janeiro.
Steward, J. H. and Faron, L. C. (1959) *Native Peoples of South America*, McGraw-Hill, New York
Steward, J. H. (ed.)(1963), *Handbook of South American Indians* (6 vols),Cooper Square, New York
Villas Boas, O. and C. (1974) *Xingu: the Indians, Their Myths*, Souvenir Press, London; Farrar, Strauss and Giroux, New York (1973)

The colonial landscape

Baudet, H. (1965) *Paradise on Earth: Some Thoughts on European Images of Non-European Man*, Yale Univ. Press, New Haven and London
Boxer, C. R. (1957)*The Dutch in Brazil 1624–54* Oxford Univ. Press, London and New York
Boxer, C. R. (1962) *The Golden Age of Brazil*, California Univ. Press, Berkeley
Boxer, C. R. (1969) *The Portuguese Seaborne Empire 1415–1825*, Hutchinson, London and New York
Burns, E. B. (ed.) (1966) *A Documentary History of Brazil*, Knopf, New York
Chiappelli, F. (1976) *First Images of America: The Impact of the New World on the Old*, California Univ. Press, Berkeley and London, 2 vols
Davies. A. (1956) 'The first discovery and exploration of the Amazon', *Trans. Inst. Brit. Geog.* **22**, 87–96
Delson, R. M. (1979) *New Towns for Colonial Brazil*, University Microfilms International, Ann Arbor.
Galloway, J. H. (1979) 'Agricultural reform and the enlightenment in late colonial Brazil', *Agric. Hist.* **53**, 763–79

Goodman, E. J. (1972) *The Explorers of South America*, Macmillan, New York and London

Greenlee, W. B. (1937) *The Voyage of Pedro Alvares Cabral to Brazil and India*, Hakluyt Society, London

Hemming, J. (1978) op. cit.

James, P. E. (1969) op. cit.

Markham, C. R. (1859) *Expeditions into the valley of the Amazons*, Hakluyt Society, London

Markham, C. R. (1894) *The letters of Amerigo Vespucci*, Hakluyt Society, London

Morse, R. M. (ed.) (1965) *The Bandeirantes*, Knopf, New York

Nash, R. (1926) *The Conquest of Brazil*, Cape, London

Parry, J. H. (1963) *The Age of Reconnaissance*, Weidenfeld and Nicolson, London

Penrose, B. (1963) *Travel and Discovery in the Renaissance 1420–1620*, Harvard Univ. Press, Cambridge, Mass

Poppino, R. E. (1968) *Brazil: The Land and the People*, Oxford Univ. Press, New York and London

Prado, C. (1969) *The Colonial Background of Modern Brazil*, California Univ. Press, Berkeley

Schwartz, S. B. (1973) *Sovereignty and Society in Colonial Brazil*, California Univ. Press, Berkeley and London

Webb, K. E. (1974) *The Changing Face of Northeast Brazil*, Columbia Univ. Press, New York and London

The African landscape

de Almeida Barbosa, W. (1972) *Negros e quilombos em Minas Gerais*, privately printed, Belo Horizonte

Bastide, R. (1978) *The African Religions of Brazil*, Johns Hopkins Univ. Press, Baltimore and London

Cohen, D. W. and Greene, J. P. (1972) *Neither Slave nor Free*, Johns Hopkins Univ. Press, Baltimore and London

Conrad, R. (1972) *The Destruction of Brazilian Slavery 1850–1888*, California Univ. Press, Berkeley and London

Curtin, P. (1969) *The Atlantic Slave Trade*, Wisconsin Univ. Press, Madison and London

Dzidzienyo, A. and Casal, L. (1979) *The Position of Blacks in Brazilian and Cuban society*, Minority Rights Group Report No. 7

Fernandes, F. (1979) 'The negro in Brazilian society: twenty-five years later' in M. Margolis and W. E. Carter (eds), *Brazil: Anthropological perspectives*, Columbia Univ. Press, New York

do Nascimento, A. (1978) 'African culture in Brazilian art', *J. Black Studies* **8**, 389–422

Pescatello, A. (ed.) (1975) *The African in Latin America*, Knopf, New York

Price, R. (ed.) (1973) *Maroon Societies*, Doubleday, New York

Ramos, A. (1956) *O negro na civilização brasileira*, Casa do Estudante do Brasil, Rio de Janeiro

Rodrigues, J. M. (1965) *Brazil and Africa*, California Univ. Press, Berkeley; Cambridge Univ. Press, London

Toplin, R. B. (ed.) (1974) *Slavery and Race Relations in Latin America*, Greenwood, Westport.

The neo-colonial landscape

The economic cycles

Associação dos Geografos Brasileiros (1962) *Aspectos da geografia carioca*, Conselho Nacional de Geografia, Rio de Janeiro
Burns, E. B. (1965) 'Manaus, 1910: portrait of a boom town', *J. Inter-American Studies* **7**, 400–21
de Castro Soares, L. (1963) *Amazonia*, Conselho Nacional de Geografia, Rio de Janeiro
Coustet, R. (1970) 'Nineteenth century Brazilian architecture', *Art and artists* **11**, 16–23
Collier, R. (1968) *The river that God forgot*, Collins, London
Franca, A. (1960) *A marcha do café e as frentes pioneiras*, Conselho Nacional de Geografia, Rio de Janeiro
Graner, E. A. and Godoy, C. (eds) (1967) *Manual do cafeicultor*, Editora Melhoramentos, São Paulo
Haring, C. H. (1966) *Empire in Brazil*, Harvard Univ. Press, Cambridge, Mass
James, P. E. (1932) 'The coffee lands of southeastern Brazil', *Geogr. Rev.* **22**, 225–44
James, P. E. (1969) op.cit.
Manchester, A. K. (1972) *British pre-eminence in Brazil*, Octagon, New York
Mindlin, H. E. (1956) *Modern architecture in Brazil*, Architectural Press, London
Momsen, R. P. (1964) *Routes over the Serra do Mar*, Taveira, Rio de Janeiro
Monbeig, P. (1952) *Pionniers et planteurs de São Paulo*, Colin, Paris
Motta Sobrinho, A. (1978) *A Civilização do café*, Editora Brasiliense, São Paulo
Porto Domingues, A. J. and Keller, E. C. de Souza (1958) *Bahia*, Conselho Nacional de Geografia, Rio de Janeiro
Russell-Wood, A. J. R. (ed.) (1975) *From Colony to Nation: Essays on the Independence of Brazil*, Johns Hopkins Univ. Press, Baltimore and London
Stein, S. J. (1976) *Vassouras, a Brazilian Coffee County 1850–90*, Atheneum, New York
Wagley, C. (1964) *Amazon Town*, Knopf, New York
Wagley, C. (ed.) (1974) *Man in the Amazon*, Florida Univ. Press, Gainsville

Immigrant landscapes

Augelli, J. (1958a) 'The Latvians of Varpa', *Geogr. Rev.* **48**, 365–87
Augelli, J. (1958b) 'A Dutch colony in Brazil', ibid. 431–3
Borges Pereira, J. B. (1974) *Italianos no mundo rural Paulista*, Universidade de São Paulo, São Paulo
de Boni, L. A. (1977) *La Mérica*, Universidade de Caxias do Sul, Caxias do Sul
de Boni, L. A. and Costa, R. (1979) *Os Italianos do Rio Grande do Sul*, Universidade de Caxias do Sul, Caxias do Sul
Cavati, J. Batista (1973) *História da imigração Italiana no Espirito Santo*, Ed. São Vicente, Belo Horizonte
Cintra, J. T. (1971) *La migracion Japonesa en Brasil*, El Colegio de Mexico, Mexico City
Hall, M. M. (1974) 'Approaches to immigration history' in R.Graham and P. H. Smith (eds) *New Approaches to Latin American History*, Texas Univ. Press, Austin and London, pp. 175–93

Lenard, A. (1965) *The Valley of the Latin bear*, Gollancz, London
Lorenzoni, J. (1975) *Memórias de um imigrante Italiano*, Livraria Sulina, Porto Alegre
Malta Ferraz, P. (1976) *Pequena história da colonização de Blumenau, 1850–83*, Fundação Dr Blumenau, Blumenau
Ramos, A. (1975) *As culturas européias e europeizados*, Ministério da Educação e Cultura, Rio de Janeiro (3rd edn)
Roche, J. (1959) *La colonisation Allemande et le Rio Grande do Sul*, Institut des Hautes Etudes de L'Amerique Latine, Paris
Stawinski, A. V. (1976) *Primórdios da imigração Polonesa no Rio Grande do Sul*, Universidade de Caxias do Sul, Caxias do Sul

The foreign contribution

Coustet, R. (1976) op.cit.
Denis, P. (1911) *Brazil*, Fisher Unwin, London
Dent, H. C. (1886) *A Year in Brazil*, Kegan Paul Trench, London
Dickenson, J. P. (1967) 'The iron and steel industry in Minas Gerais, Brazil, 1695–1965', in R. W. Steel and R. Lawton (eds), *Liverpool Essays in Geography*, Longman, London, pp. 407–22
Dickenson, J. P. (1978) *Brazil*, Dawson, Folkestone; Westview, Boulder
Duncan, J. S. (1932/1968) *Public and Private Operation of Railways in Brazil*, AMS, New York
Evenson, N. (1973) *Two Brazilian Capitals*, Yale Univ. Press, New Haven and London
Graham, R. (1968) *Britain and The Onset of Modernization in Brazil 1850–1914*, Cambridge Univ. Press, London and New York
Hall, A. (1981) 'Innovation and social structure: the sugar industry of Northeast Brazil', in S.Mitchell, *The Logic of Poverty*, Routledge Kegan Paul, London and Boston, pp. 143–56
Haring, C. H. (1966) op. cit.
Leonardos, O. H. (1970) *Geociências no Brasil – a contribuição britânica*, Forum, Rio de Janeiro
Manchester, A. K. (1972) op.cit.
Mindlin, H. E. (1956) op.cit.
Momsen, R. P. (1964) op.cit.
Müller, N. L. (1969) *O fato urbano na bacia do Rio Paraiba – São Paulo*, Instituto Brasileiro de Geografia, Rio de Janeiro
Onody, O. (1973) 'Quelques aspects historiques des capitaux etrangers au Bresil', in C. N. R. S. *L'histoire quantitative du Bresil de 1800 a 1930*, Centre Nacional de la Recherche Scientifique, Paris, pp. 269–314
Taylor, K. S. (1978) *Sugar and the Underdevelopment of Northeastern Brazil 1500–1970*, Florida Univ. Press, Gainsville

Foreign views of Brazil

Agassiz, L. and A. (1868/1969) *A Journey in Brazil*, Praeger, New York and London
Bates H. W. (1863/1975) *The Naturalist on the River Amazon*, Dover, New York
Bigg-Wither, T. P. (1878/1968) *Pioneering in South Brazil*, Greenwood, New York
Burke, U. R. and Staples, R. (1886) *Business and Pleasure in Brazil*, Field and Tier, London

Burton, R. F. (1869/1969) *Exploration of the Highlands of Brazil*, Greenwood, New York
Caldcleugh, A. (1825) *Travels in South America*, Murray, London
Codman, J. (1867) *Ten Months in Brazil*, Lee and Shepard, Boston
Darwin, C. (1839/1958) *The Voyage of the Beagle*, Bantam, New York
Edwards, W. H. (1847) *A Voyage Up the River Amazon*, Appleton, New York
Fawcett, P. H. (1953) *Exploration Fawcett*, Hutchinson, London
Fletcher, J. C. and Kidder, D. P. (1866) *Brazil and the Brazilians*, Sampson Low, London
Gardner, G. (1849) *Travels in the Interior of Brazil*, Reeve, Benham and Reeve, London (2nd edn)
Goodman, E. J. (1972) op.cit.
Hadfield, W. (1854) *Brazil, the River Plate and the Falklands*, Longman, London
Hadfield, W. (1869) *Brazil and the River Plate in 1868*, Bates, Hendy and Co., London
Hadfield, W. (1877) *Brazil and the River Plate in 1870–76*, Church, Sutton
Hamilton, C. G. (1960) 'English-speaking travellers in Brazil, 1857–87', *Hisp. Amer. Hist. Rev.* **40**, 533–47
Kennedy, W. R. (1892) *Sporting Sketches in South America*, Porter, London
Kidder, D. P. (1845) *Sketches of Residence and Travel in Brazil*, Wiley and Putnam, London
Koster, H. (1816/1966) *Travels in Brazil*, Southern Illinois Univ. Press, Carbondale
Mansfield, C. B. (1856/1971) *Paraguay, Brazil and the Plate*, H.M.S., New York
Mathison, G. (1825) *Narrative of a Visit to Brazil, Chile, Peru and the Sandwich Islands*, Knight, London
Mawe, J. (1812) *Travels in the Gold and Diamond Districts of Brazil*, Longman, London
Mulhall, M. G. (1878) *The English in South America*, Standard, Buenos Aires
Naylor, B. (1969) *Accounts of Nineteenth Century South America*, Athlone, London
Prince, H. (1971) op. cit.
Roosevelt, T. (1914) *Through the Brazilian wilderness*, Murray, London
Savage-Landor, A. H. (1913) *Across Unknown South America*, Hodder and Stoughton, London
Spruce, R. (1908) *Notes of a Botanist on the Amazon and the Andes*, Macmillan, London and New York
Wallace, A. R. (1853/1972) *A Narrative of Travels on the Amazon and Rio Negro*, Dover, New York
Walsh, R. (1830) *Notices of Brazil in 1828 and 1829*, Westley and Davis, London

The modern landscape

Plumb, J. H. (1969) 'Introduction' in C. R. Boxer *The Portuguese Seaborne Empire 1415–1825*, xiii-xxvi, Hutchinson, London

Landscapes of development

Dickenson, J. P. (1978) op. cit.
Dickenson, J. P. (1980) 'Innovations for regional development in Northeast Brazil; a century of failures', *Third World Planning Review*, **2**, 57–74.
Jaguaribe, H. (1968) *Economic and Political Development*, Harvard Univ. Press, Cambridge, Mass
Soares e Silva, E. M. (1943) 'Volta Redonda', *Foreign Commerce Weekly*, November

Townscapes

Fernandes, F. (1972) *Comunidade e sociedade no Brasil*, Cia. Editora Nacional, São Paulo
Geiger, P. P. and Davidovich, F. (1961) 'Aspectos do fato urbano no Brasil', *Revista Brasileira de Geografia*, **23**, 263–362

Small townscapes

Harris, M. (1971) *Town and Country in Brazil*, Norton, New York
Wagley, C. (1964), op. cit.

Big cityscapes

Arns, Cardinal (1978) 'Preface' in *São Paulo Growth and Poverty*, Catholic Institute for International Relations, 1978, London
Bastide, R. (1969) *Brasil, terra de contrastes*, Difusão Europeia do Livro, São Paulo
Beaujeu-Garnier, J. and Chabot, G. (1967) *Urban Geography*, Longman, London
Evenson, N. (1973), op. cit.
Governo do Estado do Ceará (1967), *As migrações para Fortaleza*, Imprensa Official, Fortaleza

Planned townscapes

Costa, L. (1966) 'Report by Lucio Costa' in Staubli, W. *Brasília*, Hill, London, pp. 12–16
Delson, R. M. (1979) op. cit.
Niemeyer, O. (1966) 'Thoughts on Brasília' in Staubli, W. *Brasília*, Hill, London, pp. 21–23
Spade, R. (1971) *Oscar Niemeyer*, Thames and Hudson, London
Tuan, Y-F. (1974) *Topophilia*, Prentice Hall, Englewood Cliffs

Company towns

Allen, J. B. (1966) *The Company Town in the American West*, Oklahoma Univ. Press, Norman
Dickenson, J. P. (1970) *Zona Metalúrgica: a study of the geography of industrial development in Minas Gerais, Brazil*, unpublished Ph.D. thesis, University of Liverpool
Instituto Brasileiro de Geografia e Estatística (1959) *Encyclopedia dos municipios brasileiros: Minas Gerais*, vol. 26, IBGE Rio de Janeiro
Porteus, J. D. (1970) 'The nature of the company town; *Trans. Inst. Brit. Geogr.* **51,** 127–42

Urban embellishments

Bullrich, F. (1969), *New Directions in Latin American Architecture*, Studio Vista, London
Niemeyer, O. (1963), quoted in P. F. Damaz, *Art in Latin American Architecture*, Reinhold, New York
Lowenthal, D. and Prince, H. (1965) op. cit.

Landscapes of poverty

Bacha, E. L. and Balthazar, M. H. F. (1980), *Essays on Brazilian growth, wages and poverty*. PREALC Working Paper no. 188, Organizacion International del Trabajo, Santiago

Banco Nacional de Habitação (1970) *BNH-70*, Banco Nacional de Habitação, Rio de Janeiro

Governo do Ceará (1967) op. cit.

de Jesus, C. M. (1962) *Beyond all Pity*, Four Square, London

Langoni, C. G. (1973) *Income Distribution and Economic Development in Brazil*, Banco Nacional de Habitação, Rio de Janeiro

Lloyd, P. (1979) *Slums of Hope*, Penguin, Harmondsworth

Perlman, J. E. (1976), *The Myth of Marginality*. California Univ. Press, Berkeley and London

Teulieres, R. (1957), 'Favelas de Belo Horizonte', *Boletim Mineiro de Geografia* (no. 1), 7–37

The frontier

Hennessy, A. (1978) *The Frontier in Latin American History*, Arnold, London

Margolis, M. (1973) *The Moving Frontier*, Florida Univ. Press, Gainesville

Ministry of Transport (1970) *Transamazonian Highways*, Ministry of Transport, Federative Republic of Brazil, Montreal

Morse, R. (1965), op. cit.

Nicholls, W. H. (1970) 'The agricultural frontier in modern Brazilian history: the State of Paraná', *Revista Brasileiro de Economica*, **24,** (no. 4), 64–91

Smith, A. (1971) *Mato Grosso*, Joseph, London

The last frontier?

Barbira-Scazzocchio, F. (1980) *Land, People and Planning in Contemporary Amazonia*, Centre of Latin American Studies, Cambridge

Delfim Netto, A. (1971) quoted in O.Duarte Pereira, *A Transamazônica prôs e contras*, Civilização Brasileira, Rio de Janeiro

Furley, P. (1980) 'Development planning in Rondônia based on naturally renewable surveys', in Barbira-Scazzocchio, op. cit. 37–45

Institute Brasileiro de Geografia e Estatistica (IBGE) (1980) *Censo demografico de 1980, Resultados Preliminares*, IBGE, Rio de Janeiro

Mahar, D. J. (1979) *Frontier Development Policy in Brazil: A Study of Amazonia*, Praeger, New York and London

Wagley, C. (ed.) (1974), op. cit.

Behind the frontier

da Costa I. B. and Mesquita, H. M. (1978) *Tipos de habitação rural no Brasil*, IBGE, Rio de Janeiro

Paiva, R. M., Schattan, S. and de Freitas, C. F. T. (1976) *Setor agricola do Brasil*, Ed. Universidade de São Paulo, São Paulo

Webb, K. (1974) *The Changing Face of Northeast Brazil*, Columbia Univ. Press, New York and London

Landscape destruction and conservation

Bicudo, L. P. and Santiago, A da C (1977) 'Recursos naturais renovávais no Estado de São Paulo' in SUPREN *Recursos naturais, meio ambiente e poluição*, IBGE, Rio de Janeiro, vol. 1, pp. 289–300
Brooks, E. *et al.* (1973) *Tribes of the Amazon Basin in Brazil 1972*, Knight, London
Costa, R. V. da (n.d.) *Demographic Growth and Environmental Pollution*. Banco Nacional de Habitação, Rio de Janeiro
Davis, S. H. (1977) *Victims of the Miracle*, Cambridge Univ. Press, New York
Dickenson, J. P. (1967), op. cit.
Florestal Acesita (n.d.) *Notícia de uma grande floresta*, Acesita, Belo Horizonte
Goodland, R. J. A. and Irwin, H. S. (1975) *Amazon Jungle: Green Hell to Red Desert?* Elsevier, Amsterdam
IPHAN (1973) *Patrimonio historico e artistico nacional: relação de bens tombados*, Ministerio da Educação, Rio de Janeiro
Sternberg, H. O'R. (1968) 'Man and environmental change in South America' in Fittkau, E. J. *et al.* (eds.) *Biogeography and Ecology in South America*, Junk. The Hague, pp. 413–45
Strang, H. E. (1977) 'Parques nacionais e reservas equivalentes' in SUPREN *Recursos naturais, meio ambiente e poluição*, IBGE, Rio de Janeiro, vol. 2, pp. 17–22
Teixeira Guerra, A. (1969) *Recursos naturais do Brasil*, Fundação IBGE, Rio de Janeiro

Media landscapes

Goodey, B. (1971) 'Perception of the environment', *Centre for Urban and Regional Studies, University of Birmingham Occasional Paper*, No. 17, Birmingham
Lowenthal, D. (ed.) (1967) op. cit.
Lowenthal, D. and Prince, H. (1965) op. cit.

Official landscapes

Brazilian Embassy (1972) *Brazil*, Brazilian Embassy, London
Brazilian Government Trade Bureau (1961) *Brazil*, Brazilian Govt. Trade Bureau, London
Federative Republic of Brazil (1974) *II National Development Plan 1975–79*, Brazilian Government, Braslia
Federative Republic of Brazil (1976) *Brazil*, Ministry of External Relations, Brasília
Lowenthal, D. (1961) op. cit.

Landscapes of mass media

Bardi, P. M. (1970) *Profile of the New Brazilian art*, Kosmos, Rio de Janeiro
Berger, J. (1972) *Ways of Seeing*, BBC, London
Brookfield, H. (1969) op. cit.
Camargo, N. and Noya Pinto, V. B. (1975), *Communication Policies in Brazil*, UNESCO, Paris
Martins, P. G. (1961) *Um dia no vida do Brasilino* (9th edn), no publisher given, Santos
McLuhan, M. (1967) *Understanding Media*, Sphere, London
Serra, J. (1972) *El milagro economico Brasileño*, Ed. Periferia, Buenos Aires
Sontag, S. (1970) 'Posters: advertisement, art, political artifact, commodity' in D.

Stermer, *The Art of Revolution*, Pall Mall Press, London, vii–xxiii
Williamson, J. (1978) *Decoding Advertisements*, Boyars, London

Landscapes of tourism

Hodgkiss, A. (1981) *Understanding Maps*, Dawson, Folkestone
MacCannell, D. (1976) *The Tourist*, Macmillan, London and New York
Quatro Rodas (1974) *Brasil Come Along*, Quatro Rodas, Rio de Janeiro
Relph, E. (1976) *Place and Placelessness*, Pion, London
Sampson, A. (1974) *The Sovereign State*, Coronet, London

Literary landscapes

(Full details of Brazilian novels mentioned in the text are not cited below unless used for quotations. Dates given in the text in such cases refer to the original year of publication.)

de Alencar, J. (n.d.) *O Guarani*, (Ed. de Ouro), Rio de Janeiro
Amado, J. (1948) 'The violent land', quoted in S. Putnam, *Marvelous Journey*, Knopf, New York
Amado, J. (1963) *Gabriela, Clove and Cinnamon*, Chatto and Windus, London
do Amaral, R. (1977) 'Terra Roxa', quoted in M. Ellis (ed.), *O café - literatura e historia*, Ed. Melhoramentos, São Paulo, pp. 46–48
Américo de Almeida, J. (1978), *A bagaceira*, Liv. J. Olympio, Rio de Janeiro. 16th edn
Aranha, G. (n.d.) *Canaã* (ed. de Ouro), Rio de Janeiro
Attwood, M. (1972) *Survival*, Anansi, Toronto
Azevedo, A. (n.d.) *Casa do pensão* (Ed. de Ouro), Rio de Janeiro
da Cunha, E. (1944), *Rebellion in the Backlands*, Chicago Univ. Press, Chicago and London
Drabble, M. (1979) *A Writer's Britain*, Thames and Hudson, London
Gilbert, E. W. (1972) *British Pioneers in Geography*, David and Charles, Newton Abbot
Guimarães, B. (n.d.a.) O garimpeiro (Ed. de Ouro), Rio de Janeiro
Guimarães, B. (n.d.b.) *A escraval saura* (Ed. de Ouro), Rio de Janeiro.
Lobato, M. (1977) 'Negrinha' in Ellis, op. cit., 77–80
Lobato, M. (1977) 'A onda verde', ibid., 35–39
Moog, V. (1951) *An Interpretation of Brazilian literature*, Ministry of Foreign Relations, Rio de Janeiro
Peregrino Jnr. (n.d.) *A mata submersa e outras histórias da Amazônia* (Ed. de Ouro), Rio de Janeiro
Pocock, D.C.D. (1978) 'The novelist and the north', *Univ. of Durham, Dept. of Geography Occ. Paper 12*
Pocock, D.C.D. (ed.) (1981) *Humanistic Geography and Literature*, Croom Helm, London; Barnes and Nobles, Totowa, N.J.
Preto-Rodas, R. (1974) 'Amazonia in literature: themes and changing perspectives' in C. Wagley (ed.), *Man in the Amazon*, Florida Univ. Press, Gainesville, pp. 181–98
Putnam, S. (1948), *Marvelous Journey–a Survey of Four Centuries of Brazilian writing*, Knopf, New York
Ramos, G. (1965), *Barren Lives*, Texas Univ. Press, Austin
Rangel, A. (1974), 'Inferno verde', quoted in Preto-Rodas, op. cit.
Ribeiro, J. (n.d.) *A carne*, (Ed. de Ouro), Rio de Janeiro

Tuan, Y-F. (1961) 'Topophilia: personal encounters with the landscape', *Landscape*, vii, 29–32

Tuan, Y-F. (1978) 'Literature and geography: implications for geographical research' in D. Ley and M. Samuels (eds.), *Humanistic Geography Prospects and Problems*, Croom Helm, London; Maaroufa Press, Chicago, pp. 194–206

Watson, J.W. (1979) *Social Geography of the United States*, Longman, London and New York

Verissimo, E. (1945) *Brazilian Literature*, Macmillan, New York

Conclusion

Dansereau, P. (1975) *Inscape and Landscape*, Columbia Univ. Press, New York and London

Dubos, R. (1980) *The Wooing of Earth*, Athlone, London

Gourou, P. (1961) *The Tropical World*, Longman, London (3rd edn)

Lewis, P.F. (1979) 'Axioms for reading the landscape' in D. Meinig (ed.), *The Interpretation of Ordinary Landscapes*, Oxford Univ. Press, New York and London, pp. 11–32

Lowenthal, D. (1968) op. cit.

Lowenthal, D. and Prince, H. (1964) op. cit.

Lowenthal, D. and Prince, H. (1965) op. cit.

Map Sources

Maps 2, 3 & 7 after Conselho Nacional de Geografia (1966), *Atlas Nacional do Brasil*, C.N.G., Rio de Janeiro, II-1 Hipsometria; II-11 Vegetação; III-6 Colonização.

Map 4 after *Handbook of South American Indians*, op. cit.

Map 5 compiled from P. Petrone 'Povoamento e colonização' in A. Azevedo, op. cit., 126–58

Map 6 compiled from A. Franca, op. cit.

Map 8 Data from IBGE (1956) *Censo Demografico Brasil*, IBGE, Rio de Janeiro, vol. 1

Map 9 Data from DNEF (1970) *Ferrovias do Brasil*, Dept. Nacional de Estradas de Ferro, Rio de Janeiro

Map 10 Data from Conselho Nacional do Desenvolvimento (1960) *Relatorio do periodo* 1956–60, CND, Rio de Janeiro (4 vols) and Banco Nacional do Desenvolvimento Economico *Exposição sôbre o programa de reaparelhalmento economico*, BNDE, Rio de Janeiro (annual, 1956–61)

Map 14 Data from Fundação IBGE (1973) *VIII Recenseamento Geral 1970, Censo Demografico – Brasil* Fundação IBGE, Rio de Janeiro, vol 1

Map 15 after Fundação IBGE (1972) *Carta do Brasil 1 : 50,000 Maringá Folha SF-22-Y-D-11-3*, Fundação IBGE, Rio de Janeiro

Index

Note: Page numbers *in italic* refer to illustrations (maps or photographs)